THE GREENWOOD ENCYCLOPEDIA OF
ROCK HISTORY

The Greenwood Encyclopedia of Rock History

Volume 1
The Early Years, 1951–1959
Lisa Scrivani-Tidd

Volume 2
Folk, Pop, Mods, and Rockers, 1960–1966
Rhonda Markowitz

Volume 3
The Rise of Album Rock, 1967–1973
Chris Smith

Volume 4
From Arenas to the Underground, 1974–1980
Chris Smith with John Borgmeyer, Richard Skanse, and Rob Patterson

Volume 5
The Video Generation, 1981–1990
MaryAnn Janosik

Volume 6
The Grunge and Post-Grunge Years, 1991–2005
Bob Gulla

THE GREENWOOD ENCYCLOPEDIA OF
ROCK HISTORY

The Rise of Album Rock,
1967–1973

CHRIS SMITH

GREENWOOD PRESS
Westport, Connecticut • London

Library of Congress Cataloging-in-Publication Data

The Greenwood encyclopedia of rock history.
    p. cm.
   Includes bibliographical references and index.
   ISBN 0–313–32937–0 ((set) : alk. paper)—ISBN 0–313–32938–9 ((vol. 1) : alk. paper)—ISBN
0–313–32960–5 ((vol. 2) : alk. paper)—ISBN 0–313–32966–4 ((vol. 3) : alk. paper)—ISBN
0–313–33611–3 ((vol. 4) : alk. paper)—ISBN 0–313–32943–5 ((vol. 5) : alk. paper)—ISBN
0–313–32981–8 ((vol. 6) : alk. paper)   1. Rock music—History and criticism.
   ML3534.G754   2006
   781.66'09—dc22   2005023475

British Library Cataloguing in Publication Data is available.

Copyright © 2006 by Chris Smith

All rights reserved. No portion of this book may be
reproduced, by any process or technique, without the
express written consent of the publisher.

This book is included in the *African American Experience* database from Greenwood Electronic Media. For
more information, visit www.africanamericanexperience.com

Library of Congress Catalog Card Number: 2005023475
ISBN 0–313–32937–0 (set)
     0–313–32938–9 (vol. 1)
     0–313–32960–5 (vol. 2)
     0–313–32966–4 (vol. 3)
     0–313–33611–3 (vol. 4)
     0–313–32943–5 (vol. 5)
     0–313–32981–8 (vol. 6)

First published in 2006

Greenwood Press, 88 Post Road West, Westport, CT 06881
An imprint of Greenwood Publishing Group, Inc.
www.greenwood.com

Printed in the United States of America

The paper used in this book complies with the
Permanent Paper Standard issued by the National
Information Standards Organization (Z39.48–1984).

10 9 8 7 6 5 4 3 2 1

CONTENTS

SET FOREWORD

Rock 'n' roll, man, it changed my life. It was like the Voice of America, the
real America, coming to your home.

—Bruce Springsteen[1]

The term *rock 'n' roll* has a mysterious origin. Many have credited legendary
disc jockey Alan Freed for coining the term. Some claim that it was actually a
blues euphemism for sexual intercourse, while others even see the term rock as
having gospel origin, with worshippers "rocking" with the Lord. In 1947,
DeLuxe Records released "Good Rocking Tonight," a blues-inspired romp by
Roy Brown, which touched off a number of R&B artists in the late-1940s providing their own take on "rocking." But many music historians point to the
1951 Chess single "Rocket 88" as the first rock record. Produced by Sam
Phillips and performed by Jackie Brenston and Ike Turner's Kings of Rhythm
(though released under the name Jackie Brenston & His Delta Cats), the
record established the archetype of early rock and roll: "practically indecipher-
able lyrics about cars, booze, and women; [a] booting tenor sax, and a churning,
beat-heavy rhythmic bottom."[2]

Although its true origins are debatable, what is certain is that rock 'n' roll
grew into a musical form that, in many ways, defined American culture in the
second half of the twentieth century. Today, however, "rock 'n' roll" is used
with less and less frequency in reference to the musical genre. The phrase
seems to linger as a quaint cliché co-opted by mass media—something that a
Top Gun pilot once said in voicing high-speed, mid-air glee. Watching MTV
these days, one would be hard-pressed to find a reference to "rock 'n' roll,"
but the term *rock* survives, though often modified by prefixes used to denote the

growing hybridization of the genre: There is alternative rock, blues rock, chick rock, classic rock, folk rock, funk rock, garage rock, glam rock, grunge rock, hard rock, psychedelic rock, punk rock, roots rock, and countless other sub-genres of rock music. It seems that musicians found more and more ways to rock but, for some reason, stopped rolling—or to paraphrase Led Zeppelin's "Stairway to Heaven," the music world opted to rock, but not to roll.

Call it what you will, rock music has never existed within a vacuum; it has always reflected aspects of our society, whether it be the statement of youth culture or rebellion against adult society; an expression of love found, lost, or never had; the portrayal of gritty street life or the affirmation of traditional American values; the heady pondering of space-age metaphysics or the giddy nonsense of a one-hit wonder, rock music has been an enduring voice of the people for over five decades. *The Greenwood Encyclopedia of Rock History* records not only the countless manifestations of rock music in our society, but also the many ways in which rock music has shaped, and been shaped by, American culture.

Testifying to the enduring popularity of rock music are the many publications devoted to covering rock music. These range from countless single-volume record guides providing critics' subjective ratings to the multi-volume sets that lump all forms of popular music together, discussing the jazz-rock duo Steely Dan in the same breath as Stravinsky, or indie-rock group Pavement with Pavarotti. To be sure, such references have their value, but we felt that there was no authoritative work that gives rock music history the thorough, detailed examination that it merits. For this reason, our six-volume encyclopedia focuses closely on the rock music genre. While many different forms of rock music are examined, including the *influences* of related genres such as folk, jazz, soul, or hip-hop, we do not try to squeeze in discussions of other genres of music. For example, a volume includes the influences of country music on rock—such as folk rock or "alt.country"—but it does not examine country music itself. Thus, *rock music* is not treated here as synonymous with *popular music*, as our parents (or our parents' parents) might have done, equating whatever forms of music were on the charts, whatever the "young kids" were listening to, as basically all the same, with only a few differences, an outsiders' view of rock, one that viewed the genre fearfully and from a distance. Instead, we present a six-volume set—one that is both "meaty" and methodical—from the perspective of the rock music historians who provide narrative chapters on the many different stories during more than five decades of rock music history.

The Greenwood Encyclopedia of Rock History comprises six information-packed volumes covering the dizzying evolution of this exciting form of music. The volumes are divided by historical era: *Volume 1: The Early Years, 1951–1959*, spans from the year "Rocket 88" (arguably the first rock single) was released to the year of the infamous "Day the Music Died," the fatal airplane crash that took the lives of Buddy Holly, Ritchie Valens, and J. P. Richardson (a.k.a. The Big Bopper). *Volume 2: Folk, Pop, Mods, and Rockers, 1960–1966,* covers the period when the British Invasion irrevocably changed the world, while such American rock scenes as Motown and surf rock held their own. In *Volume 3: The Rise of Album Rock, 1967–1973*, Chris Smith chronicles the growing experimentation during the psychedelic era of rock, from *Sgt. Pepper* to *Dark Side of the Moon* and everything in between. In *Volume 4: From Arenas to the Underground, 1974–1980*, Smith et al., record how rock became big business while also spawning hybrid forms and underground movements. *Volume 5: The Video Generation, 1981–1990* starts with the year of MTV's debut and captures the era when video threatened to kill the radio star. Finally, in *Volume 6: The Grunge and Post-Grunge Years, 1991–2005*, Bob Gulla captures the many innovations of millennial rock music and culture. Within each volume, the narrative chapters are supplemented by a timeline, discography, bibliography, and a glossary of encyclopedia entries for quick reference.

We hope that librarians, researchers, and fans alike will find endless nuggets of information within this reference. And because we are talking about rock, we hope you will find that reading *The Greenwood Encyclopedia of Rock History* will be a whole lot of fun, too.

Rock on.

Rob Kirkpatrick
Greenwood Publishing Group

NOTES

1. Rock and Roll Hall of Fame and Museum home page, http://www.rockhall.com.
2. All Music Guide entry for Jackie Brenston, http://www.allmusic.com.

PREFACE AND ACKNOWLEDGMENTS

Someone once said that to borrow the work of one author is plagiarism, but to borrow from 100 authors is research. A text with such broad scope as this could not have been accomplished if it had not been built on the backs of other scholars, as the lengthy bibliography will attest. But first, a few specifics about the contents herein.

This book seeks to follow the explosion of rock genres in the late 1960s and early 1970s. Though there is much to be said about the contributions of other countries' stylistic offshoots—particularly those of Britain—the focus here is on the United States, how American culture influenced rock music and how the music reciprocated. Though a number of British musicians are featured in the text, their early careers are generally glossed over in favor of covering in more detail their impact on American culture once they caught on in the United States.

Much of the impact rock acts made was through their records; thus the *Billboard* charts—which have been tracking album sales and radio play in the United States since 1945—play a significant role in analyzing the popularity of certain acts and releases. In fact, I often refer to albums as having an impact not when they were released but when they first charted or otherwise reached significant appeal (e.g., Frank Zappa's debut *Freak Out* was released in July 1966 but first charted in February 1967).

Album titles can occasionally be confusing, as some records are released under different names (e.g., Joni Mitchell's debut album *Song to a Seagull* was also known as *Joni Mitchell*, and the New York Dolls' debut was released as both *Introducing the New York Dolls* and *New York Dolls*). Often albums from British groups are released in the United States under a different name (e.g., the 1967 album *Happy Jack* by the Who was released in the United Kingdom as *A Quick One*). Whenever there is doubt about the appropriate title, I refer to it by its U.S. release title; otherwise, I use the best-known name. Song lyrics can also be confusing, as they often change from artist to artist and recording to recording. Whenever lyrics are presented here, they are the original lyrics penned by the songwriter or the lyrics to the specific version being discussed.

All data concerning album rankings and gold/platinum status come from the Recording Industry Association of America (www.riaa.com) and Joel Whitburn's archives of the *Billboard* charts, widely acknowledged to be the authoritative source:

> Whitburn, Joel, ed. *The Billboard Book of Top 40 Albums.* New York: Billboard, 1987.
>
> Whitburn, Joel, ed. *The Billboard Book of Top 40 Albums, 1955–1992.* New York: Billboard, 1993.
>
> Whitburn, Joel, ed. *The Billboard Book of Top 40 Hits.* New York: Billboard, 1996.
>
> Whitburn, Joel, ed. *Joel Whitburn Presents a Century of Pop Music.* New York: Billboard, 1999.

More than one hundred sources were utilized in researching this book, including historical and theoretical texts, artists' and fans' Web sites, films, recordings, personal interviews, museum archives, and firsthand reportage from the publications of the period (including *Rolling Stone*, *Creem*, the *New York Times*, the *Washington Post*, *Time*, *Newsweek*, and a number of local and regional presses). Every effort was made to ensure accuracy by finding at least three reliable sources whenever very specific information was presented. When reliable sources disagreed (for instance, I discovered that two very reputable encyclopedias have the incorrect date listed for the Concert for Bangladesh), I consulted primary sources and sometimes directly contacted individuals who had firsthand knowledge of the topic. Chapter endnotes usually refer to the most accessible source; backup sources are not cited but are noted in the bibliography.

It would have been impossible to write a book of this breadth and depth without the excellent work of the journalists and critics who came before and left such detailed and readable analysis in their wake. If I wore a hat, I would take it off to them.

A number of specific individuals deserve mention for their contributions to this project. The good folks at *Rolling Stone* opened their archives to me, allowing me to browse the first six years of the magazine and experience the thrill of watching music history unfold issue by issue—my deepest thanks to Andrew Dansby, Dave Swanson, Rodney Woodson, and Jann Wenner. It was also fortunate that the excellent *Creem* magazine began publishing again the first year I spent on this book, and I owe a debt to publisher Robert Matheu for *Creem's* online article archive and his personal replies to my queries. Overdue gratitude as well to Professors Charles L. Perdue and Nancy J. Martin-Perdue at the University of Virginia for their scholarly guidance and personal interest in my work.

I have always believed that good writing is 30 percent research, 60 percent editing, and only 10 percent skill (give or take), and without the help of trusted associates, this book would have been limping in weakly with the latter. Much thanks to Craig Jones for his valuable research assistance; Elizabeth Dunn for her honest evaluation, enthusiasm, and immeasurable patience; John Borgmeyer for lending his support and musical expertise; and Tristan Kromer for not only his insightful critical commentary but also his excellent music that always eased the 3:00 a.m. writer's block. Lastly, thanks to my superb editors: Jamie Thaman and Carla Talmadge at Westchester Book Services for their excellent copyediting, and Rob Kirkpatrick and Anne Thompson at Greenwood Publishing, who showed me many roads I would not have seen, but never forced me down them against my will.

This book is dedicated to the unstoppable Lydia Hutchinson, publisher of *Performing Songwriter* magazine, who gave me my start as a music writer and believed in me until I began to believe in myself. Thank you, Lydia, for showing us what a "nut with a good idea" is capable of.

INTRODUCTION

What is rock? Or to put it another way, what makes one piece of music rock and another something else entirely? What makes one group a rock band and another not? Barrels of ink and acres of forest have been expended analyzing the divergence of rock music styles at the turn of the 1970s, and it is this topic that lies at the heart of this book.

In the mid-1960s, barely a decade out of diapers, rock and roll went through puberty—it developed acne, it noticed girls, and it treated its parents with contempt. The decade was a time of explosive change in America: the Bay of Pigs incident; the assassinations of John F. Kennedy, Robert Kennedy, and Martin Luther King Jr.; the civil rights movement; the first moon landing; the Watts riots; the Vietnam War. And every step of the way, rock music issued its own response to the events around it: Bob Dylan, *Sgt. Pepper's*, heavy metal, Monterey Pop, *Let It Bleed*, Woodstock.

Before 1960, rock and roll was young and not nearly so complicated. The genre was fairly limited to three-minute songs that found either massive airplay or none at all, as stations spun the same thirty songs in constant rotation. Artists were generally part of a machine, only partially invested in their own performance, as often as not recording songs written for them by others. While some artists became immensely popular—Elvis Presley more than any other— rock and roll garnered little respect as a legitimate art form, generally dismissed as lowbrow entertainment for teenagers.

It was largely Bob Dylan and the Beatles, two of the greatest forces in pop culture during the 1960s, that changed all that. Bringing a new literacy and a sense of experimentalism to contemporary music, these two powerhouses literally changed the nature of rock and roll, profoundly influencing acts to step outside of the three-minute pop song boundary and see what the music was capable of. The result was a melding of musical styles like never before—blues, jazz, western, swing, classical, folk, raga, electronica, and avant-garde experimentation found their way into standard rock formats, stretching the boundaries of rock and roll.

More than musical change, the willingness to reach outside of rock and roll's limited paradigm brought about an engagement with the world beyond the front of the stage. Throughout the 1960s, rock music constantly responded to—and subsequently influenced—the culture surrounding it. Heavily impacted by the protest tradition of 1950s folk music, rock artists put themselves in the middle of the fray, providing a soundtrack to a cultural revolution in America. And nowhere was this more apparent than mid-1960s San Francisco:

"There was an interweaving of the rock and roll world and the political world, the world of labor unions and the armed forces and kids and hippies and yippies and weathermen and democrats, mods and rockers, policemen worlds and the drug world, artists, craftsmen, Sierra Clubs and Hell's Angels, women's movements and Black Panthers, gurus, Jesus freaks, punks, lawyers, doctors, and Indians—you get the picture."[1]

San Francisco rock and its accompanying anti-establishment message created an unprecedented epicenter of counterculture, drawing the nation's youth by the thousands to the ground zero of Haight-Ashbury, where bands like the Grateful Dead, Jefferson Airplane, and Big Brother and the Holding Company brought them together under the banner of communal brotherhood. Largely in response to the Beatles and the growing popularity of folk and folk rock (especially Bob Dylan and the Byrds), Bay Area groups engaged the world around them through heavily experimental music that transformed "rock and roll"—music you felt through your feet—into "rock," which expanded into the domains of the head and the heart.

San Francisco rock—known as psychedelic music, largely for the prevalence of psychotropic drugs used by bands and fans to enhance the musical experience—became a powerful social and musical force, influencing artists throughout the world, including acts like the Beatles and Bob Dylan, which had largely influenced psychedelic rock to begin with. Soon the experimental nature of psychedelia helped bring about an explosion of musical styles, including glam, heavy metal, progressive, and southern rock.

In addition to the fracturing of rock into distinct subgenres, the decade saw significant improvements in technology that would allow bands to perform for larger audiences. Sound engineers like Phil Spector and Owsley Stanley designed systems that would broadcast clearer signals over a larger range and put control of the sound in the hands of the artist—a huge improvement over the technically unsophisticated public address systems that bands had traditionally used. This increase in quality and range led to larger concerts, the advent of the music festival, and, by the early 1970s, stadium rock.

Recording technology advanced even faster than performance technology, allowing some artists (most notably those in the progressive genre) to experiment with electronics in ways that had never been dreamed of, creating complicated sonic endeavors that were difficult to reproduce on stage. Soon the album became more than a collection of a few hit singles and a lot of filler material. The Beatles, the Beach Boys, and the Who helped bury the three-minute pop song doctrine with theme albums that treated songs as interdependent elements of a greater collection. By 1967, album sales had overtaken singles sales, and artists were much more involved with the creative process, some even starting their own record labels to control every aspect of their music.

Over the six years covered in this text, album sales in the United States doubled from $1 billion in 1967 to $2 billion in 1973 (80 percent of which comprised rock music), as the multiplication of subgenres created a parallel increase in the population of rock fans.[2] Rock music became a force to be reckoned with, surpassing the financial clout of movies and sports as entertainment options.[3] Unlike sports and movies, however, the rock audience was overwhelmingly young—fans in their teens and twenties—creating a significant social force that was willing to go wherever the music took it.

This collection of young minds with common musical interests—and often concomitant social interests—created a sense of community unlike any rock had seen before. Teenagers at a Grateful Dead concert at San Francisco's Fillmore or a Mike Bloomfield performance at New York's Café Wha? or a Pink Floyd show at London's UFO club shared community-centered social experiences beyond what rock and roll stars had been able to provide them until the mid-1960s. This was particularly true in the populist San Francisco scene in which audience members were themselves treated like part of the performance.

This sense of investment on the part of the young, enthusiastic audience created a social cohesion that helped bring about mass musical gatherings like the 1967 Human Be-In in San Francisco; the 1967 Monterey Pop Festival in Monterey, California; and eventually 1969's Woodstock Music and Art Fair in upstate New York. Such regular congregations of massive, young, energetic crowds made them believe they could change the world, and the new, socially conscious rock music brought with it not only a soundtrack but, as MC5 manager John Sinclair claimed in 1972, a message: "MUSIC IS REVOLUTION. Rock and roll music is one of the most vital revolutionary forces in the West—it blows people all the way back to their senses and makes them feel good, like they're *alive* again in the middle of this monstrous funeral parlor of Western civilization."[4]

It is no overstatement to label rock music, particularly the rock of the late 1960s, revolutionary. Never before or since has rock undergone change on such a massive scale in such a short period of time, bringing about political, social, and cultural changes in its wake. It is this age that I attempt to dissect in this text, when rock was leaving the safe arms of its mother blues and striking out on its own, to be inspired and shaped by the universe around it and ultimately to make its own mark on the world.

NOTES

1. McDonough 1985, vii.
2. Friedlander 1996, 233.
3. Friedlander 1996, 101.
4. London 1984, 102.

TIMELINE: 1967–1973

1967

Annual album sales reach the $1 billion mark in the United States. Album sales are now 82 percent of the market (versus singles), and 54.1 percent of album sales are stereo, marking the labels' trend toward phasing out mono.

Rumors circulate early in the year that the Beatles are either breaking up or combining with the Rolling Stones. Individual Beatles projects include John starring in *How I Won the War*, Ringo acting in *Candy*, and George studying sitar with Ravi Shankar.

January:	The Doors release their self-titled debut album featuring "The End," "Break On Through," and "Light My Fire."
January 14:	The Human Be-In at San Francisco's Golden Gate Park ushers in the age of the rock festival.
January 15:	The Rolling Stones appear on *The Ed Sullivan Show*, changing the lyrics "Let's spend the night together" to "Let's spend some time together."
February:	Jefferson Airplane release *Surrealistic Pillow*, featuring the summer of love classics "White Rabbit" and "Somebody to Love," and creating the hippie mantra "Feed your head."
	Frank Zappa's first album, *Freak Out*, debuts on the American charts.
March:	The Velvet Underground release their Andy Warhol–produced debut, *The Velvet Underground & Nico*.

March 25:	The Who perform their first American concert in New York.
April:	Cream arrives in the United States, where guitarist Eric Clapton is influenced by his exposure to the San Francisco psychedelic scene.
April 7:	Tom Donahue debuts FM "underground radio" at KMPX in San Francisco, challenging the state of affairs in Top 40 radio, which played the same thirty singles over and over.
May:	Scott McKenzie's "San Francisco (Be Sure to Wear Flowers in Your Hair)" becomes a worldwide smash, marking the beginning of the summer of love.
May 1:	Elvis Presley marries Priscilla Anne Beaulieu, the daughter of his commanding officer in Germany.
May 17:	D. A. Pennebaker's Bob Dylan documentary *Dont Look Back* premieres in the United States.
June:	The Beatles release *Sgt. Pepper's Lonely Hearts Club Band*, hailed by many critics as the greatest rock album of all time. Moby Grape release their debut, *Moby Grape*.
June 2:	The KFRC Fantasy Faire and Magic Mountain Music Festival brings 15,000 people together for a concert at San Francisco's Mount Tamalpais.
June 7:	Moby Grape members are arrested for possession of marijuana.
June 16–18:	The Monterey Pop Festival introduces Jimi Hendrix, the Who, Ravi Shankar, Otis Redding, and others to a receptive American audience.
June 25:	The Beatles record "All You Need Is Love" live via satellite from Abbey Road Studios for more than two hundred million viewers.
July:	After a powerful performance at Monterey, Big Brother and the Holding Company receive a $250,000 record deal for *Cheap Thrills* and sign with Bob Dylan's manager, Albert Grossman.
July 17:	Jazz great John Coltrane dies of liver failure.
August 22–September 3:	Cream plays a two-week residency at San Francisco's Fillmore, the basis for the live half of *Wheels of Fire*.
August 26:	Jimi Hendrix's first album, *Are You Experienced?*, debuts on the charts, where it sets a record by remaining in the Top 40 for seventy-seven weeks.
August 27:	Beatles manager Brian Epstein dies of a drug overdose, marking the beginning of the end of the Beatles.
September 17:	The Doors perform on *The Ed Sullivan Show*. After Jim Morrison ignores a lyric change that Sullivan had asked for, they are banned from the show.

October:	Joan Baez and more than 100 others are arrested for blocking the entrance to the Armed Forces Induction Center in Oakland, California. After her release, Baez is arrested in December for doing it again.
October 3:	Folk legend and Bob Dylan mentor Woody Guthrie dies in New York of Huntington's chorea.
October 6:	Locals carry an empty coffin down San Francisco's Haight Street, in a mock funeral marking "the death of the hippie."
October 17:	The rock musical *Hair* opens at New York City's Shakespeare Festival.
October 18:	The first issue of *Rolling Stone*, dated November 9, rolls off the press.
October 22:	Members of the Grateful Dead are arrested on drug charges in San Francisco.
December 9:	Doors frontman Jim Morrison is arrested at a show in New Haven, Connecticut, for obscene references to the policemen in attendance.
December 10:	The twenty-six-year-old Otis Redding is killed in a plane crash, three days after recording "(Sittin' on) the Dock of the Bay," which would become his first No. 1 hit the following March.
December 21:	Mike Nichols' film *The Graduate* premieres with a chart-topping Simon and Garfunkel soundtrack.

1968

Eight rock/pop groups are chosen for the 1968 edition of *Who's Who in America*, signaling an elevation of status of rock performers (previously the Beatles and Elvis Presley were the only rock personalities to make the cut). The new listing includes the Grateful Dead, Jefferson Airplane, Country Joe and the Fish, the Doors, the Mamas and the Papas, the Monkees, the Rolling Stones, and Donovan.

Promoters in London attempt a "great rock and roll revival," booking tours for top 1950s American acts like Bill Haley and the Comets; releasing singles by Bill Haley, Elvis Presley, and Buddy Holly; and attempting to bring back styles associated with the era and its music, such as leather jackets and motorcycles.

| January: | The Beatles launch their entertainment company Apple Corps, featuring a record label, a recording studio, and a clothing store. |
| January 7: | Bob Dylan is elected president of the United States in a "Grass Ballot" poll conducted by KMPX San Francisco. Other winners: |

vice president Paul Butterfield, ambassador to the UN Paul McCartney, attorney general Grateful Dead, secretary of defense Country Joe McDonald.

February 1:   Elvis and Priscilla Presley have their only child, Lisa Marie Presley, in Memphis, Tennessee.

February 12:   Jimi Hendrix receives the key to the city of Seattle and an honorary diploma from Garfield High School, where he had dropped out when he was fourteen.

March 2:   Jim Morrison exposes himself at a show in Miami, Florida, to a crowd of 12,000. Six warrants are filed against him.

March 8:   Bill Graham opens the Fillmore East in New York City.

March 9:   American heavy metal's first two albums, Iron Butterfly's *Heavy* and Blue Cheer's *Vincebus Eruptum*, simultaneously premiere on the U.S. charts.

March 20:   Eric Clapton, Neil Young, Jim Messina, and a dozen others are arrested in Los Angeles for "being at a place where it is suspected marijuana is being used." All are fined and released.

April: Simon and Garfunkel release their finest album, *Bookends*, which spends seven weeks at No. 1, replacing their soundtrack for *The Graduate*, which held the top spot for nine weeks.

April 29:   The rock musical *Hair* makes its Broadway debut at the Biltmore Theater.

May 5:   Buffalo Springfield perform their last concert together.

June: Cream release their double album *Wheels of Fire*, featuring one disc recorded in the studio and one live at the Fillmore in San Francisco.

June 1:   Simon and Garfunkel's "Mrs. Robinson" rises to the top of the singles chart.

July: The Band release *Music from Big Pink* after hiding out with Bob Dylan for several months in upstate New York.

July 1:   Bill Graham renames the Carousel Ballroom the Fillmore West.

July 14:   The film *Easy Rider* debuts in American theaters with one of the first hard-rock soundtracks.

August: Big Brother and the Holding Company release their debut with Janis Joplin, *Cheap Thrills*.

               The Byrds release their seminal country-rock album *Sweetheart of the Rodeo*.

               The Beatles form Apple Records.

	Jimmy Page re-forms the Yardbirds as the New Yardbirds with John Paul Jones, John Bonham, and Robert Plant.
September 28:	The Beatles song "Hey Jude" takes the No. 1 spot for nine weeks—the longest stay for any Beatles song and, at more than seven minutes, the longest song to reach the top spot up to that point.
October:	The New Yardbirds change their name to Led Zeppelin.
October 30–31:	Early Detroit punk band MC5 record two shows for their seminal live album *Kick Out the Jams*.
November:	The Beatles release *The Beatles* (aka *The White Album*) in the United States.
	Janis Joplin leaves Big Brother and the Holding Company.
November 8:	John Lennon and his wife, Cynthia, divorce.
November 13:	The Beatles' animated film *Yellow Submarine* is released in the United States.
December:	Joan Baez releases *Any Day Now*, a tribute album to her friend Bob Dylan.
December 3:	Elvis Presley mounts an impressive comeback performance on NBC that revitalizes his career for years.
December 26:	The festival documentary *Monterey Pop* is released in the United States.

1969

Jerry Wexler and Phil Walden found Capricorn Records in Macon, Georgia, launching the Allman Brothers Band and southern rock to national stardom.

January:	Led Zeppelin release their self-titled debut album.
January 30:	The Beatles give their last performance from the roof of Apple Studios, filmed for the documentary *Let It Be*.
March:	The rock magazine *Creem* debuts in Detroit, Michigan.
	Quicksilver Messenger Service release their finest album, *Happy Trails*.
March 12:	Paul McCartney marries Linda Eastman.
March 20:	John Lennon marries Yoko Ono.
March 25–30:	John Lennon and Yoko Ono hold their first "bed-in" for peace in their Amsterdam hotel room.
April:	The jazz-rock band Chicago release their debut, *Chicago Transit Authority*.
	Bob Dylan makes his foray into country rock with his album *Nashville Skyline*.

April 2:	Twenty-five thousand fans riot at a poorly executed rock festival in Palm Springs, California.
May:	The Who release *Tommy* in the United States, hailed as the first rock opera.
May 3:	Jimi Hendrix is arrested in Toronto for possession of narcotics.
June 7:	Blind Faith launch their short career with a 100,000-strong free concert in London's Hyde Park.
June 20:	A riot at a Los Angeles rock festival results in more than 300 injuries and $50,000 worth of damage.
June 27:	Dozens are arrested and several injured by overzealous police in riot gear at the Denver Pop Festival.
July:	Blind Faith release their only album, *Blind Faith*.
July 3:	Rolling Stones guitarist Brian Jones is found dead in his swimming pool.
August:	Santana release their debut album, *Santana*.
	The Stooges release their self-titled debut album.
August 15–17:	The Woodstock Music and Arts Fair draws more than 400,000 fans to a dairy farm in upstate New York.
October:	The Beatles release *Abbey Road* in the United States.
	Captain Beefheart releases his most celebrated—and most derided—recording, *Trout Mask Replica*.
	Led Zeppelin release *Led Zeppelin II*, their first No. 1, which spends seven weeks at the top.
November:	The Grateful Dead release their seminal live album *Live/Dead*.
	The Rolling Stones release their most acclaimed album, *Let It Bleed*.
November 1:	Elvis Presley reaches the No. 1 spot—his first in seven years and the last in his lifetime—with "Suspicious Minds."
December 6:	The Rolling Stones play the last show of their American tour in Altamont, California, where 850 spectators are injured and four killed, one of them murdered by Hell's Angels right in front of the stage.
December 20:	Peter, Paul and Mary chart their only No. 1 hit and last single, John Denver's "Leaving on a Jet Plane."

1970

February:	James Taylor releases his breakthrough debut album, *Sweet Baby James*.

February 28:	Simon and Garfunkel's most popular song, "Bridge over Troubled Water," begins a six-week stay on top of the charts.
March 5:	The FCC issues a warning to FM radio stations to beware of drug references in the songs they play on the air.
March 11:	Crosby, Stills, Nash & Young release their masterpiece *Déjà vu*.
March 20:	David Bowie marries Angela Barnett.
March 26:	The documentary *Woodstock* is released in American theaters, winning the Academy Award for Best Documentary.
April 11:	The Beatles' "Let It Be" debuts at No. 6 on the charts, the highest entry position by any act to date.
April 26:	Jean-Luc Godard's Rolling Stones documentary *Sympathy for the Devil* finally reaches American theaters two years after it is finished.
May:	Black Sabbath release their debut album *Black Sabbath*.
	The Beatles release their final album *Let It Be* (though much of it was recorded before their 1969 *Abbey Road*).
May 13:	The film *Let It Be* premieres in the United States, marking the end of the Beatles as a group.
July:	Creedence Clearwater Revival release their most acclaimed album, *Cosmo's Factory*.
July 4:	250,000 fans gather for the Atlanta International Pop Festival, one of the last major rock festivals of the period.
September:	Santana release their second album, *Abraxas*, featuring their memorable songs "Black Magic Woman" and "Oye Como Va."
September 18:	Jimi Hendrix passes away after taking too many sleeping pills and choking to death.
October 4:	Janis Joplin dies of a heroin overdose in a Los Angeles motel room.
November:	Eric Clapton releases *Layla and Other Assorted Love Songs* with Derek and the Dominos.
November 27:	George Harrison releases his first post-Beatles album, *All Things Must Pass*, which spends seven weeks at No. 1.
December 6:	The film *Gimme Shelter* is released in the United States, chronicling the Rolling Stones' tragic 1969 concert at Altamont Speedway.
December 26:	George Harrison's "My Sweet Lord" peaks at No. 1—making him the first Beatle to reach the top after the band's breakup.

1971

January:	Alice Cooper releases his first Top 40 album, *Love It to Death*, featuring the hit song "Eighteen."
	Black Sabbath release their breakthrough album *Paranoid*.
March 1:	James Taylor appears on the cover of *Time* magazine with the subtitle: "The New Rock: Bittersweet and Low."
March 12–13:	The Allman Brothers Band record four shows in New York that become one of the greatest live albums in rock, *Live at Fillmore East*.
April 10:	Carole King's *Tapestry* begins a fifteen-week stay in the No. 1 spot on the charts, eventually becoming the fifth longest charting album in any genre.
April 23:	The Rolling Stones release *Sticky Fingers*, featuring the classics "Brown Sugar" and "Wild Horses."
May:	The term "heavy metal" first appears in the press in *Creem* magazine.
May 20:	Marvin Gaye releases his soul-stirring *What's Going On*, one of Motown's most successful albums.
June:	Joni Mitchell releases her critically praised album *Blue*.
June 27:	The Fillmore East closes in New York City.
July:	The Allman Brothers Band release *Live at Fillmore East*.
July 3:	Jim Morrison dies of a heart attack in Paris soon after retiring from music.
August 1:	George Harrison's Concert for Bangladesh at Madison Square Garden begins a trend of benefit concerts to bring an end to third-world poverty.
October 29:	The Allman Brothers Band guitarist Duane Allman dies in a motorcycle accident in Macon, Georgia.
November:	Led Zeppelin release their seminal album *Led Zeppelin IV*, featuring the classic "Stairway to Heaven."
November 10:	Frank Zappa releases the bizarre tour documentary *200 Motels* in America.
December 7:	A fire at Montreux Casino in Switzerland destroys all of Frank Zappa and the Mothers of Invention's equipment, inspiring the Deep Purple song "Smoke on the Water."

1972

January:	Jackson Browne releases his debut, *Jackson Browne: Saturate Before Using*.

January 15:	Don McLean's "American Pie" reaches the top of the charts for a four-week stay.
January 27:	Gospel singer Mahalia Jackson dies—40,000 attend her funeral in Chicago.
February:	Neil Young releases *Harvest*, one of the best-selling albums of the year and one of his most critically praised.
April:	Deep Purple release *Machine Head*, featuring the heavy-metal classic "Smoke on the Water."
May:	Jethro Tull release their first U.S. No. 1, *Thick as a Brick*.
May 12:	The Rolling Stones release their eclectic album *Exile on Main St.*
June:	David Bowie releases *The Rise and Fall of Ziggy Stardust and the Spiders from Mars*.
July 1:	The rock musical *Hair* closes on Broadway after 1,742 shows.
November 6:	Billy Murcia, drummer for the New York Dolls, dies during their first European tour.
November 11:	Berry Oakley, bass player for the Allman Brothers Band, dies in a motorcycle accident eerily similar to that of Duane Allman one year earlier.
November 25:	Los Angeles radio station KROQ ushers in the era of "stadium rock" with a concert at the L.A. Memorial Coliseum.

1973

Annual album sales in the United States pass the $2 billion mark.

January 14:	Elvis Presley's *Aloha from Hawaii* is seen by more than one billion viewers around the world.
March 8:	Ron "Pigpen" McKernan of the Grateful Dead dies of a stomach hemorrhage.
March 17:	Pink Floyd's *Dark Side of the Moon* debuts on the American charts, where it remains in the Top 200 for a record 741 weeks.
July 3:	David Bowie retires his character Ziggy Stardust at a show in London, captured on film by D. A. Pennebaker for his documentary *Ziggy Stardust and the Spiders from Mars*.
July 28:	The Watkins Glen concert in upstate New York sets an attendance record with more than 600,000 fans who came to see the Grateful Dead, the Allman Brothers Band, and the Band.
August:	The New York Dolls release their self-titled debut album.
September:	Lynyrd Skynyrd release their debut album *Pronounced Leh-Nerd Skin-Nerd*, which includes their signature song "Freebird."

September 19: Gram Parsons, who took the Byrds in a country-rock direction, dies of a heroin overdose.

December: *Creem* magazine readers vote the New York Dolls both the Best New Group and the Worst New Group of the year.

THE PSYCHEDELIC EXPERIENCE

San Francisco has always been a bellwether of cultural revolution in America. As early as the environmental and labor movements of the 1900s and as recent as the digital revolution of the 1990s, California's Bay Area often seems to be riding the first wave of change.

Part of this phenomenon rests with the fact that San Francisco has spent the better part of the last century as the center of the nation's counterculture ideology, and it is from the well of counterculture that popular culture springs forth. Change, simply put, comes from those who want change and are willing to rebel against the status quo to get it. It was this rebellious spirit, this thirst for change, that inspired a small number of local bands in 1965 to take San Francisco by storm and create an entirely new form of blues-based rock called psychedelic music—an experimental, drug-enhanced, free-form style that pushed the three-minute pop song envelope and set fire to the American music scene.

The pioneers of psychedelic music were the ideological children of the San Francisco beatniks, who dubbed them "a little hip" and thus, "hippies." The chemical and sexual experimentation the beatniks were known for, as well as their left-wing politics and liberal attitudes concerning personal freedoms, were passed down to their sixties counterparts, and their musical attitudes reflected their lifestyle—music was a communal activity, belonging to everyone, and its practitioners were beholden to no one.

Amid the highly charged political and social climate of mid-1960s San Francisco, with the Vietnam War, union strife, Berkeley activism, equal rights debates, and the specter of McCarthyism still looming large, the hippies were born. Their doctrine of individualism and personal freedom spoke to a generation of young people eager to break free of conformist expectations, and at the center of it all, carrying the message, was the music.

IN THE BEGINNING, THERE WERE THE CHARLATANS

Few genres of music can trace their origins back to a single person, place, or date that can be said to have started it all. Jazz may have begun with faceless dixie musicians on Mississippi riverboats, folk with wandering rail and dam workers, and heavy metal with any number of British hard-rock bands, but critics and historians generally agree that psychedelic music started with a band called the Charlatans on June 1, 1965, when they played their first gig at the Red Dog Saloon in Virginia City, Nevada.

The Charlatans were born in 1964, two years after Richard Olsen, a music major at San Francisco University, met George Hunter, who was dabbling in electronic music at the Tape Music Center in the Haight-Ashbury district—a neighborhood that would later become the heart of the psychedelic scene. The two formed the group with guitarist/vocalist Mike Wilhelm—Hunter's childhood friend—and pianist Michael Ferguson, who at the time owned an antique store. With Olsen on bass and Hunter learning the tambourine and autoharp, the quartet picked up drummer Sam Linde (who was quickly replaced by Dan Hicks) and became one of San Francisco's first rock bands.

The group was short on talent but long on presentation. Hunter, the group's leader, banked their success on their style as much as their music. The band members dressed like they were appearing as extras in an early John Wayne movie—long hair, boots, vests, string ties, wing collars, and cowboy hats—and their repertoire ranged from folk standards like "Wabash Cannonball" and "Alabama Bound" to covers of Chuck Berry and the Coasters. Hunter was hoping that the nostalgic visuals combined with their loose, bluesy renditions of folk/rock songs would land them a film or television deal.

In early 1965, Chandler Laughlin, the Red Dog Saloon's bartender, came to San Francisco to book the Byrds for a gig at his venue but happened upon the Charlatans instead, and invited them back to Virginia City for a stint as the house band. The Red Dog was perfectly suited to the band's style—a mellow venue in an Old West town. "It was the first hip commune, I mean, like before acid was big," recalled Olsen in a 1970 *Rolling Stone* interview. "It was so groovy. It was like the beginning of this movement."[1]

It was, indeed, the beginning of psychedelic rock, also known as acid rock for reasons that will become clear. The Charlatans' first performance at the Red Dog was essentially an audition for the staff of thirty. The band members took acid (LSD) before the show—most of them for only the first or second time—and could barely play their instruments, but proved to be highly entertaining nonetheless. The Red Dog hired them for $100 a week plus room and board to play three or four sets six nights a week, plus a Saturday matinee.

As the band's reputation grew, other musicians and "long-hairs" from all over the West Coast began to visit the town, and for a brief period the city was the new scene, until just after Labor Day when police began coming down hard on the Red Dog for its alleged role as the center of a drug culture. But the Charlatans were essentially a San Francisco band, and with frequent trips back to the Bay for shows or recording attempts, they became underground heroes in the city's infant rock scene, spawning a major cultural movement that changed the face of rock music.

Unfortunately, the group was not terribly talented or commercially appealing, and though they were the first psychedelic rock group to sign with a major label (in late 1965), they got almost nothing from the contract, and released only one album before they broke up in 1969, after four years of standing still while the scene exploded around them. Besides pioneering an offbeat visual style and incorporating drugs into their musical performances, the group introduced the use of psychedelic posters, which became a cultural phenomenon of its own (see Psychedelic Posters). The Charlatans were, according to legendary promoter Bill Graham, "what San Francisco really was."[2]

 PSYCHEDELIC POSTERS

The first stirrings of psychedelic music that started with the Charlatans in 1965 were accompanied by a new art form that the band used to promote its shows. Bands had used handbills and posters for years to get the word out, but early psychedelic artists employed highly stylized posters that were not just promoting the art of music—they were art forms themselves.

George Hunter and Michael Ferguson are generally credited with creating the first psychedelic concert poster—known among graphic aficionados as "the Seed"—advertising their band as "The Amazing Charlatans" opening the Red Dog Saloon in Virginia City, Nevada, in June 1965. The black-and-white hand-drawn design features renderings of each band-member's face as well as a group drawing, and text that uses a mix of different fonts, sizes, and upper- and lowercase letters, surrounded by elaborate doodling to give the poster a busy, detailed look. Although the poster is rather tame by the standards of later psychedelic art, it was a whole new direction in design for concert-promotion paraphernalia, which up to that point was merely informative—featuring the names of the acts in uniform fonts, with maybe a photo of the feature artist at the top—and thus visually uninteresting.

By 1966, Family Dog and Bill Graham, the two main concert promoters in San Francisco, were hiring local artists to design exciting posters to match the mood of the experimental shows they were presenting. Wes Wilson was their first regular designer of psychedelic concert posters, designing two- or three-color

PSYCHEDELIC POSTERS *(continued)*

text-heavy bills that often incorporated wavy lettering wrapping itself around heavily distorted faces or bodies. It was rumored that Graham complained about the illegibility of some of the posters, but Wilson's designs were progenitors of the form and have since become valuable collector's items.

Family Dog soon began hiring Stanley "Mouse" Miller and Alton Kelley of Mouse Studios to design posters for their shows at the Avalon Ballroom. Miller and Kelley reversed Wilson's style by using large animations in the center of a poster and augmenting them with stylized text flowing all around, making the posters easier to read than Wilson's crowded text collages. Miller and Kelley designed most of the Family Dog posters through 1966, drawing on graphics and photography they found in art books, and eventually designing the cover art for a number of Grateful Dead albums.

By the end of 1966, Family Dog was also employing a well-known local artist named Victor Moscoso, whose posters—though sometimes as difficult to read as Wilson's—were almost able to hypnotize the viewer with vivid colors and incredibly detailed graphics that foreshadowed the acid-rock trips they were advertising. Inspired by Miller and Kelley's work, a surf artist named Rick Griffin began designing witty and clever posters for the Avalon Ballroom, featuring stunning, sometimes zany graphics that eventually became famous, like the "flying eyeball" advertising a Jimi Hendrix performance, and an Avalon poster for a Grateful Dead show that became the cover art for their 1969 album *Aoxomoxoa*.

Wilson, Miller, Kelley, Moscoso, and Griffin were the "big five" San Francisco artists who brought a unique visual art form to the world of psychedelia, and just like the music, the posters quickly became an international phenomenon. In Detroit, Gary Grimshaw was designing posters for the Grande Ballroom similar to those of Miller and Kelley, creating some stunning visual promotions for Motor City's proto-punk band MC5. In Boston, Massachusetts, and Santa Cruz, California, Jim Phillips designed vivid, almost frightening posters for the Doors, Moby Grape, and many others. From Texas to Canada and on both coasts, local artists were imitating and evolving psychedelic poster art. The practice even spread to London, where Michael English and Nigel Weymouth used metallic ink to create very slick designs for the UFO club, the Saville Theatre, and the Middle Earth Club, places where psychedelic-influenced musical styles such as glam rock and art rock took root.

Just as psychedelic music became an international commodity and hippie symbols became marketing slogans, by the early 1970s, the original hand-drawn psychedelic posters had become glossy, overused advertising tools, losing much of their status as individual works of art. Though psychedelic-inspired graphics continued to appear on posters and album covers, the form was no longer new, and thus its heyday had passed.

OUT OF THE BASEMENTS AND INTO THE HALLS

Psychedelic music took another major step on October 16, 1965, when the first large local rock show was held in Longshoreman's Hall in San Francisco, featuring Jefferson Airplane, the Marbles, the Great Society, and the Charlatans. Until then, local promoter Chet Helms held small dance parties in Big Brother and the Holding Company's basement at 1090 Page Street in the Haight-Ashbury district. Helms was the promoter for The Family Dog, a local commune-turned-production company that put on small, multiband shows. The October show, titled "A Tribute to Dr. Strange," was the advent of San Francisco's dance-hall scene, a crucial step in bringing psychedelic music to the masses.

Family Dog sponsored two more events by the end of the year featuring the Charlatans, the Lovin' Spoonful, and Frank Zappa and the Mothers of Invention. In December, the career of rock's greatest promoter, Bill Graham, was launched when he rented the Fillmore Auditorium, a second-story ballroom in one of the city's rundown neighborhoods. Graham was manager of the avant-garde San Francisco Mime Troupe, and rented the hall for a fundraising concert featuring Jefferson Airplane, the Great Society, and the Warlocks. Once he got a taste for it, Graham decided to go into concert promotion full time, and his name became synonymous with the Bay Area ballroom scene.

Initially Graham and Family Dog alternated weekends at the Fillmore Auditorium, but Graham was a much more savvy businessman, and he soon rose to dominate the live scene in the Bay Area. By early 1966, dance-hall performances had spread to other local ballrooms, including Avalon, Winterland (a converted ice-skating rink), and Carousel (which Bill Graham renamed Fillmore West when he bought it in 1968).

Dance-hall shows quickly became more than mere concerts; they were sensual extravaganzas incorporating the defining elements of psychedelic music: light shows, LSD, and hours of musical improvisation by bands that were often as drugged as their audience. This scene was a world away from the three-minute Top 40 rock of 1965, played by short-haired or mop-topped lads with matching outfits and innocent love songs. The experiments being played out in basement jam sessions in the Haight carried over into the ballrooms for a wider audience, drawing hippies to San Francisco in droves.

SAN FRANCISCO BALLROOMS

The San Francisco sound was born in the basements and living rooms of local bands living in Haight-Ashbury communes, such as Big Brother and the Holding Company at 1090 Page Street, the Grateful Dead at 710 Ashbury, and Jefferson Airplane at 2400 Fulton. Jefferson Airplane also performed as house band at the Matrix, a small folk club owned by one of their guitarists, Marty Balin. When the sound became popular enough to attract larger audiences, promoters began booking run-down ballrooms for small performances, often serving as fundraisers for local arts organizations or political causes.

After organizing a small show at the Ark in Sausalito in 1965, a local commune dubbed themselves The Family Dog and began organizing larger performances, with Chet Helms serving as their promoter. The first large show, titled "A Tribute to Dr. Strange," was held on October 16, 1965, at Longshoreman's Hall, with Jefferson Airplane, the Marbles, the Great Society, and the Charlatans performing.

The following month, Bill Graham featured Jefferson Airplane at a fundraising concert for his radical performance group San Francisco Mime Troupe, held at the Calliope Ballroom on Howard Street. In December, Graham held another fund-raiser with Jefferson Airplane, the Great Society, and the Warlocks at the Fillmore Auditorium in one of the city's poorer neighborhoods. Graham and Family Dog began sharing the Fillmore for shows and soon branched out to other venues, including Avalon, Winterland, and Carousel. Ken Kesey and his Merry Pranksters collaborated with shows they called acid tests, captured in Tom Wolfe's 1968 classic *The Electric Kool-Aid Acid Test*.

The key feature of these venues was that they were ballrooms rather than concert halls, so they had large, open spaces for dancing and mingling rather than fixed seating. Audiences were participating in the music rather than acting as passive recipients, an important factor in the evolution of the psychedelic scene. Performances soon included light shows, slide shows, costumes, theater sets, microphones in the audience area, and of course, plenty of LSD. Over the next few years, similar ballrooms would spring up around the country, including the Electric Factory in Philadelphia, the Kinetic Playground in Chicago, the Grande Ballroom in Detroit, and the Boston Tea Party in Boston.

Throughout 1966 and 1967, there were shows almost every weekend at at least one of the Bay Area venues. Family Dog proved to be mediocre at the business end of the music industry, and soon disappeared to leave the hard-nosed Graham as chief promoter and one of the most pivotal figures in the San Francisco music scene. In 1968 he bought the Carousel Ballroom and renamed it Fillmore West, opening a Fillmore East in New York only weeks later, converting a vacant movie house on Second Avenue. During the short time they were open, some of the most memorable concerts in America were held at these venues, including an eleven-night residency for Cream that became half of their memorable 1968 release *Wheels of Fire*.

SAN FRANCISCO BALLROOMS *(continued)*

Graham used his status and connections to continue hosting social and political benefits, as well as to bring artists such as B. B. King, Ravi Shankar, Miles Davis, and Muddy Waters to receptive white audiences. He also managed or helped bring to fame a number of significant San Francisco musicians, including the Grateful Dead, Quicksilver Messenger Service, Big Brother and the Holding Company, Santana, and Jefferson Airplane. In 1971 Graham closed both Fillmores and ran shows out of Winterland—a converted ice-skating rink—for the next decade, ending an era of ballroom shows that served as an important link between the basements of the Haight and the arenas of the world.

THE PSYCHEDELIC CONNECTION

Few would dispute that the psychedelic movement would have developed much differently—or not at all—without the widespread use of drugs. Marijuana was as common as cigarettes among local bands and their followers, and hardly a month went by that some performer or another was not jailed for its use, and in the case of harsh sentences, many a promising musical career ended with a poorly timed joint.

The mover of the movement, however, was lysergic acid diethylamide—also known as LSD, or acid—which was not only a powerful hallucinogen but also fairly new in the 1960s and still legal to own until late 1966. Because of its heavy use in the burgeoning psychedelic scene by performers and audience members alike, and because of the effect it had on the music of the period, one of the most important contributors to psychedelic music was not a musician at all but a local chemist and sound engineer by the name of Augustus Owsley Stanley III.

Owsley—the name Stanley was best known by, though he was called "Bear" by local musicians—was a regular in the Berkeley scene in 1963, where he began producing methedrine until his lab was raided in 1965. After relocating to Los Angeles for a short period of time during which he started to make LSD in large amounts, he returned to San Francisco and began supplying the drug to Ken Kesey, a local writer (author of *One Flew over the Cuckoo's Nest*) and veteran of the Stanford University LSD experiments. Kesey was the leader of a bizarre assemblage of folks who called themselves the Merry Pranksters, a wild bunch of LSD prophets who enjoyed dressing in Day-Glo colors and pulling stunts such as their famous cross-country trip in a painted school bus to meet East Coast LSD guru Timothy Leary, an event chronicled in vivid detail by Tom Wolfe in *The Electric Kool-Aid Acid Test*.

In November 1965, Kesey, supplied by Owsley, sponsored the first of a series of LSD parties known as acid tests, which became the format for many of the area's psychedelic shows. Often using the Warlocks as a house band (soon renaming themselves the Grateful Dead), the acid tests were the original all-night raves, featuring hypnotic light shows, hour after hour of improvisational rock (sometimes a single song would last forty-five minutes), and copious amounts of LSD. In January 1966, Kesey's bunch put on the Trips Festival at Longshoreman's Hall. With Native American imagery, slide shows, strobe lights, theater, and of course rock bands, it is remembered as the most elaborate of the acid parties.

Owsley and Kesey brought to the psychedelic scene a visceral quality, influencing musicians and fans to experience the music beyond its immediate aural sensation. The word "psychedelic" comes from the Greek, meaning "to reveal or make manifest the mind and soul." Early writers of the psychedelic experience, mainly scientists and philosophers, describe it as bringing forth the ability to see sounds as colors, in essence, enabling "synesthesia"—the ability to cross the senses. This is what musicians were trying to capture in their music; using heavily distorted sounds, drones, feedback, the atonal qualities of Indian raga, and long, wandering improvisations that did not begin or end as much as slip into and out of being, psychedelic musicians were out to make music so pure that listeners would be able to see it.

By late 1966, LSD was outlawed, though it continued to play a large part in psychedelic performances. Kesey soon moved to Mexico to escape jail for miscellaneous drug charges. Owsley was not so lucky; his lab was eventually raided, and he spent two years in prison. But before he was arrested, he convinced the Grateful Dead to pay attention to how their sound reached the audience, and after he was released, he designed one of the most complex and high-quality sound systems in the country for the band's live performances, recentering control of the sound on the musicians so that they could hear what the audience was hearing—a major step forward in the advancement of live music.

THE SAN FRANCISCO SOUND

Although San Francisco bands were out to re-create the psychedelic experience with music, that does not mean every group sounded alike. One of the motives of the larger movement was nonconformity, and there were as many styles of psychedelic music as there were bands that claimed to play it. A shortlist of acts that were the earliest and most influential purveyors of the San Francisco sound would include not only the Charlatans but Jefferson Airplane, the Grateful Dead, Moby Grape, Big Brother and the Holding Company, Country Joe and the Fish, and Quicksilver Messenger Service. Many of these bands evolved out of folk outfits that had been influenced by the recent experimental sounds of the Beatles, and as they took up electric instruments, they found that they would soon influence the Liverpool quartet themselves in ways they had not imagined.

Jefferson Airplane

Jefferson Airplane—borrowing their name from a friend's dog, Blind Thomas Jefferson Airplane—were one of the driving forces behind the San Francisco scene, seeming to accomplish what the Charlatans could not. The Charlatans created the sound, but Airplane made it sound good. The Charlatans got almost nothing out of their label deal, but only two months later, in December 1965, Airplane became the first band on the scene to win a major recording contract, signing with RCA for a $25,000 advance. Airplane brought commercial appeal to psychedelic music with a trio of talented guitarists—Marty Balin, Paul Kantner, and Jorma Kaukonen—and, after their first release, their new vocalist Grace Slick, who joined the group in 1966 from the Great Society.

Balin owned the Matrix, a local folk-rock club at which Airplane performed regularly in 1965. The band actually started out as folkies, as many of the psychedelic groups did. Balin and Signe Anderson would sing for the group as they covered standards and electric versions of folk ballads in an early Beatles style. As the band experimented more and slid into their role as rockers, they became a popular local attraction—but they were still just a local band, even after their first album in 1966. Anderson then became pregnant and left the group, replaced by Grace Slick, whose fiery voice and dominating presence would bring the group to national prominence with *Surrealistic Pillow*

Jefferson Airplane performing in California, circa 1967. Courtesy of the Library of Congress.

in 1967, for some the theme album to the summer of love. Featuring the hits "Somebody to Love" and "White Rabbit"—the latter banned from some radio stations for its blatant drug references—the album went to No. 3 and has since become a classic of the era.

Jefferson Airplane got more national recognition after their appearance at the Monterey Pop Festival later that year (a launching pad for many Bay Area artists) and became the San Francisco ambassadors of hippie goodwill, repeatedly calling for brotherhood and open-mindedness through their flower-power music. After a few successful years playing major festivals like Woodstock and Altamont in 1969, and releasing excellent albums such as *Crown of Creation* and *Volunteers*, the band fell apart in 1971, but was re-formed by some members later as Jefferson Starship, a popular sci-fi themed band through the 1970s.

The Grateful Dead

Jefferson Airplane were the biggest of the area's bands, but none of the groups could match the Grateful Dead for stamina. Renowned for their seemingly endless jam sessions as well as their thirty-year touring schedule, the tireless band left an indelible mark on the pages of rock history and America's counterculture movement.

As the Warlocks, the group was essentially an electrified version of their earlier folk/blues/bluegrass outfit, Mother McCree's Uptown Jug Champions. Led

The Grateful Dead, 1968. Courtesy of the Library of Congress.

by guitarist/singer Jerry Garcia (a beloved teddy bear of a man who, to many, *was* the Grateful Dead) and featuring guitarist Bob Weir and keyboardist/harmonica player Ron "Pigpen" McKernan, the Jug Champions picked up bassist Phil Lesh and drummer Bill Kreutzmann in 1965. As the Jug Champions, gigs were hard to find, so when a music-store owner offered to loan them equipment if they became a rock band, they jumped at the chance and, with their recently acquired members, became the Warlocks.

For about six months they were an average rock-and-roll outfit, playing blues and rock standards for straitlaced crowds. After they got a regular gig in a Fremont club in 1965, they began to play longer, louder sets, experimenting with their sound and, as often as not, driving listeners right out of the room. They had begun to take acid, and it quickly seeped into their music. Before long, Ken Kesey invited the group to jam for a weekend at his house in La Honda with the Merry Pranksters. This was essentially the first acid test, and a coming-out party for the new, experimental Warlocks.

The band stopped playing standard gigs altogether and devoted themselves almost exclusively to acid tests. By spring of 1966, they had outgrown all former pretensions and become underground celebrities. To celebrate this rebirth, they decided to change their name by opening up an *Oxford English Dictionary*, immediately spying *grateful dead*—a folklore term for deceased who must walk the earth performing good deeds—and adopting the moniker for their new incarnation.

By 1967 the Dead were major cult figures and signed to Warner Brothers Records for their self-titled debut album, which unfortunately failed to capture their unique live presence—an oversight corrected on subsequent recordings, especially their first fully live album, the seminal 1969 release *Live/Dead*. At the turn of the decade, the group was a unique phenomenon, inspiring such loyalty from their fans that they drove around from show to show and created a whole lifestyle based on the populist, community-centered example of their musical heroes. The Dead often played shows for free, and sometimes declined major performance opportunities to protest promoters who took unfair advantage of fans. The group's focus on their listeners paid off in spades, as the band became one of the most successful touring acts in history, listed as one of the top grossing tours in North America even in their last few years in the 1990s—all this despite the fact that their songs rarely reached the charts, with zero albums and only one song making the Top 10 in their thirty-year history.

Many students of the rock era believe that the psychedelic movement was short-lived, lasting essentially until 1967 when San Francisco was "discovered" by the wanna-be hipsters, and all of the real bands moved away or broke up. It's true that few of the psychedelic impresarios remained by 1970, but for decades—until 1995, when Jerry Garcia died of a heart attack—fans could get a taste of the time and its mood by becoming "Deadheads"—following the Grateful Dead from show to show, living in a supportive, community-driven time capsule that strove to adhere to the original populist ideals of the psychedelic era.

Moby Grape

Moby Grape, a talented act that formed in the Bay in 1966, were as fleeting as the Dead were eternal. Featuring guitarist Skip Spence (originally the guitarist for Quicksilver Messenger Service and then Jefferson Airplane's drummer before joining Moby Grape), L.A. folkie Peter Lewis, and a trio that played in the Frantics in Seattle—Jerry Miller, Bob Mosley, and Don Stevenson—the Grape burst onto the scene in 1967 with a stunning, self-titled debut album. In one of the most egregious marketing blunders in rock history, the band's label CBS Records released five singles (plus B-sides) simultaneously, flooding the market with excellent but over-hyped songs that made it impossible for sales to live up to expectations.

Had the label released the singles one at a time, as was customary, several of them could have easily been smashes, as the band demonstrated tight, beautifully composed psychedelic blues that showed strong commercial appeal. The group never lived up to the hype of their first album, but the record did reach No. 24 on the charts, and their excellent follow-up *Wow* reached No. 20 a year later. Though national fame eluded them, the band became one of the most popular local groups until the downward spiral begun by their ill-fated first release, coupled with poor label decisions and Spence's slide into mental illness, ended the group by 1970. A certain amount of myth sprung up around the band in the decades since, as it is hard to listen to their first album and not imagine, if the group had been handled differently, what might have been.

Janis Joplin, 1969. Courtesy of Photofest.

Janis Joplin/Big Brother and the Holding Company

For another San Francisco band, a management decision gave a relatively unknown blues ensemble more fame than they probably expected. Big Brother and the Holding Company was, along with the Warlocks and Airplane, one of the first psychedelic groups to grow out of the Haight-Ashbury scene in 1965. Their house at 1090 Page was the site of some of the early jam sessions that became the psychedelic ballroom scene. Chet Helms, who coordinated the gigs for Family Dog productions, suggested to Big Brother that they get a female lead singer and recommended his friend Janis Joplin.

Joplin was originally a coffeehouse singer from Port Arthur, Texas, who had come to San Francisco in 1963, playing regularly at the North Beach Coffee Gallery. After becoming addicted to amphetamines, Joplin returned to Texas in 1965 to dry out and give college another try, but was induced to return to the Bay to front Big Brother in 1966. After a limited debut album on a small label, the group caught national attention with a stunning performance at 1967's Monterey Pop Festival, after which Joplin was hailed as one of the most talented white blues singers in the country.

The sudden fame was both good and bad news for the band. On the one hand, they were stars, and their subsequent recording, *Cheap Thrills*, was a smash hit and an enduring classic, thanks largely to Joplin's wild, full-throated delivery. On the other hand, much of the media focus was on Joplin, a relative newcomer to the band, which irked its long-standing members and caused such tension during the recording of *Cheap Thrills* that Joplin left the group soon after its release to pursue solo projects.

To what extent Big Brother deserved its success is still open to debate. The group clearly owes a debt to Joplin, as it is doubtful they would have been remembered as anything more than a local band without her extraordinary talent, which garnered them such widespread attention. Indeed little was heard from them after Joplin left, even though they stayed together for several years following her departure. On the other hand, those who were there recall Big Brother as an entertaining blues ensemble in their own right, and before Joplin came along, the group had secured their place as one of the founding bands of the psychedelic scene.

Quicksilver Messenger Service

Perhaps the least successful band of the period, Quicksilver Messenger Service, most typified the San Francisco sound. Not dissimilar in style to the Grateful Dead, with long, improvised jam sessions and live performances overshadowing their recording work, the two groups often played shows together, billed as "The Quick and The Dead." Constant roster changes, however, limited the group's development, with their guitarist Skip Spence defecting to Jefferson Airplane to play drums, and their lead singer Dino Valenti imprisoned for several years on a drug charge. Even though the group formed in 1964, it was only after a successful performance at the Monterey Pop Festival that they began recording, releasing *Quicksilver Messenger Service* in 1968 and the highly acclaimed *Happy Trails* in 1969. Only two of the original members remained in the group for these albums, and subsequent recordings were largely ignored, with all of the original band members gone by 1972.

Country Joe and the Fish

One of the more locally popular—but commercially unsuccessful—of the founding San Francisco bands was the outspoken and politically charged folk-rock act Country Joe and the Fish. Country Joe was local activist Joe

McDonald, who established the Instant Action Jug Band in 1965 with guitarist Barry Melton. Rounding out the group in 1966 to create a full-on psychedelic rock ensemble, CJ and the Fish maintained deep ties to the Berkeley community and its culture of protest. The fact that the band focused on societal issues at the cost of self-promotion contributed to their limited commercial success, but they were widely admired for their use of music to effect social change.

Country Joe and the Fish were a lively, imaginative group with a strong local following, but they are remembered best for their "I Feel Like I'm Fixin' to Die Rag," a Vietnam-protest ditty that made "One, two, three, what are we fighting for?" a popular antiwar slogan. The line, unfortunately, did not seem to apply to the group members, who constantly fought among themselves through their short history, ending the band's run by 1970.

ARE YOU GOING TO SAN FRANCISCO?

The newly born San Francisco scene barely got out of diapers when it began attracting musicians from all over the country, drawn by rumors of unbridled experimentation (both musical and chemical); sudden media attention lavished on the city's scene in 1966 and 1967 by *Time*, *Newsweek*, and *Life*; the recording contracts Bay-Area bands were receiving; and, of course, the incredible music. Songs about the city filled the airwaves, including the Flowerpot Men's "Let's Go to San Francisco"; Eric Burdon's "San Franciscan Nights"; and, most famously, Scott McKenzie's popular "San Francisco (Be Sure to Wear Flowers in Your Hair)." The first wave of psychedelia was a local phenomenon, but by late 1966 it was being exported around the globe as new artists were being imported to the Bay, bringing their own styles of blues-based improv and adding to the city's already swelling musical appeal.

The Steve Miller Band

One of the early newcomers was a young Wisconsin guitarist named Steve Miller, who came to the Bay by way of Chicago with his childhood friend Boz Scaggs, setting up shop as the Miller Blues Band in 1966. Within a year, the talented duo added three more members and earned a large local following as the Steve Miller Band, signing with Capitol Records for the extraordinarily large sum of $50,000 after an excellent performance at the Monterey Pop Festival. Miller not only was a gifted guitarist—taught from a young age by family friend Les Paul—but managed to translate his clean playing and smooth voice into commercially appealing tunes. Four of his first six albums managed to break into the Top 40, and while his more commercial releases were not true psychedelic improv-fests, his heavy-hitting status brought even more attention to San Francisco music and elevated the status of other bands, who could now demand more from the record companies that seemed to suddenly be signing every string-plucker in town.

Santana

One aspect of psychedelic music that is, unfortunately, overshadowed by the drug use is the diversity of musical styles involved; from Indian raga to electronic experimentation to heavily distorted guitars to bluegrass, psychedelic music is the product of whatever instrument the musician walks into the room with. Carlos Santana brought a high-energy combination of jazz, funk, and Afro-Latin sound to the psychedelic scene with his band's break-out performance at Woodstock in 1969, making them instant Latin rock gods.

Carlos Santana formed his band in 1967 San Francisco, while the scene was burning at its brightest. The Mexican-born leader augmented his precise, imaginative guitar work with two conga drummers, giving the band a distinct sound that earned them

Carlos Santana, 1969. Courtesy of Photofest.

prominence locally. Their well-timed debut album, *Santana*, released immediately after their Woodstock appearance, put them on the charts early, reaching the No. 4 spot; their follow-up albums *Abraxas* and *Santana III* topped the charts in 1970 and 1971, respectively. Though latecomers to the scene, Santana brought with them exotic polyrhythms and powerful, emotive guitarwork that made their sound—in the true spirit of psychedelic music—as much felt as it was heard.

Creedence Clearwater Revival

On the other side of the Bay, a different type of music was stirring. The Oakland-based Creedence Clearwater Revival are more associated with straight-up blues rock than with psychedelia, but they too were part of the scene. To the followers of the

Creedence Clearwater Revival, 1972. Courtesy of Photofest.

counterculture movement in San Francisco, CCR were little more than radio-play sellouts, garnering massive hits with quick, polished songs about American life and the value of home. In their short, three-year recording career, they managed five Top 10 albums and nine Top 10 singles. They did, however, record war-protest songs and the occasional long-playing tune—not enough to call them a psychedelic band, but it is worth mentioning the diversity of musical styles in such close proximity.

The Doors

It was not long before bands outside of the Bay Area picked up on the San Francisco sound and remade it in their image or, in some cases, pioneered original psychedelia with little help from the Haight. In 1965 Los Angeles, Jim Morrison and Ray Manzarek created a Southern California psychedelic sound in their band the Doors, taking the name from Aldous Huxley's book *The Doors of Perception*. Though Morrison's lyrics and Robby Krieger's creative guitar work made many of their songs the right length and sound for radio play—which garnered them some major hits and national attention—they were also replete with sex and drug references, and Morrison's words, like Jerry Garcia's guitar in the Grateful Dead, would often glide around the song during live shows looking for a place to land.

The Doors, 1967. Courtesy of Photofest.

Much like Garcia, Morrison relied heavily on mind-expanding drugs for insight, and his style fit one of his favorite quotes from William Blake (by way of Huxley): "If the doors of perception were cleansed, everything would appear to man as it is, infinite."[3] Morrison sought to be spiritually—and sometimes physically—naked on stage, his particularly sexual brand of altered consciousness focusing on darker themes of death and desperation rather than the feel-good exploration of musical bliss sought by his hippie neighbors to the north. After five years of exhaustive soul searching, a spent Morrison retired to Paris to escape his role as a teen idol and become a novelist, only to die of a heart attack—brought on by years of drug abuse—soon after his arrival in 1971.

Jimi Hendrix

A similar career trajectory and tragic end met another icon of late-1960s psychedelia, an artist whose name is synonymous with brilliant improvisation aided by unchecked drug use—Jimi Hendrix. Hailed by many as rock's greatest guitarist, Hendrix was a master of sonic experimentation. Although he was originally from Seattle and was making a name for himself in England, his big splash came in the United States the same way it came for Janis Joplin, Steve Miller, Quicksilver Messenger Service, and several other Bay Area groups— through an electric performance at the Monterey Pop Festival in 1967, at which he set his guitar on fire to top the Who, a band that smashed its instruments as dangerously (and as often) as they played them.

After Monterey, Hendrix was the new psychedelic and hard-rock phenom, improvising complex licks with an intuition for creative use of distortion, volume, and feedback, in a style that stayed true to his background in southern blues and soul (see Chapter 2, "Hard-Rock Lightning, Heavy-Metal Thunder"). His rainbow outfits and wiry hair tied in headbands gave him the look of a Merry Prankster, and his copious drug use and improvisational style would have put him in good stead with San Francisco groups, but his skills far outweighed anything coming out of the Bay, or anywhere else for that matter. Much like Jim Morrison, his creative improvisation skyrocketed him to the top of the charts—all five of his albums between 1967 and 1970 reached the Top 10—and made him a living rock icon. The sad corollary is the similarity of their deaths, both at the tender age of twenty-seven, both caused at least indirectly by years of drug abuse.

Psychedelia beyond the Bay

The psychedelic movement was by no means limited to the West Coast. In Austin, Texas, the 13th Floor Elevators played an unusual acid-infused jug-band blues that was ill-received by conservative local tastes. The avant-garde scene in New York City found their mind-expanding music in the Velvet Underground, a darker, more brooding psychedelia than their West Coast flower-power contemporaries (see Chapter 3, "Glamour Kings: The Birth of Glitter Rock"). The band found sponsorship and fame through their association with counterculture icon Andy Warhol, in some ways the East Coast version of Ken Kesey. In England, meanwhile, psychedelic-inspired performances were surfacing in underground groups such as Pink Floyd and David Bowie, artists that would be enormously influential in new genres such as art rock and glam. All over the western world, groups as diverse as the Rolling Stones, the Beach Boys, and the Byrds were finding at least an occasional opportunity to incorporate such psychedelic hallmarks as distortion, Eastern instruments, and improvisation into their music.

1967 AND THE SUMMER OF LOVE

In retrospect, psychedelic music endured a surprisingly small gestation period. It was only months between the first Charlatans performance at the Red

Dog Saloon and the advent of San Francisco's ballroom parties, followed quickly by Kesey's acid tests, the sudden migration of musicians to the city, and the widespread influence it carried elsewhere. By late 1966, barely a year after the music moved out of Haight-Ashbury basements, national magazines like *Newsweek*, *Time*, and the *New York Times Magazine* were running stories on the burgeoning scene in the Bay. All of the native talent coupled with the swarm of musicians and fans clogging the ballroom entrances made the scene ripe for a major musical revolution, and the map for its rise—as well as its demise—can be drawn on the back of 1967.

The Gathering of the Tribes

It started early in the year, on January 14, with one of the events most emblematic of hippie ideals, the Gathering of the Tribes. The Gathering, also known as the Human Be-In, was a simple affair—in fact, its goal was simplicity itself: to assemble a large group of artists and supporters to forget about the tribulations of the day, the race and gender wars, the Vietnam conflict, the union movement, the protests, and just "be." It was an unqualified success. Between twenty and thirty thousand people gathered under friendly skies on a Sunday afternoon at Golden Gate Park's polo grounds. According to all accounts of the event, it was transcendently peaceful, with only two police officers on horseback, and no fights or arrests (see Chapter 7, "The Festival Is Born").

The Be-In was not the largest, the most well-attended, or the most famous musical gathering of the period, but it was the hallmark of a new kind of community experience, one in which the audience was more than a gathering of customers on the receiving end of an entertainment transaction. Those assembled at the Be-In were the focus of the event, invested members rather than passive recipients. In a way, they owned the moment, and they made the most of it. The Gathering of the Tribes ushered in a new era of audience participation, and without it there may have been no Monterey, Woodstock, or other of the countless festivals that suddenly sprang up over the next few years. The event made the hippie into a living myth and—riding the wave of national press features on the hippie phenomenon—brought a whole new flood of immigrants to San Francisco looking for some good music and a little enlightenment.

Psychedelia on the Radio

In February, Jefferson Airplane released their best-selling and most enduring work, as well as their debut with singer Grace Slick, *Surrealistic Pillow*. Promoted by a heavy touring schedule, the album went to No. 3 on the charts and established the band as a major act. Two songs on the album, "White Rabbit" and "Somebody to Love," both of which Slick brought with her from the Great

Society, landed in the Top 10 and became anthems for the psychedelic movement. "White Rabbit" was particularly controversial, retelling the classic Alice in Wonderland story as a drug parable wherein Alice's adventures become a product of chemical stimulation. Both a paean to experimentation and a challenge to America's pretentious authority system, the song brought yet another slogan to the psychedelic scene meant to address both issues: Feed Your Head.

Surrealistic Pillow was one of the few major psychedelic albums to make a splash on AM radio. At the time, AM radio dominated the market, carrying a homogeneous Top 40 format, and there was little airplay for underground music such as psychedelia. Albums were not themed but just collections of songs, and AM stations generally played a small, impenetrable list of high-performing singles, which meant little variety and almost no experimental new sounds. The FM stations of the day generally carried local or specialty programming, and were not known for their music.

This all changed on April 7, 1967, when Tom Donahue debuted "underground radio" on San Francisco's KMPX, a foreign-language station with a rather limited audience. Inspired by Larry Miller, who had begun an eclectic mix for his midnight–6:00 a.m. slot in February, Donahue challenged the Top 40 policy of playing the same thirty singles over and over by creating a rock-oriented show for his 8:00 p.m.–midnight slot. Donahue's show was enormously popular, increasing revenues for the station 1,000 percent in the first year (see Chapter 8, "Rock and the Media"). It helped that Donahue was already a major figure in the local scene, promoting Rolling Stones and Beach Boys concerts, managing several bands, and running a small record label. Thanks to his efforts, by the end of that spring, local alternative music had a home on the airwaves, and with news of upcoming events whetting the appetite of the now bloated hippie population, locals began billing the coming months in San Francisco by the name it is now famously remembered for: the summer of love.

Though one can trace the origins of the summer of love back to January's Be-In, the actual summer kicked off in late April with the song that became the summer of love's unofficial anthem, "San Francisco (Be Sure to Wear Flowers in Your Hair)." This smash hit for former New York folkie Scott McKenzie was written by John Phillips of the Mamas and the Papas to promote the upcoming Monterey Pop Festival, for which Phillips was a major organizer. Even though it was recorded in Los Angeles by a New Yorker, it set all eyes on San Francisco just as the phrase "summer of love" was spreading like a grassfire through the national press. The song hit No. 3 on the American charts and was a worldwide success, reaching the No. 1 spot on charts in at least a dozen countries, including Britain, Australia, Germany, Israel, Norway, and Malaysia. By this time the hippie phenomenon was world-renowned, and a bus company started "Hippie Hop Tours" through San Francisco's more alternative neighborhoods, calling it "the only foreign tour within the continental limits of the United States."[4]

Sgt. Pepper's Lonely Hearts Club Band

Within weeks of McKenzie's release, arguably the most famous psychedelic album of all time hit the shelves, not by a San Francisco band but by a British group. The Beatles' *Sgt. Pepper's Lonely Hearts Club Band* was a landmark album and a milestone in experimental production. Entire books have been written about the recording, reception, and larger impact of this single album.

Though *Sgt. Pepper's* was officially released June 1, 1967, the events leading up to the band's tour de force stretch back three years and several albums. As early as 1964, members of the group—John Lennon in particular—began experimenting with alternative instrumentation in their songs, using such instruments as the flute, French horn, strings, and, thanks to George Harrison's eastern travels, sitar in their songs. These were instruments not normally found on rock albums, and their use led to more creative experimentation, not just with instruments but with electronic and ambient sounds such as feedback on "I Feel Fine" in 1964, coughing on *Revolver's* "Taxman," and a backward-tracked vocal (believed to be the first use of the technique) on the 1966 single "Rain" (the B-side to "Paperback Writer").

The experimental use of alternative instruments links the Beatles—in a small way, perhaps—to the psychedelic sound coming out of mid-sixties San Francisco. But a much stronger link, which had a profound impact on their subsequent releases, is rooted in an August 1964 meeting the band had with

The partial cover of the Beatles' revolutionary album, *Sgt. Pepper's Lonely Hearts Club Band*, 1967. Courtesy of Photofest.

Bob Dylan in New York, where the groovy folkie introduced the naive young lads to their first drug experience—a marijuana cigarette. Within a year, the group had made marijuana part of their musical diet, as hours of footage left on the cutting-room floor from their 1965 film *Help!* will attest—mostly pot-induced giggling fits. A further round of mind-expanding direction came in spring of 1965 when John, George, and their wives were given LSD at a dinner party, after which the whole band became patrons of the drug. According to Harrison, "It was like gaining hundreds of years of experience within twelve hours. It changed me, and there was no way back to what I was before."[5] Their music soon showed the effects.

The band's use of LSD made the group take traditional rock formulas less seriously but their music more seriously. On 1965's *Rubber Soul* and 1966's *Revolver*—the two albums leading up *Sgt. Pepper's*—we see a band transformed. In place of bouncy tunes about young love and rock 'n' roll, we find more insightful, solemn, and abstract lyrics in songs like "Nowhere Man," "For No One," and "Norwegian Wood." Even on their less serious tracks, such as "She Said She Said" and "Good Day Sunshine," there are unusual rhythms and chord changes that indicate the band's shifting direction. In "Tomorrow Never Knows," the last song on *Revolver*, heavy electronic effects augmenting Zen-like lyrics foreshadowed *Sgt. Pepper's* LSD-inspired revolution. Such lyrics certainly match the mind-set of those who organized the Be-In the following January, and in retrospect, there was plenty of evidence that something like *Sgt. Pepper's* was on the horizon.

The actual recording of the album was a Herculean effort, taking 700 hours to produce over 129 days. (By comparison, the Beatles' 1963 debut *Please Please Me* was recorded in under ten hours.) The cover included a staged photo of the foursome with standups of every figure they could think of that had influenced their music, including Mae West, Bob Dylan, Carl Jung, Edgar Allan Poe, Albert Einstein, and Elvis Presley. The record packaging included not only the first gatefold album but also the first instance of printed lyrics, and a page from which the listener could cut out props such as a moustache and a badge to fit the theme of the album, which was a fictional band with characters played by the Beatles. Since the group had already decided not to tour anymore, they created an album that would tour for them by simulating this fictitious ensemble and their touring experience.

The fact that the Beatles had stopped touring also opened up the production possibilities of the recording, since they would not be required to reproduce the songs on stage. One track, "Within You Without You," takes the unusual step for a rock band of dismissing all but one artist—the song is simply George singing and playing the sitar. The original use of sound effects is probably the most obvious feature, with employment of vocal echo, oscillators, variable-speed tape recorders, a steam organ, forty-two classical musicians, various farm animals, and a pack of foxhounds. As a final stab at convention, the album's closing track, "A Day in the Life," ends in a booming piano chord that fades into a drone that ends at fifteen kilocycles (at Lennon's request, so that only dogs can hear it), followed by a concentric groove at the end of the album that would repeat nonsensical snippets of studio chatter ad infinitum until someone lifted the arm of the record player. If *Sgt. Pepper's* is not, as many critics have hailed it, the greatest rock album of all time, then George Martin at least wins the gold medal for production of the album *London Times* critic Kenneth Tynan called upon its release "a decisive moment in the history of Western civilization."[6]

Though recorded at Apple Road studios in London, *Sgt. Pepper's* was, stylistically, a stone's throw from San Francisco. The album was partly inspired by a trip Paul had taken to California in 1966, where he was exposed to a musical community that existed beyond the boundaries that separated individual bands, and musical styles that defined themselves by how much they were willing to borrow from other styles rather than which mold they wanted to fit into. "People were no longer the Beatles or the Crickets," claimed Lennon in a later interview about the Bay Area scene. "[T]hey were suddenly Fred and His Incredible Shriveling Grateful Airplane."[7]

Monterey Pop

June 1967 was the benchmark month for the psychedelic scene with Scott McKenzie's homage to San Francisco getting airplay all over the world, and *Sgt. Pepper's* beginning its fifteen-week stay at the top of the charts and another eleven months in the Top 40. The year's events were leading up to something magical, it seemed—a moment that would define the summer of love in San Francisco. That moment came on the weekend of June 16, with the first and last Monterey International Pop Festival.

There were music festivals before Monterey—just two weeks earlier San Francisco bussed 15,000 concertgoers up Mount Tamalpais for the Fantasy Faire & Magic Mountain Music Festival—but nothing on this scale; nothing with this much musical talent that became this influential. While the Be-In five months earlier was the first shot across the bow of musical convention, Monterey was the volley that sank the whole ship. The open-air concert festival was a relatively new idea, and at Monterey it was done on a grand scale, with total attendees exceeding the expected 50,000—approximately 200,000 people came from all over the globe, considered a massive gathering at the time for any entertainment event. As Scott McKenzie crooned over the airwaves at the time, "If you come to San Francisco, summertime will be a Love-In there."

The three-day festival, held at the Monterey County Fairgrounds between San Francisco and Los Angeles, was as close as there came to being a definitive moment in psychedelic music. Two years later, the Woodstock Music and Arts Fair would become the cultural apex of this chapter in rock history, but Monterey was the musical apex. With Paul McCartney serving as the talent consultant, and Lou Adler (president of Ode Records) and John Phillips (of the Mamas and the Papas) producing the event, the musical lineup was a cornucopia of talent, featuring the best of psychedelia (the Grateful Dead, Jefferson Airplane, Country Joe and the Fish, Moby Grape, Quicksilver Messenger Service), blues (Steve Miller, the Butterfield Blues Band, Al Kooper), folk (Laura Nyro, Simon and Garfunkel, the Mamas and the Papas, Buffalo Springfield, Scott McKenzie), and soul (Otis Redding, Booker T and the MGs, Lou Rawls), as well as many more remarkable acts—a good deal of them relatively unknown at the time but destined to change rock music.

The performances at Monterey would be remembered and reminisced about for decades: the Who and the Jimi Hendrix Experience engaged in a note-bending, guitar-smashing battle of the bands during the Sunday evening lineup; Big Brother's lead singer Janis Joplin was said to raise people out of their seats with her hand during each crescendo in "Ball and Chain"; Otis Redding, who would tragically die only months later in a plane crash, used his stunning performance at Monterey to successfully cross over to predominately white audiences, adopting the position of honorary soul ambassador to the hippie community; and Indian artist Ravi Shankar, the lone act on Sunday afternoon, mesmerized audiences with a sitar marathon that earned him a standing ovation that started well before his set ended, allowing him to come out of the shadows of the major acts he had influenced—the Beatles, the Rolling Stones, the Byrds—and become an icon in his own right (see Chapter 7, "The Festival Is Born").

Monterey was, all in all, a catalyst for a proliferation of new, experimental sounds. Many of the bands were signed for albums and tours following their performances, and the festival itself set a new standard for rock concerts, inspiring copycat shows around the country, just as Haight-Ashbury was inspiring alternative music communities around the country. For the decade leading up to 1967, the top albums in the United States were by "respectable" or barely controversial bands like the Monkees, Herb Alpert and the Tijuana Brass, Andy Williams, Barbra Streisand, and Elvis Presley, not to mention a host of film soundtracks. This trend took a radical turn after Monterey and the popularization of FM radio. The chart-toppers in 1968 included Big Brother and the Holding Company, the Jimi Hendrix Experience, Simon and Garfunkel, the Doors, and Cream; 1969 saw Blind Faith, Creedence Clearwater Revival, Led Zeppelin, and Blood, Sweat & Tears all reach No. 1—along with the soundtrack to the hippie musical *Hair*. Although they did not perform at Monterey, the Beatles were the only top act of the period to survive the change because they changed themselves, from innocent skiffle-and-blues teenagers to LSD-enlightened experimentalists. The Beatles had a No. 1 album every year from 1964 to 1970 because they were capable of changing with the times.

And how, to paraphrase Dylan, the times were a'changin'. Monterey was a double-edged sword; although the attention it garnered for San Francisco music would quickly change the face of rock, it also changed the face of San Francisco itself. The large presence of psychedelic and psychedelic-inspired artists at Monterey brought even more attention to the Bay Area, already overcrowded with counterculture types and more arriving every day. Many of the local bands that had made the city famous went on large tours after Monterey, or moved out of the suddenly very public Haight and into nearby Marin County. In the early scene, many of the local hippies had been college educated, sharing strong ties with nearby University of California at Berkeley—a school always at the forefront of protest among colleges in the United States—whereas a large number of the new arrivals were high-school dropouts looking to escape to a paradise free of responsibility. Suddenly crime went up, heroin and methamphetamines became as common as LSD, and many of the counterculture gurus were no longer around to guide the energy of aimless youth in creative directions.

Within a year of Monterey, San Francisco—at least the local scene in San Francisco that created, nurtured, and exported a countercultural revolution—was a corporate shadow of its former self. Much of the original talent had moved out of the area, replaced by outsiders looking to tap into the Haight magic, and what remained of Haight-Ashbury's dignity was commodified in Madison Avenue advertisements and slogans painted on fighter planes, and swept away in city "health inspections" that tried to rid the district of communes. Many members of top acts in California were arrested on drug-related or indecency charges, including those in the Grateful Dead, Electric Flag, Jefferson Airplane, Canned Heat, the Charlatans, and the Doors. An attempt to repeat the Monterey festival in 1968 was scrapped amid news that an accountant had absconded with much of the proceeds from the original. Cities like London, New York, and Los Angeles would soon steal headlines with their own versions of psychedelia-inspired rock forms such as punk, glam, and heavy metal.

It is inevitable that when a local musical flavor tickles the national or international palate, the taste becomes more bitter locally as it is altered for more commercial buds. The San Francisco sound no longer belonged to San Francisco—it was an international commodity—and the original hippies longed for the days when they owned the style that had spread worldwide in two short years. Psychedelia was now an international scene, and local reaction was decidedly moribund. On October 6, 1967, a small cadre of locals carried a coffin down Haight Street in a mock funeral procession, declaring—in the minds of the locals, at least—the death of the hippie.

BEYOND THE BAY: PSYCHEDELIA AND THE BRAVE NEW WORLD

Since the early days of psychedelia, the allure of the San Francisco rock scene was more than the music; it was the lifestyle. Youth culture had stepped up and asserted itself as a creative, independent force. Even *Time* magazine had, for the first time, given its Man of the Year honor to a generation rather than an individual, awarding it to "Twenty-five and Under" in 1966. *Time* recognized the potential of this new force: "That generation looms larger than all the exponential promises of science or technology. It will soon be the majority in charge."[8]

The inmates, it seemed, had taken over the asylum. Rock was inextricably tied to the artistic and social movements of the day, and other art forms took on the open-minded, experimental character of psychedelic music. An anti-establishment, youth-oriented music magazine called *Rolling Stone* debuted in San Francisco in October 1967, writing mostly about the Bay Area scene but also rock music worldwide. At the same time, the rock musical *Hair* was opening off-Broadway at the New York Shakespeare Festival's Public Theatre, later moving to Broadway where it would become one of the all-time top moneymakers. Psychedelic music helped bring about a newer, harder rock that dominated the charts and began to take over the airwaves as Tom Donahue's FM rock format was copied in cities like Los Angeles, St. Louis, Detroit, and New York (see Chapter 8, "Rock and the Media").

Far from simply copying San Francisco styles, alternative communities around the United States and in some European countries created their own branches of experimental sounds. There were some failed experiments, such as an effort in Boston to create "the Bosstown sound" with local bands Ultimate Spinach, Beacon Street Union, and Orpheus. But elsewhere artists began to fuse jazz, country, classical, raga, electronica, and other styles with rock to influence various fusion genres such as glam, heavy metal, southern rock, and art rock. From 1967 to 1970, psychedelia exploded in many different directions, influencing further variations of the original blues-based rock sound.

Out of England came a British form of psychedelia called "art rock," or "progressive rock," from bands such as Pink Floyd, King Crimson, Genesis, Yes, Jethro Tull, and the Moody Blues. Art rock combined complex classical forms with psychedelic experimentation to create lush, thickly layered, rock-orchestral works. Some art-rock bands incorporated surreal and fantastical lyrics into their songs, such as in the early Moody Blues hit "Nights in White Satin," whose spoken-word interlude became one of their better-known lyrical creations. The Moody Blues also helped pioneer the use of the mellotron (though it had already been employed by the Beach Boys in the United States)—an electronic instrument that can be used to simulate orchestral sounds—soon employed by a number of art-rock groups. Jethro Tull created a distinctive sound for themselves with flute leads by frontman Ian Anderson, who borrowed from classical, jazz, and avant-garde styles to augment the band's blues-revival roots. Groups such as Pink Floyd and the Electric Light Orchestra (ELO) created elaborate stage productions and light shows to enhance their live performances. Pink Floyd especially attracted audiences prone to the use of psychoactive drugs to enhance the visual and aural experience (see Chapter 6, "Rock Goes Progressive").

Also out of Britain came "glam rock," or "glitter rock," which differed little from art rock except that glam focused much more on the artist's persona as an element of musical identity. Where art rock borrowed from San Francisco's psychedelic multimedia presentations, glam rockers borrowed liberally from the theater, using over-the-top stagecraft to bring characters and plots to their performances. The originator and king—or, as he might prefer, queen—of glam rock was Londoner David Bowie, whose memorable characters Major Tom and Ziggy Stardust set the standard for a future evolution in American psychedelic with theatrical bands like the New York Dolls, Kiss, and Alice Cooper. The androgynous nature of early glam artists, especially Bowie, influenced glam rockers like Gary Glitter and Elton John to adopt desexualized characters as well (see Chapter 3, "Glamour Kings: The Birth of Glitter Rock").

Heavy metal and hard rock only partially descended from the psychedelic phenomenon, sharing a common value in their use of distortion and feedback as a musical tool. Although such techniques date back to at least 1964 with the Kinks' "You Really Got Me" and the Beatles' "I Feel Fine," Jimi Hendrix's highly sophisticated sonic experimentation influenced a generation of hard rockers. The Grateful Dead also played a role with their emphasis on the importance of mastering the sound as well as the music. While many bands— even top acts—were satisfied with whatever PA systems local promoters had on hand, the Dead were traipsing around the country with twenty-three tons of equipment designed by their sound engineer Owsley, determined to milk the very best sounds out of their instruments (see Chapter 2, "Hard-Rock Lightning, Heavy-Metal Thunder").

The Beatles' *Sgt. Pepper's Lonely Hearts Club Band* was enormously influential for the future of rock, its presence felt in a number of subsequent releases. Jefferson Airplane delayed their much-anticipated follow-up to *Surrealistic Pillow* because they felt the need to return to the studio after hearing *Sgt. Pepper's*, eventually emerging in December 1967 with *After Bathing at Baxter's*. The Rolling Stones attempted their own *Sgt. Pepper's* with their late-1967 release *Their Satanic Majesties Request*, a laudable, if somewhat limited, attempt at sonic experimentation. For decades after *Sgt. Pepper's*, bands continued to experiment with effects like backmasking, distortion, feedback, and ambient noise, ensuring a lasting place for improvisation in almost every musical genre.

Psychedelic music did more than mutate into different forms during its waning years of 1968 and 1969. With the United States embroiled in a very unpopular war in Vietnam, the antiestablishment nature of psychedelia led some bands to momentarily augment the "sex, drugs, and rock 'n' roll" themes of their music with antiwar sentiments, creating a spike in the prevalence of protest songs to complement the general disenchanted-with-the-mainstream nature of psychedelic music. The catch, of course, was that now psychedelic music *was* mainstream, which made protest music popular, as it came with a built-in audience. Newly minted superstars like the Grateful Dead and Jefferson Airplane were appearing at rallies for causes ranging from removing American forces from Vietnam to saving a small park in Berkeley. Country Joe and the Fish, the most politically active musical group of the time, saw minor national success with their antiwar music between 1968 and 1970, by which time American forces in Vietnam had reached almost half a million.

Although San Francisco was the center of the American rock world in 1968, it was no longer considered the local scene it once was, due to the large influx of outsiders and the music industry asserting its might in the Bay. Rock music was becoming big business, and it didn't take long for much of it to take on a corporate feel. In 1967 album sales in the United States had hit the $1 billion mark for the first time ever, and would reach $2 billion by 1973.[9] San Francisco, and the rock revolution it produced, had gone from the center of musical counterculture to the center of musical culture.

Psychedelia gave its last major gasp in a recognizable form at the Woodstock Music and Arts Fair in August 1969. With improvisation, drug use, and audience interaction three of the hallmarks of psychedelic music, the large outdoor festivals spawned by the Human Be-In and Monterey were central to the music's identity. Woodstock is remembered, if in a somewhat overly romanticized fashion, as the culmination of five years of rock revolution, with more than 400,000 fans gathering in the muddy hills of upstate New York to hear one of the greatest lineups of the decade, including Jimi Hendrix, Creedence Clearwater Revival, the Band, Jefferson Airplane, Janis Joplin, the Who, Canned Heat, Ravi Shankar, the Grateful Dead, Santana, and a score of other top acts (see Chapter 7, "The Festival Is Born").

This would be the last time many of these bands would play together. Most of the original San Francisco supergroups would be gone by 1970, replaced by hard rockers and glamour gods that took the focus off the audience and recentered the music on the artist. Woodstock marked not only the end of the decade but the end of the personal interaction between artist and audience. Festivals grew to be large, corporate events, and with the exception of the Grateful Dead and the occasional smaller event, the remaining psychedelic acts largely reached their audiences not through personal performances but through their albums and large concerts and festivals. The doors of perception that psychedelic music had opened would close behind them by 1970, but psychedelia's extraordinary influence on other musical styles would be felt indefinitely, marking the psychedelic revolution as one of the most creative periods in American rock.

NOTES

1. Geoffrey Link, "The Charlatans," *Rolling Stone*, February 21, 1970, 31.
2. *Rolling Stone*, February 21, 1970, 32.
3. Huxley 1963, introduction.
4. Sculatti and Seay 1985, 99.
5. DeCurtis 2005, 68.
6. Kenneth Tynan, *London Times*, June 1967.
7. Sheff and Golson 1981, 166.
8. *Time* magazine Web site, www.time.com/moy.
9. Friedlander 1996, 233.

HARD-ROCK LIGHTNING, HEAVY-METAL THUNDER

In rock critic Albert Goldman's 1992 book *Sound Bites*, he recalls an interview in which he asks Jimi Hendrix, "What is the difference between the old blues and the new?" to which Hendrix responds, "Electricity."[1]

Electricity, both literally and figuratively, is power. In the literal sense, advances in electric instruments and amplification techniques during the first few decades of rock and roll allowed musical acts not only to play for bigger audiences but to treat volume itself as an instrument. From the earliest electric guitars and basses at the turn of the 1950s to Jim Marshall's advances in amplifier technology in the mid-1960s to the stadium-rock "walls of sound" in the 1970s, increased volume meant increased access to the audience. By the time hard rock and heavy metal had taken full hold of the concert halls and *Billboard* charts, fans of harder, louder music did not have to be content with just hearing the songs—they could now feel them reverberating throughout their body. "The 'sound' became all-encompassing, and the experience of music became a jolting activity—the body a conductor of electric energy transmitted through amplified sound."[2]

In the figurative sense, electricity provided artists with a new dimension for their instruments. Although amplified instruments were initially treated as simply louder versions of their acoustic predecessors, artists soon used techniques such as feedback, distortion, and increased dynamic range to capture previously unavailable sounds with their instruments—particularly their electric guitars. It was electricity that turned blues into rock, and it was taking electricity to the brink of chaos that turned rock into heavy metal.

A word must be said here about the differences between hard rock and heavy metal. Subgenres of rock are invariably linked by common factors, and although almost all acts display the features of several genres, artists and bands are usually labeled as belonging to a specific genre by virtue of the predominant characteristics they display. And while it is sometimes difficult to assign a label to a band or artist, it is not impossible, and the reasons are not arbitrary.

In this case, hard rock and heavy metal are closely related and share a number of features: a focus on volume as a technique to be manipulated; the use of distortion and feedback to bring new sounds into the repertoire; the electric guitar as a centerpiece of the band (usually) and guitar solos as a common showpiece; extensive use of short, repeating bass riffs; and an overall thematic fixation on rebellion, often manifesting itself in themes of sex, drugs, uninhibited behavior, and other elements of the rock-and-roll lifestyle.

These very similar styles nonetheless contain attributes that differentiate them and make it relatively easy to put bands into their proper categories. As a rule, hard rock predates and largely created heavy metal as a separate genre, so while loud, guitar-driven bands prior to 1969 may contain elements of heavy metal, they are essentially hard-rock acts. With regard to the use of volume, hard-rock acts tend to exhibit some degree of control over their dynamic techniques, whereas heavy-metal acts will push the sonic envelope to the brink of chaos. Thematically, heavy-metal lyrics tend to explore a fairly narrow scope of material limited to anarchy, rebellion, gothic themes of death and hell, and the immortality of rock and roll, while hard-rock acts include a much wider range of tropes. By extension, the lyrics to heavy-metal songs are not as central to the overall presentation—the words are usually screamed instead of sung, and wordplay comes second to powerful vocal delivery. Finally, hard-rock acts remain mired in their blues and folk roots, with the wide range of lyrical themes complemented by frequent appearances of instruments such as the organ and acoustic guitar. Heavy-metal bands almost exclusively include guitars, bass, and drums, and when the occasional alternative instrument appears, it stands out specifically because of its rarity.

Thus—with the caveat that there are many common traits—it is not difficult to assign bluesy, multithemed, late-1960s bands like the Yardbirds, the Who, and Cream to the category of hard rock, and turn-of-the-1970s bands like Iron Butterfly, Black Sabbath, and Alice Cooper to the realm of heavy metal. Clearly the categories are not perfect or rigid—some bands simply defy definition. The Detroit group MC5 is claimed by both heavy-metal and punk fans as essential forebears. The British rockers Deep Purple are considered one of the first heavy-metal acts, but much of their early work was profoundly influenced by classical music, and some of their material is pure art rock (see Chapter 6, "Rock Goes Progressive"). And of course Led Zeppelin, though gods in the heavy-metal world, were extraordinarily multifaceted, and while they produced some of the biggest early metal hits, their albums are littered with music from folk, blues, Indian, and reggae traditions, just to name a few.

The term "hard rock" is simply an extension of the 1960s catchall "rock music," which came from the more dance-oriented "rock and roll" of the 1950s, but the origin of the term "heavy metal" has for years been the subject of much debate. Many have mistakenly attributed the expression to author William Burroughs' mid-fifties, heroin-fueled novel *Naked Lunch*, though the phrase does not appear anywhere in the text. However, Burroughs does use the idiom in his mid-1960s Nova trilogy, made up of *The Soft Machine*, *The Ticket That Exploded*, and *Nova Express*—a series that features "Uranium Willy, the Heavy Metal Kid," and even makes a reference to "metal music" long before there was such a thing.[3] With the trilogy's dark, anti-establishment themes of alienation in a mechanical world, the connection to later heavy-metal music is not too much of a stretch.

A more popular—but equally questionable—source of the term is the hit 1968 Steppenwolf song "Born to Be Wild." Steppenwolf, a Canadian hard-rock band, claimed the No. 2 spot for three weeks with the song, which later became the theme to the popular film *Easy Rider*. The lyrics use the phrase "heavy-metal thunder" to capture the feeling of riding a motorcycle across a barren plane. Though the term is not directly referring to a musical genre, Steppenwolf was one of the early loud rock bands that relied on intense, distorted guitars and full-throated vocal delivery, a style that brought about heavy metal only a few years later.

The origin of the term as specifically referring to a musical genre probably rested with the rock critics around the turn of the 1970s, when music journalism was enjoying a heyday, as various rock genres were being born more or less after every meal. Former Black Sabbath bassist Geezer Butler claims that the term was first used in the pejorative around 1972 to describe his band's music as "the sound of heavy metal crashing," a phrase similar to a mythical blurb in a 1967 issue of *Rolling Stone* describing Jimi Hendrix's guitar playing.[4] However, the earliest textual reference that can be verified is a May 1971 review in *Creem* magazine of Sir Lord Baltimore's album by journalist Mike Saunders, in which Saunders claims "Sir Lord Baltimore seems to have down pat most all the best heavy metal tricks in the book," and entices readers to "be the first on your block to have your brains blown out."[5]

ELECTRICITY AS NOISE

Critics and historians generally agree that the earliest known example of intentional distortion in rock music was created by guitarist Link Wray in his 1958 gangfight-themed hit "Rumble," in which he achieved a crunching effect by poking a hole through his amplifier with a pencil. Perhaps foreshadowing the later chaotic rock that the sound inspired, "Rumble" faced censorship for the song's sound as well as its subject matter, but made Wray a godfather to later rock, metal, and punk artists.

In 1964, the Kinks got into the act with their Top 10 single "You Really Got Me"—a song that has been referred to many times as the birth of heavy metal for its simple lyrics, unpredictable guitar solo, off-key singing, and gravelly feel. In creating this track, Ray and Dave Davies use an amplifier they had slashed with a razor blade. Only a month later, distortion appeared on the much perkier No. 1 hit "I Feel Fine" by a band that popularized a number of unconventional sonic techniques, the Beatles. As rock musicians began to discover the possibilities of electronic amplification as a playing technique that could be manipulated, crude new devices surfaced in the studio and on stage, such as the fuzz box (which increased the guitar's distortion), the Octavia (which echoed the played note at different octaves), and the wah-wah pedal (which made a tone quiver between slightly higher and lower ranges, in the right hands making the guitar sound like it was singing), allowing musicians to deliver sonic variation at will.

In 1962 a British music-store owner named Jim Marshall—later nicknamed "the Father of Loud"—began selling amplifiers of his own design that increased the volume available to musicians. Marshall amplifiers soon became a trademark for loud acts, and the higher you piled them (known as "Marshall stacks"), the louder you were. While performing in Britain in the mid-1960s, an unknown Seattle native named Jimi Hendrix had Marshall customize some of these early models to give him the greatest output possible. Hendrix was one of the first—and arguably the greatest—masters of alternative sonic techniques, and in his short career, he pushed his equipment into realms of noise no one had ever dreamed of.

Since many of the advances in performance technology in the 1950s and 1960s were centered on the electric guitar, the instrument emerged as the voice of rock. Early rockers like Bill Haley's guitarist Francis Beecher, Elvis Presley's Scotty Moore, solo-artist Duane Eddy, and the Beatles' George Harrison slowly drew the spotlight from the rhythm guitarist to the newly emerging position of lead guitarist. Rockers of the 1960s like Hendrix, Dave Davies, and Eric Clapton also drew the focus away from the vocals until the rock guitar—particularly the improvisational solo—became the sound of a louder, harder rock and a symbol of the rebel lifestyle, giving birth to that most unfortunate of rock legacies, the air guitar.

FROM HIPPIE IDEALISM TO HEAVY METAL

The groovy sounds of 1960s psychedelia and its many predecessors and variations (especially folk rock) were as much about power as hard rock and later heavy metal, but in a different sense. The sweet strains that filled the San Francisco air were about social power, the power of people to come together and make the world a better place. By the height of the hippie movement in 1967 and 1968, millions of flower children across the country were riding a wave of love-your-neighbor vibes produced by politically and socially charged rock acts such as the Grateful Dead, Jefferson Airplane, and Country Joe and the Fish (see Chapter 1, "The Psychedelic Experience").

Perhaps the most oft-cited evidence of the social power of rock was the 1969 Woodstock Music and Arts Fair, a grossly underplanned event that nonetheless embodied the spirit of communal cooperation advocated in positive, socially conscious rock lyrics of the period. But if Woodstock was the model of rock's social idealism, the disaster at Altamont only months later marked its antithesis (see Chapter 7, "The Festival Is Born"). The failure of rock's seemingly inherent goodwill coincided with a number of political and social setbacks, such as the escalating war in Vietnam, the increasingly violent nature of antiwar and civil rights protests, the brutal police response to demonstrators at the 1968 Democratic National Convention in Chicago, the assassinations of Robert Kennedy and Martin Luther King Jr. in 1968, the shootings of students by police and national guardsmen at Kent State and Jackson State in 1970, and the 1970 invasion of Cambodia by the United States. Despite their best efforts, the nation's youth were losing their battle, and by the turn of the decade, according to Deena Weinstein, "heavy metal was born amidst the ashes of the failed youth revolution."[6]

Not that American youth had an exclusive claim to societal ennui, nor to these new rock forms that sprung from their alienation—many of hard rock's and heavy metal's founding groups were British. But as the promises of the psychedelic gurus went unfulfilled and the movement waned amid the breakup of nearly all of San Francisco's top acts, both American and British bands whose music displayed something of an edge found easy access into the minds of American teenagers through the burgeoning FM radio format, and into their hearts through their vulnerable spirits. The sheer volume and discord of louder, harder rock music empowered its fans that were being alienated by a violent, conformity-driven society. If flower-power music could not cure society's ills, then at least the louder rock could drown them out.

The troubled turn of the 1970s made rock angry. More than any other form of rock music, heavy metal is about power and the funneling of aggression. The new rock singers did not croon about peace and love; they screamed about its demise. As the Beatles—the good kids, compared to the emerging Who and Rolling Stones—slid down the slope of drugs, animosity, and eventual breakup through the late 1960s, a darker movement waited on the horizon to fill their shoes. Rock bands didn't have to be pretty anymore, they just had to be loud, and falling in love with the bad boys was still the best way to anger one's parents and demonstrate contempt for the social order.

THE BANDS

Unlike genres such as southern rock and psychedelic music, which began as local phenomena and spread outward, hard rock and heavy metal reared their heads over a short period of time in a number of places in the United States and Britain. So rather than a chronologically or geographically organized breakdown of the events that led to heavy metal, it might be better to view the movement through the individual stories of the bands that made it happen.

The Kinks

The Kinks are widely believed to be the first band to display an approximation of the heavy-metal sound. Though they are rightly held to be progenitors of the punk-rock movement in the 1970s, they also displayed a number of the traits that later became heavy-metal staples, such as distorted guitar, harsh vocal delivery, a simple guitar/bass/drums lineup, and a tendency toward drunken violence a decade before Led Zeppelin were trashing $1,000-a-night hotel rooms at every stop.

Despite the band's enormous success in their native England from 1964 to 1970 and the celebrated songwriting of frontman Ray Davies, the band experienced only mediocre notice on the American charts, with their albums dancing around the Top 100 throughout the 1960s. This was mostly due to the group's inability to tour the states after being banned for several years early in their career for their rowdy behavior. Nonetheless, several of their 1964 and 1965 singles, including the classics "You Really Got Me," "All Day and All of the Night," and "Tired of Waiting for You" made their way into the Top 10 in the United States with almost no tour support.

The group reemerged in the American Top 10 in 1970 with their surprise hit "Lola," and spent much of the next two years performing packed

The Kinks, 1967. Courtesy of Photofest.

shows in the United States and earning a tremendous following, though their chart success changed little otherwise. Oddly, as heavy metal was arriving on the international scene, the Kinks' material was much more lyrical and subdued than the earlier, harder music they had made as teens. The closest they got to being a heavy-metal group was with their first few albums, which were more raw and energetic than their releases from the late-1960s on. The band continued to tour and record through the 1990s, scoring albums both brilliant and forgettable, but it was the garage-band style of their early releases that marked their contribution to the edgier rock soon to follow.

The Rolling Stones

For millions of fans over the past forty years, the Rolling Stones have epitomized the rock-and-roll band as an icon of bad-boy rebellion. Marketing themselves as a foil to the Beatles' clean-cut persona—a journalist once asked, "Would you let your daughter go with a Rolling Stone?"[7]—the group pioneered the image of rock musicians as obnoxious, misogynistic party boys whose music was too loud and whose lyrics were too controversial. As with many British rock groups of the period, their sound was built on the shoulders of American blues pioneers like Muddy Waters, Bo Diddley, and Chuck Berry (the band's moniker even came from the Waters tune "Rollin' Stone"). Lead singer Mick Jagger also copied the stage stylings of energetic powerhouses like James Brown and Little Richard to give the Rolling Stones' performances an uninhibited sexual appeal that drove their largely female audience crazy, often leading to hysteria and even riots.

The band's fuzzed-out guitar intro on their 1965 hit "(I Can't Get No) Satis-faction"—which may have simply been the result of a blown amplifier—captured the imagination of edgier acts that followed, and established a gritty, blues-based sound for the band that was copied by dozens of later groups. The Rolling Stones were soon an icon of trouble coming over the horizon. As their star was rising in the United States, a critic commented that there was "some-thing elegantly sinister about the Rolling Stones. They sit before you at a press conference like five unfolding switchblades, their faces set in rehearsed snarls, their hair studiously unkempt and matted, their clothes part of some private conceit, and the way they walk and the songs they sing all become part of some long mean reach for the jugular."[8]

Enhancing the band's status throughout their first decade was their ability to capture the unique qualities of other groups—such as the Beatles' use of the sitar and the LSD-fueled wanderings of psychedelic music—and integrate them into their own blues-based work (as evidenced by their 1966 No. 1 single "Paint It Black," which contains both of these elements). The group often seemed to live in the shadow of the Beatles, on the one hand setting themselves up as the "anti-Beatles" in the minds of American teens, while on the other borrow-ing elements of their music and even parodying their work, such as their lesser 1967 album *Their Satanic Majesties Request*, a quick response to the Beat-les' *Sgt. Pepper's Lonely Hearts Club Band*. Their ability to remain on the cutting edge of rock's increasingly diverse stylistic offshoots, coupled with the sexual ur-gency of their lyrics and lead singer Mick Jagger's stage struts, made them one of the most popular touring acts in the United States throughout the 1960s and 1970s.

Even the band's poor luck paid off for them. Whenever one of their songs was banned in the United States, it just enhanced their image as purveyors of revolution that teenagers craved. When their shows were canceled for fear of rioting, it only served to increase their status as dangerous rebels. News reports of the members' numerous arrests, ranging from drug possession to urinating in public, were free publicity for the group, feeding the mythology they were try-ing to build around themselves. Album after album of songs about sex, vio-lence, and alienation found their way near the top of the charts between 1965 and 1970. A 1971 review of the band claimed, "The Stones confronted the

Poster for the Rolling Stones concert at the Oakland Coliseum in San Francisco, 1969. Courtesy of the Library of Congress.

public with a completely individual approach of insult and insolence that matured from juvenile art student fuck-you-all to a cult of militant decadence that drew on the libertine anarchy of a de Sade nobleman. Bad guys in the James Dean/Brando tradition, they surpassed both for teen rebel nastiness. They were the group that caused a national Press debate on whether or not they smelt. They were the group that got themselves photographed being brought from jail in handcuffs. People got shot at their concerts."[9]

The band's reckless habits caught up with them at California's Altamont Speedway on December 6, 1969, at the final performance of a massive U.S. tour. Eighteen-year-old Meredith Hunter was knifed and beaten to death by Hell's Angels, whom the group's manager had hired as security for the event. The murder took place right in front of the stage as the Rolling Stones played, one of 4 deaths and 850 injuries suffered that weekend (see Chapter 7, "The Festival Is Born"). Although footage of the event shows that Jagger had tried to calm the crowd several times during the band's set, many in the press blamed the band for the event's poor organization and chided them for refusing to acknowledge any responsibility for the catastrophe. The sex and violence in their songs was reason enough for mainstream America to dislike the Rolling Stones, but played out in actuality at their performances, the music ceased to be an outlet for the frustrations of disenfranchised youth and became instead the stuff of privileged rock stars who thought themselves above blame and reproach.

The heavy publicity surrounding the Altamont debacle overshadowed one of their finest efforts, the incredible *Let It Bleed* that was released in November 1969 as they were winding up their American tour. Coming at a low point in the band's career—the drowning of their rhythm guitarist Brian Jones that summer, the attempted suicide of Jagger's girlfriend Marianne Faithfull soon after, and the events at Altamont—the album was a heavy-handed indictment of flower-power naivety. Dark and powerful tunes like "Let It Bleed," "You Can't Always Get What You Want," and "Gimme Shelter" signaled an end to the era of hippie optimism and the advent of a certain realism in pop lyrics.

The events of 1969 took a toll on the shaken band. Although they disavowed responsibility for the Altamont nightmare, they spent 1970 unusually quiet, releasing only one album (compared to the two or three per year they normally produced)—the live *Get Yer Ya-Ya's Out!*, which was recorded in Madison Square Garden only weeks before Altamont. The year also saw the release of the film *Gimme Shelter*, a documentary of their otherwise successful 1969 tour, leading up to shocking footage of Hunter's death, captured by the tour's cameramen.

But, as the Rolling Stones would do again and again in their career, the group rebounded, this time with two of their most memorable records: 1971's *Sticky Fingers* and 1972's double album *Exile on Main St.*, each of which spent four weeks in the No. 1 spot. Musically, from 1968's *Beggars Banquet* to 1972's *Exile* was the band's zenith, with guitarist Keith Richards creating riff after riff that would find solid footing in the memories of rock fans for decades. Their heavily layered percussion bits, Richards' aggressive playing style, and the public airing of taboo subjects in their lyrics gave the band a somewhat primeval and menacing tone. Wrote Paul Williams, editor of the fanzine *Crawdaddy!*, "Dylan has his own incredible power, but it's not the straight-down-the center, get-out-of-my-way-or-I'm-going-to-kill-you, rock 'n roll power of the Rolling Stones. . . . The sound is so strong and appealing, we are almost forced to receive the song on a profound level, to find a profound level to receive it on. And we do."[10]

The group particularly enjoyed touring and recording in the United States, which, at a time of extreme social unrest and political upheaval, provided ample fodder for their continuing motifs of sex, drugs, death, alienation, and rebellion. After their peak at the turn of the decade, however, these themes were common in rock, and the Stones found themselves further challenged by the likes of David Bowie and Elton John on one side (more feminine than Jagger's strutting sexuality) and Led Zeppelin and the Who on the other (more masculine than Richards' guitar riffs). Although their slice of the pie became smaller, the Rolling Stones continued a several-decades-long career as one of the top acts in rock and one of the most influential marketers of teenage rebellion.

The Yardbirds

The Yardbirds might be considered the most dangerous rock group of their era if for no other reason than they contained, over a short career from 1963 to 1968, three of the finest guitarists rock has ever known. With Eric Clapton, Jeff Beck, and Jimmy Page playing in the band at different times (except for a six-month overlap between Beck and Page), the group pioneered a sophisticated rhythm and blues that coupled prepsychedelic improvisation and technical mastery.

The Yardbirds' sound was by turns peppy, gritty, psychedelic, and catchy, depending on what song you were listening to. Although they saw limited chart success in the United States, with only their 1967 *Greatest Hits* album breaching the Top 40, they deeply influenced heavy metal with their skilled guitar pyrotechnics, a staple of later metal bands. Beck in particular was rivaled only by Jimi Hendrix in his innovative fretwork, capable of squeezing almost any sound imaginable from his guitar. "Mention his name to a musician," said one critic, "and any guitarist worth his weight in guitar strings will start to shake."[11] Unfortunately, Beck's habit of missing performances got him expelled from the group during a U.S. tour in 1966. The band remained a quartet and achieved underground status in America, but dissolved in 1968. But even in their disbanding the Yardbirds were influential, as Page formed the New Yardbirds shortly thereafter, soon renaming themselves Led Zeppelin—one of heavy metal's most beloved acts and inarguably the most popular hard-rock band of the 1970s.

The Who

Many fans of 1960s rock remember the Who as the first "angry" band, a group that destroyed its instruments during performances, which by itself is a characteristic copied by heavy-metal and punk-rock artists in the 1970s. But more central to the Who's legacy is the message their onstage antics related and the audience for whom they were intended. The Who were the third wave of the British invasion, following closely on the heels of the Rolling Stones, who lagged just behind the Beatles. But while tempo cued the Beatles' nods and the Stones' struts, the Who embarked on a hard-driving sermon bordering on chaos, with only the irregular cadence of public disorder keeping the beat.

Much that should be remembered about the Who is summed up in the eponymous hit off their first album, *My Generation*. Though released in 1965—several years before the band found a home on the U.S. charts—the song was tailor-made for increasingly estranged American youth. The Who assumed the voice of alienated teens who felt disenfranchised from their future, expressing their

cohort's rage with heavy, stuttering, power-chord-driven diatribes at a callous society. The direct lyrics of "My Generation" cut to the heart of teen angst, especially in the anthemic line "Hope I die before I get old." These sentiments were the prototype of later heavy-metal lyrics that focused to a large degree on youth rebellion.

Depending on one's perspective, there are many events that could be interpreted as "the birth of heavy metal" in the United States, and the 1967 Monterey Pop Festival is as good as any. At the Sunday evening finale, both the Who and Jimi Hendrix performed wild, instrument-smashing sets, an uncommon theatric device at the time (see Chapter 7, "The Festival Is Born"). Monterey was the stepping-off point for both acts in the United States, the watershed moment that lit

The Who, 1973. Courtesy of Photofest.

a match to their fame in America. The concert was one of a number of high-profile appearances the Who were making in the states after several years of relative anonymity outside of England. Their electric presentation of Pete Townshend's dangerous guitar antics, singer Roger Daltrey's acrobatic leaps, Keith Moon's thrashing drums, and John Entwistle's blur of fingers on bass set new standards for rock presentation and caught the imagination of a whole new string of power bands. "They have been creeping up," said one critic from the period. "If you don't see them by now then you won't know it till your whole room explodes with their dynamite."[12]

As a demonstration of how far the band was willing to go on stage, consider their appearance on *The Smothers Brothers Comedy Hour* during their 1967 American tour. The band secretly added extra flash powder to their special effects to highlight their "explosiveness" on stage. According to biographer

Richard Barnes, "The explosion at the end of 'My Generation' was enormous. Pete temporarily lost his hearing and singed his hair, a fragment of flying cymbal embedded itself in Keith's leg, and show guest [movie star] Bette Davis fainted into Mickey Rooney's arms."[13]

The Who followed their successful appearances in America with four incredible albums between 1969 and 1973 that would be the finest work of their career: *Tommy, Live at Leeds, Who's Next*, and *Quadrophenia*. The first, *Tommy*, was a tour de force of teenage estrangement, one of the first "concept albums" in which each song serves as a chapter in a larger text. This particular style was dubbed "rock opera" for its narrative format, and paved the way for similar albums by 1970s supergroups like Pink Floyd and Jethro Tull (see Chapter 6, "Rock Goes Progressive"). *Tommy* was the final nail in the coffin for the three-minute pop song, which had dominated radio play and record sales for too long. The album was perfectly timed on the heels of loosely narrative groundbreakers like the Beach Boys' 1966 *Pet Sounds* and the Beatles' 1967 *Sgt. Pepper's Lonely Hearts Club Band*, which accompanied the advent of album sales outpacing singles, a trend that soon became the status quo.

Following their 1969 appearance at Woodstock (at which Townshend famously knocked Abbie Hoffman off the stage for stealing his microphone for a political diatribe), the Who rattled off a number of successful tracks that lambasted commercialism and continued operating as a voice for disaffected youth. Songs like "Won't Get Fooled Again," "Behind Blue Eyes," "Love, Reign O'er Me," and resurfacing tracks from *Tommy* like "I'm Free" and "Pinball Wizard" kept the band in constant airplay and became enduring rock classics. Every original album the band released in the United States since *Tommy*—nine in all between 1969 and 1982—reached the American Top 10, but amazingly the band never had a record or single top the charts, despite their widespread popularity and enormous influence on 1970s rock, punk, and heavy metal.

Between 1965's *My Generation* and 1973's *Quadrophenia*—the band's second rock opera—one can discern many of the elements that would make heavy metal what it is. Artistically, the Who served as a template for passionate, chaotic, shake-your-fist-at-the-sky songs driven by aggressive drumming, power chords, and technical prowess. Thematically, the band functioned as an embodiment of frustrated youth, a message that this generation had something to say; and with Pete Townshend as one of the most versatile and imaginative lyricists of his time, it was well worth hearing.

Eric Clapton and Cream

Eric Clapton was one of the most incongruous rock musicians of the 1960s and 1970s—a young, white, British guitar virtuoso who worshiped aging black musicians from Chicago and the Delta; a blues purist who wrote numerous enduring pop hits; and a major celebrity in an egocentric rock world who dodged fame at every corner. Clapton was also one of the most important musical figures of his time, a central character in two of hard rock's seminal bands—the Yardbirds and Cream.

After Clapton left the Yardbirds in 1965, he joined John Mayall's Bluesbreakers, one of the top blues outfits in England. At the tender age of twenty-one, he was considered among the finest guitarists in rock, earning him a nickname that could not lack any more in subtlety: God. During a performance, it was not unusual to hear a shout from the audience, "Give God a solo!" After one album with the Bluesbreakers, Clapton invited bassist Jack Bruce and drummer Ginger Baker to form the power trio of Cream, one of the first rock supergroups and hailed by some critics as the best rock group in the world.

Because they saw themselves as a blues band, Cream soon targeted the United States for their new home to be close to blues's roots. They did not even consider themselves a rock group at first, but their April 1967 arrival in the United States was timed for the explosion of psychedelic jams that included hour-long improvised solos.

Eric Clapton in a movie still. Courtesy of Photofest.

Clapton especially liked the summer-of-love San Francisco scene and jumped right into the fray, with his early jazz background making it easy for him to improvise, and his dexterity as a blues player giving the group a truly unique sound. Bruce took on vocals, but it was Clapton the fans came to hear. "Cream was the first of a new species—the high-voltage superblues group. By channeling their 'amplified heat' through traditional blues, they created a clean, lean, sensual sound which fused their audiences together in a virtual cult of electricity, with Eric Clapton as its god."[14]

Cream released only four albums in their short, two-year career, the debut *Fresh Cream* charting high in England but barely breaking the Top 40 in America. During their 1967 tour of the United States, the band played a two-week residency at San Francisco's hottest venue, the Fillmore Auditorium, often jamming until after sunrise. Their performance was as powerful as anything the Fillmore had seen, and by the end of the gig, Cream had been elevated in the American rock world (centered at that time in San Francisco) from just another British invasion band to bona fide rock gods.

Success in the states soon followed with their sophomore album *Disraeli Gears*. Though the band's songs had limited success on the charts—with only

"Sunshine of Your Love" and "White Room" breaking the Top 10—their records fared much better. *Disraeli Gears* rose to No. 4 on the strength of their live shows in the United States (where they spent most of their time), and their 1968 follow-up *Wheels of Fire* spent four weeks in the top spot. A double record, *Wheels of Fire* featured an album's worth of live cuts from their stay at the Fillmore, now considered to be one of the best live performances ever captured on vinyl.

Before the release of their fourth album, *Goodbye* (which spent two weeks in the No. 2 spot), Cream dissolved in 1968, partially from personality clashes between Bruce and Baker and partially from pure exhaustion at being the top live performers in the game. The perennially shy Clapton especially resented being such a public figure, preferring to play guitar in the shadows and let others garner the press clippings. But the band had made such an impact on the burgeoning hard-rock scene in America that a post-breakup *Best of Cream* reached No. 3, and two subsequent live albums in 1970 and 1972 made the Top 40. The pioneering power-trio format that Cream and the Who invented was copied by many metal bands, as was Clapton's penchant for memorable blues riffs and Cream's dynamic interplay between guitar, bass, and drums (rather than designated lead and backup instruments).

After Cream, the tortured Clapton continued to fail miserably at avoiding the spotlight. Between 1969 and 1970 he formed two short-lived bands—Blind Faith and Derek and the Dominos—both attempts to retire to obscure blues-bar gigs, both enormously successful despite Clapton's best efforts. Each band spit out one quick album, both of which have become classics. *Blind Faith* spent two weeks in the No. 1 spot and spawned the single "Can't Find My Way Home." Derek and the Dominos (essentially a backing band for Clapton, though even the name was created as something for Clapton to hide behind) recorded *Layla and Other Assorted Love Songs*, the eponymous track one of rock's most enduring backstories—both because the song was a collaboration with legendary southern rocker Duane Allman and because it was a masked confession of Clapton's unrequited love for Pattie Harrison, the wife of ex-Beatle and close friend George.

After several mediocre solo efforts, Clapton gave up music and disappeared into a three-year heroin stupor in the early 1970s, eventually rescued by George Harrison and the Who's Pete Townshend. He returned to making music, garnering many more hits over the following decades as one of the more enduring musical figures of the 1960s rock revolution. One reviewer, upon seeing one of Clapton's return-from-the-grave concerts in 1973, could only mutter in his column, "God damn, you should have been there."[15] Clapton's masterful understanding of the blues and his gift for distorted, improvised solos, especially during his tenure with Cream, inspired numerous hard-rock and heavy-metal copycats, despite his reticent personality in an egocentric genre.

Jimi Hendrix

If one were to provide a list of 1960s hard-rock attributes to the genre's die-hard fans, and then asked them to associate a name with each attribute, the list might look something like this: most skilled guitarist—Eric Clapton; most creative guitarist—Jeff Beck; loudest group—the Who; most sexual performer—Mick Jagger; most influential band—the Yardbirds; most intimidating stage presence—Alice Cooper; and so on. But if one were to ask fans to provide two names for each category, it would be a fair bet that most of those spots, and in some cases the top spot, would belong to Jimi Hendrix.

Seattle native Johnny Allen Hendrix spent his childhood in the 1940s and 1950s shuttled between relatives and foster homes—abandoned by his mother when he was ten, and in irregular touch with his military father (who renamed him James Marshall Hendrix). Hendrix buried himself in his father's collection of blues and jazz records, creating a surrogate parent-

Jimi Hendrix, 1969. Courtesy of Photofest.

age out of Muddy Waters, Elmore James, Robert Johnson, B. B. King, and Howlin' Wolf. At fourteen, Hendrix picked up an acoustic guitar and within a year was playing in a band, spending his teen years performing small gigs along the West Coast.

After several years working as a session player, Hendrix settled into the New York City scene in 1965, keeping one foot in the blues and soul houses in Harlem and the other in the Dylan-happy folk and prepsychedelic venues in Greenwich Village.

Upon spotting Hendrix at Café Wha?, acoustic blues guitarist John Hammond Jr. recruited Hendrix for some gigs of his own. Soon rock guitarists were flocking to see Hammond's new discovery. Mike Bloomfield, who was one of the top guns in the country as guitarist for the Butterfield Blues Band and regular backup for Bob Dylan, recalls his first time seeing Hendrix perform. "I was the hot shot guitarist on the block. . . . Hendrix knew who I was and that day, in front of my eyes, he burned me to death. I didn't even get my guitar out. H-bombs were going off, guided missiles were flying. . . . He just got right up in my face with that axe, and I didn't even want to pick up a guitar for the next year."[16]

After Animals manager and bassist Chas Chandler saw Hendrix perform, he convinced him (partially on the promise that he could introduce him to Eric

Clapton) that he should play the circuit in England. In September 1966, Chandler brought Hendrix to London, where he helped him form the Jimi Hendrix Experience with bassist Noel Redding and drummer John "Mitch" Mitchell. Hendrix was an instant sensation, drawing the top names in Britain—John Mayall, Paul McCartney, Pete Townshend, Eric Clapton—to see his chops. By December the Experience had recorded their first single, "Hey Joe," which made the British Top 10 and primed audiences for an explosive debut album, *Are You Experienced?*, featuring instant classics such as "Foxey Lady," "Manic Depression," "The Wind Cries Mary," and, perhaps his most memorable hit, "Purple Haze."

Are You Experienced? was a smash in England, making Hendrix the talk of English rock, though its May 1967 release was soon overshadowed by the groundbreaking Beatles' album *Sgt. Pepper's Lonely Hearts Club Band*. Hendrix's debut was held off in the United States, where he was relatively unknown, until after his appearance at the Monterey Pop Festival in June, which, according to a *Los Angeles Times* critic, graduated him "from rumor to legend."[17] Hendrix mesmerized the audiences at Monterey in 1967, playing his guitar between his legs, behind his back, and with his tongue, and setting the instrument on fire after the set, upstaging even the Who's explosive performance only an hour earlier (see Chapter 7, "The Festival Is Born"). When *Are You Experienced?* was released in America a week later, it climbed to No. 5.

Not everyone was thrilled with Hendrix, even beyond the usual uptight establishmentarians who always decried "that loud rock and roll." Music critics were split—some praising Hendrix as the most creative guitarist in rock, others portraying him as an Uncle-Tom-variety sell-out, intentionally manipulating stereotypes of black sexuality and exoticism to entertain white audiences. Though Hendrix learned his stage antics by copying previous black stars like Little Richard and James Brown, he was the first black artist to attract mostly white audiences, and as an innovative interpreter of the blues, he was accused of betraying blacks as blues originators.

As is so often the case when politics is brought into the art world, critics argued about the image while the musicians talked about the music. Hendrix was well aware of the Chicago and Delta roots of his musical heritage, as well as the innovations wrought by the British rockers and the San Francisco psychedelics, but for him, rock was not about race; it was about change. "America is divided into two definite divisions. . . . The easy thing to cop out with is sayin' black and white. . . . But now to get down to the nitty-gritty, it's gettin' to be old and young—not the age, but the way of thinking."[18] Hendrix knew he was on the forefront of a musical revolution, and the new "way of thinking" about rock music brought about unimagined transformations in sound.

After Monterey, Hendrix was in demand all over the country, as promoters rushed to supply fans with a glimpse at this popular newcomer's electric performances. Hendrix did not disappoint, on constant tour in the United States and Europe, and charting two excellent albums in 1968: *Axis: Bold as Love* and *Electric Ladyland* (his only U.S. album to top the charts). With his new-found fame and fortune, he was able to draw artists such as Al Kooper, Steve Winwood, Buddy Miles, and Jefferson Airplane's Jack Casady into his recordings, and was free to experiment with the ever-increasing repertoire of sonic toys, creating a whole new language on his guitar. His sound was a mix of the old and the new—field hollers, call and response, and the chords and scales of the blues tradition, coupled with unusual audio effects and the free-ranging solos of psychedelia.

Hendrix's music also reflected the swelling disaffection with mainstream society that so many American youth were experiencing in the late 1960s. His raw, wandering solos and powerful, high-volume delivery centered on the guitar helped establish a model for later heavy metal. "Lots of young people now feel they're not getting a fair deal," he said. "So they revert to something loud, harsh, almost verging on violence; if they didn't go to a concert, they might be going to a riot."[19] A *Newsweek* reporter, shortly after Hendrix's Monterey performance, saw the same inexorable quality in Hendrix's music that Hendrix saw in the youth who idolized him. "The Experience's destruction is inevitable rather than accidental, the surfacing of a violent streak, the spontaneous and impulsive violence of the young."[20]

After an extremely successful 1968, Hendrix faced a more difficult 1969, with drug charges interfering with his tour schedule and the eventual breakup of the Experience in June when Redding felt he could no longer subsume his own talents with those of the guitar master. Chas Chandler, who had been managing the band since he helped them form, also withdrew from Hendrix's side. Hendrix formed a short-lived outfit to back him up for the remainder of the year, most notably at the Woodstock festival in August, where the guitarist is best remembered for his electric version of the Star Spangled Banner. Despite his successful albums, sold-out performances, and new celebrity status, Hendrix suffered from punishing management and label contracts and made relatively little money from his stardom.

Jimi Hendrix was always known for his exoticism—a half-black, half–Native American outcast who was often billed as a "wild man," a caricature he lived up to with his eccentric performances. As his career bloomed at a meteoric rate, he resented that his presence was appreciated by most fans more than his skills. After attempting to put together another failed backing band, Band of Gypsies, Hendrix decided to focus on his own sound in 1970 and built the $250,000 Electric Lady studio, where he could experiment in peace. Electric Lady was packed with every gadget Hendrix could find, and he would spend hours attempting to manipulate a single sound.

Electric Lady was a landmark in studio design and innovation, but Hendrix's involvement with his new toys would be short-lived. On September 18, 1970, following a European tour, Hendrix ate a late dinner with a British girlfriend and then took too many sleeping pills. His stomach rejected the drugs, and Hendrix drowned in his own vomit. His career as a known figure in the rock world barely spanned three years, but his ability to combine blues and psychedelia into a sort of controlled sonic chaos made him extraordinarily influential on hard rock and heavy metal, and arguably the single most influential artist of the period.

Blue Cheer

The thin boundary between hard rock and heavy metal has fueled a continuous argument among critics and fans about which group first crossed the line and became the original heavy-metal band. Since heavy metal as a genre developed independently in the United States and Britain, a claim could be made for each country—in Britain, Deep Purple, Black Sabbath, and Led Zeppelin vie for the title, while in the United States, it comes down to Iron Butterfly and the San Francisco power band Blue Cheer.

The predecessor to the term "heavy metal" was simply "heavy" music or "heavy" rock. It was rock that felt weighted, with harmony and melody brought low by thick power chords and strong distortion. At the height of San Francisco's psychedelic circus, Blue Cheer brought this weighted edge to hippie love. Taking the band's name from one of Augustus Stanley's more potent strains of LSD (see Chapter 1, "The Psychedelic Experience"), Blue Cheer's members—guitarist Leigh Stephens, bassist/vocalist Dickie Peterson, and drummer Paul Whaley—began as a conventional rock group before Jimi Hendrix's performance at Monterey opened their eyes to the possibilities of distorted sound. The band began hiding their relative lack of talent (in a period of guitar virtuosos) under driving rhythms and intense volume, bringing the chaos of Hendrix to psychedelic San Francisco, if not his skills.

The original lineup lasted for only the first two albums, both released in 1968—*Vincebus Eruptum* and *Outsideinside*. Their debut (peaking at No. 11)—roughly translated from the Latin as "breaking out of the chains"—featured a thundering rendition of Eddie Cochran's "Summertime Blues" that reached No. 14, the closest thing the band had to a hit song. The sophomore *Outsideinside* was true to its name—the recording was moved outdoors when the volume destroyed the monitors in the studio. None of their follow-up albums were as memorable as their first, and by 1971 the band had dissolved to join respectable company in the history books as early purveyors of a new genre.

Iron Butterfly

Blue Cheer's competition for the honorific of "America's first heavy-metal band" fared a bit better in rock's institutional memory, and are oft-credited as edging out Blue Cheer for the title. Though Iron Butterfly's first album, *Heavy*, charted the same day as Blue Cheer's debut *Vincebus Eruptum* (one might say that heavy metal in the United States was born on March 9, 1968), and both albums offered the weight of metal from their titles to their vibes, Iron Butterfly struck gold with their second release only months later, *In-A-Gadda-Da-Vida*.

The title track—seventeen minutes of gothic organ, thick bass, screeching guitars, pounding drums, and deafening feedback—represented a stoned mumbling of "in the garden of Eden" and is believed to be heavy metal's first hit song, helping the album become Atlantic Records' biggest seller for several years.

Iron Butterfly, 1971. Courtesy of Photofest.

The Southern California outfit, initially featuring singer Darryl DeLoach, organist Doug Ingle, drummer Ron Bushy, guitarist Danny Weis, and bassist Jerry Penrod (Weis and Penrod soon to be replaced by Erik Braunn and Lee Dorman), toured with and emulated bands such as the Doors and the Who, and for a brief time seemed destined to join their rock-god stratosphere. But despite a strong 1969 follow-up album, *Ball*, Butterfly could not maintain a large fan base as louder, more talented heavy-metal acts began streaming out of England. A few forgettable releases followed *Ball* until the band broke up in 1971, shortly after *In-A-Gadda-Da-Vida* finally fell from the charts. Several reunions have been attempted, all fairly dismal, as the song that made them famous and helped establish heavy metal in the United States slowly turned into a parody of its own genre.

Black Sabbath

As heavy metal in the United States was erupting from the strained amplifiers of California's psychedelic outfits, the British version of the genre simultaneously exploded in the form of Black Sabbath—a Birmingham, England, blues band described by one critic as having the "sophistication of four Cro-Magnon hunters who've stumbled upon a rock band's equipment."[21]

Though slightly predated by fellow English bands Led Zeppelin and Deep Purple, Black Sabbath was the first English group that was pure metal: loud, heavily distorted, guitar-driven rock with anarchic themes (Zeppelin's albums demonstrated mastery of many genres, and Deep Purple was as much progressive rock as heavy metal in its early years). Sabbath began in 1968 under the name Polka Tulk, with Ozzy Osbourne on vocals, Bill Ward on drums, Tony Iommi on guitar, and Terry "Geezer" Butler on bass. The group soon changed their name to Earth and finally Black Sabbath, reputedly borrowed from a movie poster for the Boris Karloff film of that name.

Largely influenced by hard rockers like Cream, the Yardbirds, the Jimi Hendrix Experience, and the burgeoning powerhouse Led Zeppelin, the group's new name was meant to echo their heavy sound and gothic lyrics. Dark themes such as drugs, insanity, and the occult powered their albums and set the standard for heavy-metal lyrics to follow. Their brooding music brought them an immediate audience of frustrated youth, making the band's 1970 self-titled debut—recorded for about $1,200—an instant success in Britain and the United States. The band's cultish lyrics brought charges of Satanism, which more than anything lent an air of mystery to the group that helped increase album sales and concert grosses. Relentless touring and recording during their first few years also helped the band find an international audience.

Only six months after *Black Sabbath* reached No. 23 on the American charts in 1970, their second effort, *Paranoid*, hit No. 12, followed six months later by *Master of Reality* at No. 8. Extensive touring in the United States in the early 1970s earned them a devoted following. Now firmly ensconced in the American charts, concert halls, and the shelves of teenagers, the band was a model for all heavy metal to follow. The weighty power chords, the plodding bass lines, the lyrical fixation on themes of doom, the black leather outfits with heavy crosses slung about the neck—the group, if not for their remarkable talent, was a horror film with a tour bus. "It's all about raw, musical energy," wrote an early critic, "and if Sabbaths' music happens also to be a shade more vengeful and violent than any previous rock, it's because they mean what they say about releasing the tension in their audiences. With few of the trappings and affectations common to all too many groups, Black Sabbath deliver."[22]

Despite their gloomy themes, Sabbath sent a subtle positive message to their listeners, another quality imitated by many of the group's descendants. Though heavy metal seems to be the antithesis of flower-power music, they are both forms of social discourse. Country Joe and the Fish evoked cheerful applause and shouts with their antiwar "I Feel Like I'm Fixin' to Die Rag," while Black Sabbath garnered head bobs and fists in the air with "War Pigs." But ultimately music for hippies and metal heads shared the same message: society is in a sorry state, but brotherhood can bring it together. Behind Black Sabbath's world-weary dress and sound, the band channeled the spirit of Bob Dylan as much as anyone. This call for unity was answered by heavy-metal devotees, who found in the company of others like themselves a brotherhood of sorts, largely male and young, who would imitate their musical heroes in style and manner and bond over themes of doom, all the while finding relief in those very themes by virtue of sharing the experience with like-minded friends.

By 1972, Black Sabbath was the quintessential metal band, rivaled only by Led Zeppelin and the American group Grand Funk Railroad for album sales, intensity, and sheer volume. But hot on their heels, bands like Alice Cooper, Deep Purple, Aerosmith, and dozens of others who wanted to be the loudest kids on the block began to rival Sabbath and cut into their audience even as they copied Sabbath's sound. Though the group left the Top 20 after their fourth and fifth albums (1972's *Black Sabbath Vol. 4* and 1974's *Sabbath Bloody Sabbath*), they continued to tour and record successfully for several decades, and in the minds of many metal fans, they were the first truly great heavy-metal band.

Led Zeppelin

Widely hailed as one of rock's finest acts, Led Zeppelin owned the 1970s like the Beatles owned the 1960s and Elvis owned the late 1950s. All nine of their albums between 1969 and 1979 charted in the Top 10, with six of them reaching the No. 1 spot for a total of twenty-eight weeks at the top. According to the Recording Industry Association of America, Led Zeppelin ranks just behind the Beatles and Elvis as the third best-selling musical act in American history (including genres outside of rock).[23] Although considered one of the first metal bands, Zeppelin was a veritable grab bag of surprises, demonstrating facility with hard rock, folk, reggae, eastern, blues, and classical genres often on the same album, and sometimes in the same song.

Originally named the New Yardbirds when they formed in late 1968 (to fulfill remaining dates contracted by the Yardbirds), the group only contained one member of their recently defunct namesake, guitar phenom Jimmy Page. Page and well-known bassist/keyboardist John Paul Jones were unable to fill out the band with the musicians they wanted, so instead settled on relative unknowns—the vocalist Robert Plant and his friend, drummer John Bonham. The two proved to be a perfect fit. While on their first tour supporting the Who, legend has it that Who drummer Keith Moon and bassist John Entwistle told them their band would go over like a lead zeppelin. The New Yardbirds liked the sound of the phrase, if not its intent, and after changing the spelling of "lead" to avoid pronunciation confusion, they embarked on a career that rivaled even that of the Who.

After a 1969 American tour supporting Vanilla Fudge, the band released *Led Zeppelin*, a major work of hard English blues that showcased not only the talents of the individual members but Page's producing prowess, which gave every song the rich, textured feel of a classic (which many of them have become). Effused one critic about his early Zeppelin experience, "I played the first Zep LP three times a day for three months until I saw them on the second US tour and was so awestruck by it all that I could never bring myself to play the album again."[24] From this first release, the band lured the largely young and male audience that would be their bread and butter throughout their career. Using lyrical innuendo, orgasmic shrieks, and masturbatory guitar runs, the songs played on the teen whimsy of becoming a potent rock Adonis dripping with sexuality. Though the group did not consider themselves Satanists, themes of the occult showed up regularly in their songs, further endearing their young listeners who knew their parents would not approve. From their early U.S. tours (no less than six in their first eighteen months together), Led Zeppelin lived an almost animalistic lifestyle that would become the stuff of rock legend and adolescent fantasy—tearing apart hotel rooms, indulging in drugs and women at will, and leaving trashed performance venues in their wake. They quickly outshined the Who and the Rolling Stones as the bad boys of rock, and would soon prove to be unstoppable.

Led Zeppelin, 1972. Courtesy of Photofest.

Led Zeppelin reached No. 10 on the American charts, and was followed over the next two years by 1969's *Led Zeppelin II* and 1970's *Led Zeppelin III*, which spent a combined eleven weeks in the No. 1 spot. By the end of 1970, the band was one of the hottest acts in the world, selling out tours with the dynamic interplay between Plant's powerful voice and Page's imaginative fretwork, aided in no small part by the driving energy of Bonham's forceful drumming and the solid anchor that Jones' bass lines provided to many of their songs. Their first three albums were so powerful and well rounded that the band's single sales actually suffered as a result—only one song, "Whole Lotta Love" off of *Led Zeppelin II*, found its way into the Top 10. The range of material offered made the band's records must-haves for serious rockers, and the first three releases produced a litany of classic headbangers— "Communication Breakdown," "Babe I'm Gonna Leave You," "Dazed and Confused," "Good Times Bad Times," "Immigrant Song," just to name a few— that only a handful of acts have rivaled.

In late 1971, the group issued what would become its signature release and a benchmark in rock history. The untitled album (usually referred to as *Led Zeppelin IV*) was a masterwork, ranging from the driving energy of "Rock and Roll" to the sleepy acoustic balladry of "Going to California" to the multilayered rock anthem "Stairway to Heaven." Amazingly, the album only peaked at No. 2, trapped for four weeks behind Santana's excellent *Santana III*. But while most of the band's other albums reached the top spot, *Led Zeppelin IV* set a record for longevity, spending 259 weeks on the charts (among rock albums, second only to Pink Floyd's 1973 *Dark Side of the Moon*) and eventually going platinum more than a dozen times over.

What set Led Zeppelin apart from other bands was their range of talents. Robert Plant could sing louder and higher than most of his contemporaries. Jimmy Page could play faster, but also more melodically. Their lyrics explored a wide array of themes, and were supported by an extreme variety of musical styles. The band was driven to constantly explore their musical potential, and every record demonstrated a stab at something new. After their fifth and sixth albums, 1973's *Houses of the Holy* and 1975's remarkable double album *Physical Graffiti*, the group established their own label, Swan Song, gaining them even more artistic freedom. In 1976 they released their weakest album, *Presence*, and soon followed up with the film soundtrack *The Song Remains the*

Same. These were their two poorest sellers, but still managed to go double platinum.

A few setbacks for Plant in the mid-1970s—an automobile accident in 1975 and his son's death in 1977—threatened to break up the band, which had spent countless hours touring and recording since 1969. It was three years before they returned to the studio for their final album, 1979's *In through the Out Door*, a much-anticipated release that spent seven weeks in the top spot. Though the group had been largely inactive before the release, plans were made to return to the road for another United States tour. The idea was scrapped in September 1980 when John Bonham was found dead after a night of heavy drinking. That December, the band officially announced their retirement, later releasing one more album of archived material called, appropriately, *Coda*.

Despite their remarkable career, Led Zeppelin were rarely appreciated by the critics as much as they were by their fans, another attribute that became characteristic of heavy-metal groups. Extreme volume and screamed lyrics were seen by many critics as a substitute for talent, despite the obvious skills Page and Plant brought to the table. Reviewing the band's first album, the respected San Francisco rock journal *Rolling Stone* called Page "a very limited producer and a writer of weak, unimaginative songs," and Plant "as foppish as Rod Stewart, but he's nowhere near so exciting, especially in the higher registers."[25] But the reviews did not stop the audiences. After their third album in 1970, Led Zeppelin was voted the most popular band by the *Melody Maker* public opinion poll, the first time in eight years the Beatles had not won. In 1973 the band broke the Beatles' 1965 single-act attendance record (see Chapter 7, "The Festival Is Born"), bringing 56,000 fans to a Florida venue, making a record $309,000 for the show and ushering in the era of stadium rock. "Records are made to be broken," wrote one reporter at the event, "but if there's any shattering to be done at this point, Led Zeppelin will probably be the ones to crack the mark again. Like their namesake, they defy gravity to ride a core of flaming vapor, the acknowledged heavyweight band champions of the world."[26] More importantly, the band popularized a new genre, according to critic Ken Tucker, "[changing] the landscape against which rock is played. And so the basic formula for heavy metal was codified . . . high-pitched male tenor vocals singing lyrics that ideally combined mysticism, sexism, and hostility."[27]

Deep Purple

Though British group Deep Purple had begun in 1968 as more or less a pop cover band, scoring minor hits with reworkings of "Hush" and "Kentucky Woman" in 1968, they did not really get going as a heavy-metal act until after their third album in 1969, when they added vocalist Ian Gillan and bassist Roger Glover to a lineup that included drummer Ian Paice, keyboardist Jon Lord, and guitarist Ritchie Blackmore. Their first outing with this quintet, considered the classic Deep Purple lineup, was a partnership with the London

Philharmonic Orchestra called *Concerto for Group and Orchestra*, a squarely progressive-rock feat penned by Lord (see Chapter 6, "Rock Goes Progressive").

The album was well received, but the band wanted to try out their metal legs (impressed by what Led Zeppelin was getting away with), and released a very different *Deep Purple in Rock* in 1970 to enthusiastic British audiences, instantly reaching the British Top 5 and making them a popular attraction. Deep Purple would hold steady as one of the top metal acts in England for several years, but cracking the American market would prove to be more difficult. It was not until their seventh release, 1972's *Machine Head*, that the group made it in the United States, largely on the strength of their No. 4 single "Smoke on the Water." The song—a true story of the 1971 fire at Montreux Casino, where Deep Purple was playing with Frank Zappa and the Mothers of Invention—became a heavy-metal staple, its opening power chords the first notes played by preteen guitar wanna-bes for years to come.

Although *Machine Head* reached No. 7 in America and spent 118 weeks on the charts, the band's two follow-up albums did not fair as well, until 1973's double-live *Made in Japan* and 1974's *Burn* returned the group to the Top 10 for the last time. Though not as successful in the United States as other metal acts, Deep Purple contributed significantly to the growth of the genre. Lord and Blackmore were technical virtuosos with deep respect for classical music. As influenced by Bach and Vivaldi as by any blues artist, the duo copied baroque techniques to play extremely fast while still sounding comprehensible to listeners, a hallmark of metal bands to follow and a key component in the birth of speed metal in the 1980s. Combining speed with volume—the group was listed in the Guinness Book of World Records as the world's loudest band—was a signature of Deep Purple and had a major impact on later artists, influencing 1980s giants such as Eddie Van Halen, Randy Rhoads, and Yngwie Malmsteen. After membership changes through the 1970s (eventually leading to the band's demise in 1976), Deep Purple's artists continued to be influential in the bands Whitesnake, Rainbow, and Black Sabbath.

Jeff Beck

One of a handful of guitarists that can be compared to Jimi Hendrix and Jimmy Page was Page's fellow Yardbird and Englishman Jeff Beck. Though Beck never reached the height of fame and fortune his talent deserved, his incredibly imaginative fretwork was celebrated in music circles, and for a brief time in the early 1970s he earned public appreciation for his work with artists like Rod Stewart and Ron Wood (in the Jeff Beck Group) and Tim Bogert and Carmine Appice (both from Vanilla Fudge).

Beck first made a name for himself in 1965 as Eric Clapton's replacement in the Yardbirds—a massive pair of shoes to fill, which the unknown guitarist managed surprisingly well, though his tastes were more eclectic than Clapton's preference for straight-up blues. His attention, unfortunately, wandered as rapidly as his fingers, and he constantly stood the band up for gigs when other events interested him more. Jimmy Page was brought in to back Beck up, creating fiery duo performances on the occasional dates that Beck showed up to play. After Page had been in the band for six months, Beck walked out during a U.S. tour and was asked not to return. His unreliability turned a potentially brilliant career into one of unrequited genius, playing in and out of groups for years; associating with the performers he wanted to on his own terms; even turning down a job playing for the Rolling Stones in 1975, when they were one of the top acts in the world.

Still, one can imagine that whatever guided his lack of consistency also contributed to his extraordinary penchant for productive experimentation. Beck was a master of integrating blues, jazz, pop, and rock with unique instrumental prowess that some critics believe, in retrospect, has not been equaled since. "With the Yardbirds, his search for new sounds bridged the gap between R&B and art-pop/psychedelia, while he later helped to sow the seeds of British hard rock and heavy metal with his own group. Only Jimi Hendrix and Eric Clapton can rival the invention and the influence of Jeff Beck."[28] Beck continued to play for decades, occasionally experiencing spikes in the popular forum, but more often comfortable in his role of independent recluse, completely lacking in direction but paving roads as he went. Even Jimmy Page, though constantly frustrated with his poor social skills, admitted that though Beck was an inconsistent musician, "when he's on, he's probably the best there is."[29]

Alice Cooper

More than most early metal acts, the band Alice Cooper was as interested in theatrics as the music they were making. The band was founded in 1968 by Detroit native Vincent Furnier (who soon adopted the band's moniker as his own name) when he was a teenager living in Phoenix. Alice Cooper was an early incarnation of "shock rock," a type of hard rock that seeks to alarm and provoke its audiences as part of the entertainment. The band was known for pulling Frank Zappa–like stunts, such as staging guillotine and electric-chair executions on stage, and Furnier singing with a live snake wrapped around him.

Alice Cooper, 1973. Courtesy of Photofest.

It was Zappa, in fact, that gave the band its break by signing them to his fledgling Straight Records label, a subsidiary of Warner Brothers (which Cooper switched to for their third album in 1970). Not surprisingly, the band's bizarre style did not immediately attract the attention of the charts, but as their adolescent-targeted lyrics began to speak to rebellious youth, the band developed a following. Their biggest hits were rebel anthems that spoke directly to teenagers, such as 1971's "Eighteen" and 1972's "School's Out," their first song to break the Top 10. Buoyed by these themes, which fed teenage desire for independence, Cooper issued a string of Top 10 releases between 1972 and 1975 with the albums *School's Out*, *Billion Dollar Babies*, *Muscle of Love*, *Alice Cooper's Greatest Hits*, and *Welcome to My Nightmare*.

With his thick black makeup that long predated KISS and other theater bands of the late 1970s, Furnier and his onstage antics gave the band the feel of a dark-fantasy show, where teens could indulge themselves in visions of the occult and the supernatural. By 1975, however, Furnier had fired his band and essentially gone solo under the name Alice Cooper, beginning a long, slow descent into mediocrity and ridicule (partly fueled by his appearance on the 1970s puppet comedy *The Muppet Show*), with only two singles and no albums breaching the Top 10 over the following decades. But hindsight has proved just to both Furnier and Alice Cooper, as they are now regarded as the originators of shock rock as well as major influences on the theatrical trappings of later metal acts.

LESSER GODS

There were so many personalities at the outset of hard rock, so many originators, so many influences on so many disparate styles, that it would be impossible to detail them all. The strains of Davies, Beck, Hendrix, Page, and Clapton spread across the United States like a virus, infecting local music scenes and revolutionizing the rock world in a relatively short period of time. The late 1960s and early 1970s were ripe for an explosion of musical variety, giving birth to punk, southern, metal, progressive, and other minor forms of rock, all based largely on the power of the electric guitar.

Two major artists of the era whose names have been buried behind the short-lived acts in which they participated are Chicago guitarist Mike Bloomfield and New York organist Al Kooper. Bloomfield, largely considered the finest white American blues guitarist of his time, leaped into the spotlight in 1965 when, at twenty-one years of age, he mesmerized audiences with his emotional playing in the Paul Butterfield Blues Band, and the same year backed up Bob Dylan at the Newport Folk Festival when the folkie first played electric guitar in public. In 1967, Bloomfield left to form the brief but influential Electric Flag, combining soul, blues, and a horn section—very unusual for rock bands at the time. After more collaborations with Dylan, Bloomfield produced his best work in 1968 with Stephen Stills and Al Kooper on the album *Super Session*, then with Kooper on 1969's *The Live Adventures of Mike Bloomfield and Al Kooper*. Bloomfield was wary of success, though, and spent much of the next decade as a recluse, scoring film soundtracks, releasing very good to mediocre collaborations and solo efforts, and indulging his drug habit before eventually dying of an overdose in 1981.

Al Kooper's path to fame was not dissimilar to Bloomfield's. The two were close friends, both working with Dylan in 1965 (though Kooper, a session guitarist, turned to the organ when Bloomfield had already filled the guitar seat). Kooper's first step into the spotlight was playing a memorable organ on Dylan's "Like a Rolling Stone" and its accompanying album *Highway 61 Revisited*, earning him work on other Dylan albums like *Blonde on Blonde* and *New Morning*. After a brief period with the Blues Project, Kooper formed the seminal group Blood, Sweat & Tears in 1968, which, much like Electric Flag, incorporated horns into its blues-based rock. Kooper left the group after only a year, just before they experienced major success with their second and third albums, which spent a combined nine weeks at No. 1.

Though mainstream success kept eluding him, Kooper was a talented arranger and a seminal figure behind other major stars, not only collaborating with Dylan but also performing on albums such as Jimi Hendrix's *Electric Ladyland* and the Rolling Stones' *Let It Bleed*. Inspired by what he was hearing from Phil Walden's Capricorn Records (see Chapter 4, "The South Rises Again"), Kooper moved to Atlanta in 1972 to found the Sounds of the South label, discovering the seminal southern-rock group Lynyrd Skynyrd. In the thirty-plus years since, Kooper has continued to work behind the scenes, producing albums and film soundtracks and occasionally surfacing with a release of his own. In the world of popular appreciation, however, both Bloomfield and Kooper have largely been denied their rightful places as major forces during a period of rock innovation.

Just as Kooper and Bloomfield influenced rock through their collaborations with other artists, bands in England and the United States regularly traded members, aiding in the spread of certain styles and themes. The British power rockers Uriah Heep have gone through more than two dozen lineup changes since debuting in 1970, its members also playing with acts like Elton John, Ozzy Osbourne, Rainbow, King Crimson, and David Bowie. Though Heep was much derided by the critics for their cheesy lyrics and cliché themes, they were part of the exchange of ideas in the early 1970s that gave heavy metal its distinct style.

Also in England, the group Free spread their own form of unpolished, good-timey hard rock that influenced their British contemporaries as well as bands in the United States. Formed during London's 1968 blues explosion, Free combined the expressive singing of Paul Rodgers with Paul Kossoff's piercing guitar in a raw, energetic style that celebrated rock's rough edges, influencing not only hard rock and heavy metal, but also southern rockers like Lynyrd Skynyrd and the Allman Brothers Band. Though the group had only one Top 40 record in the United States—1970's *Fire and Water*—a single from the album, "All Right Now," reached No. 4 on the charts and became an enduring classic. After leaving the band in 1973, Rodgers and his drummer Simon Kirke formed the 1970s powerhouse Bad Company.

Adding spice to the mix were New York bands Vanilla Fudge and Mountain. Vanilla Fudge, a brief pop-cover band between 1966 and 1970, gained a hard edge in their last years, which proved influential to American metal acts, with their members going on to play with Jeff Beck, Alice Cooper, Rod Stewart, and Cactus. It was on the coattails of a popular Vanilla Fudge that a nascent Led Zeppelin rode into the American market, touring the United States as their opening band shortly before releasing *Led Zeppelin*. A harder sound was brought to bear by guitarist/vocalist Leslie West and his 1970 act Mountain. West's singing was as heavy and powerful as his guitar, further popularizing screeching lyrics in the heavy-metal genre. A highly respected guitarist, West and bassist/producer Felix Pappalardi created a sound compared—both favorably and unfavorably—to Eric Clapton's supergroup Cream, a band Pappalardi produced and performed with.

Grand Funk Railroad, 1973. Courtesy of Photofest.

But not all of rock's major acts came from New York, California, and London. In Detroit, the proto-punk band MC5 were cranking the distortion and offending audiences as early as 1964, before finally releasing a live album in 1969, the seminal *Kick Out the Jams*. Unlike many hard-rock acts, MC5 were overtly political, openly aligning themselves with the radical White Panther Party, a move that made them Detroit's most popular underground act but guaranteed their limited success. Never a band to be pushed around, the group took out advertisements in the local paper criticizing a large chain store that refused to stock the powerful and controversial *Kick Out the Jams*, leading them to be dropped from their label. Two follow-up albums fared poorly, and the band wisely broke up in 1972 while they were still adored by the underground. Praised as instigators by 1970s punk bands, MC5 were the less-successful American version of the Kinks, playing controlled chaos long before it was cool.

Also hailing from Michigan were the less innovative but much more successful Grand

Funk Railroad, a brash party band that made up in popularity what it lacked in critical acclaim. GFR's commercial success was based largely on the platform that music just needed to be fun and loud—a theory that worked for the band, as it placed a remarkable eight albums in the Top 10 between 1970 and 1974. Also a popular live attraction, Grand Funk was the first band to sell out Shea Stadium since the Beatles did it in 1965. Their first No. 1 single, 1973's "We're an American Band," summed up their philosophy and legacy perfectly: "We're coming to your town, we'll help you party it down, we're an American band."

Steppenwolf, 1970. Courtesy of Photofest.

A similarly successful but more respected power band was the L.A.-based Steppenwolf, named after the Herman Hesse tale of alienation and individuality, themes that regularly surfaced in the group's music. Originally hailing from Toronto, Steppenwolf adopted the persona of outlaw bikers with guitars, an image fueled by their first major hit—1968's "Born to Be Wild"—being used in the opening sequence of the cult biker film *Easy Rider* a year later. Other socially conscious, heavy blues hits like "Magic Carpet Ride," "The Pusher," and "Rock Me" earned the band admiration as an act that could deliver shrewd social commentary in the form of raw, vigorous blues.

The ingredients these many acts contributed to the stew of early 1970s music helped popularize hard rock and earn a place for heavy metal as a genre unto itself. Largely born out of psychedelic and proto-punk bands of the mid-1960s, the constant sonic experimentation in which these groups indulged partly or wholly inspired revolutions in punk, funk, disco, southern, and other forms of rock popular in the later 1970s. Heavy metal itself shortly fell into a variety of subcategories such as speed metal, thrash metal, death metal, lite metal, and hair metal. Though some of these forms are virtually indistinguishable from one another, they each spawned numerous bands that dominated the airwaves in the 1970s and 1980s, all of which subscribed to heavy metal's earliest revelation: that volume is power.

NOTES

1. Goldman 1992, 87.
2. Waksman 1999, 182.
3. Burroughs 1964, 112.
4. "Metal Shop: Black Sabbath 20th Anniversary Special," WVVX, April 7, 1990.

5. Mike Saunders, "Sir Lord Baltimore: *Kingdom Come*," *Creem*, May 1971.

6. Weinstein 2000, 13.

7. CBC Television, November 14, 1965.

8. Flippo 1985, 37.

9. Mick Farren, "The Rolling Stones: Millionares With Nasty Habits," *Ink*, May 1, 1971.

10. Paul Williams, "The Stones: It Wasn't Only Rock and Roll (And I Liked It)," *Crawdaddy!*, November 1974.

11. Steven Rosen, "Jeff Beck . . . In Retrospect," *Los Angeles Free Press*, December 1973.

12. Barry Miles, "The Who: From the Marquee to the Met: Watching the Who," *Crawdaddy!*, September 1970.

13. Friedlander 1996, 126.

14. Dalton and Kaye, 1976.

15. Charles Shaar Murray, "Eric Clapton: Rainbow Theatre, London," *Creem*, February 1973.

16. Friedlander 1996, 221.

17. Hopkins 1983, 118.

18. Waksman 1999, 170.

19. Szatmary 1996, 200.

20. *Newsweek*, October 9, 1967, 90–92.

21. Halfin and Makowski 1982, 5.

22. Mike Saunders, "A Dorito and 7-Up Picnic with Black Sabbath," *Circular*, September 25, 1972.

23. www.riaa.com.

24. Jonh Ingham, "Led Zeppelin: *Houses of the Holy*," *Let It Rock*, June 1973.

25. Friedlander 1996, 237.

26. Dalton and Kaye 1976.

27. Friedlander 1996, 242–243.

28. Hibbert 1983.

29. Lescroart 1978, 151.

3

GLAMOUR KINGS: THE BIRTH OF GLITTER ROCK

The turn of the 1970s was a dynamic and chaotic period in rock. The psychedelic movement centered in San Francisco rose and fell within a period of four years, leaving in its wake numerous and complicated questions concerning "identity" in rock music, questions for which there seemed to be as many answers as there were performers. Was rock an exploration of the possibilities of sound (Pink Floyd, Jeff Beck, Jimi Hendrix) or a link to the sounds of our past (the Moody Blues, Yes, King Crimson)? Was it a force for social change (Country Joe and the Fish, the Grateful Dead, the Who) or just an excuse to party (Grand Funk Railroad, the Monkees)? Was it an endeavor that deserved serious attention (Janis Ian, Jethro Tull) or was rock music, in the end, just one big joke (Alice Cooper, Frank Zappa, Captain Beefheart)?

With the chart and concert popularity of masculine hard rock, the birth of testosterone-driven heavy metal, and the extraordinary celebrity status bestowed on potent and openly sexual idols like Jimi Hendrix, Jimmy Page, Robert Plant, and Mick Jagger, one aspect of rock seemed to be beyond question: rock and roll had no doubt about the proper placement of gender roles. Rock was an assertion of power—a traditionally male domain—and when rock stars were explicitly feminine, such as with Mick Jagger's pouty stage struts, it was more an assertion of sexual potency (an echo of Elvis Presley's ungentlemanly hip thrusts) than it was a surrendering of one's privileged gender authority.

Another, more practical, truism of turn-of-the-decade rock was a renewed emphasis on spectacle to complement the music. Major leaps in amplifier technology and increasingly sizable crowds at large-capacity venues meant performers had to put on grander shows to hold audience attention, and with more tickets sold per show, artists could afford more elaborate sets to carry out this task. The leap into the 1970s was a headlong dive into rock spectacle. When the Who and Jimi Hendrix engaged in a showdown at the 1967 Monterey Pop Festival—Pete Townshend smashing his guitar and Hendrix setting his on fire—they unwittingly fueled an ever-increasing emphasis on presentation over music (see Chapter 7, "The Festival Is Born").

The fixity of masculinity in rock and the escalating place of spectacle in rock performance led to something of a coup in late 1960s Britain and early 1970s America. A new form of showmanship called "glam," or "glitter rock," capitalized on the audience's desire for exhibition, while also challenging the masculine nature of rock music. Glam was not so much a new kind of music as it was a new way for rock artists to present themselves: as creatures who were simultaneously asexual, in that they eschewed established gender categories, and highly sexualized, in that their sexual presence became a part of their act through onstage and offstage bisexuality and transvestitism. Whether the phenomenon was a real sociological stand for a postmodern rethinking of gender or just a clever marketing ploy to appeal to alternative tastes—though probably a bit of both—there is little doubt that the man who transformed it from a local trend to a bona fide rock genre was an enigmatic Londoner named David Bowie.

QUEEN BITCH: THE IRREPRESSIBLE DAVID BOWIE

If it weren't for the rise of the New York Dolls in 1970s Manhattan, David Bowie might have encapsulated—in his performance and persona—everything that needs to be said about glitter rock. He certainly wasn't the only glam performer, but he was one of the first and by far the biggest in both Britain and the United States. Every major glam artist was indirectly influenced or directly touched by Bowie's stage presence, and his aura and authority reached into the decades to come, shaping other genres such as punk and new wave.

Born David Jones in post–World War II London in 1947, Bowie's status as an otherworldly figure—an image he would later cultivate with great success—got an early start when he was stabbed in the eye with a compass during a schoolyard fight, resulting in a paralyzed pupil and different-colored irises. In his early career, however, he was relatively tame, listening to jazz and establishing himself as a minor folk singer and modster in early 1960s England.

Passing through several unsuccessful rock and R&B outfits during the 1960s—the King Bees, the Manish Boys, the Lower Third—Bowie began to reinvent himself in 1966, starting with his name. Wishing to avoid confusion with the popular Monkee Davy Jones, he changed his last name to Bowie (ostensibly after the Bowie knife, because he wanted to "cut like a knife through lies").[1] A series of unsuccessful singles and a poor-selling debut album left him an unlikely candidate for pop-star success, leaving Bowie to immerse himself in other arts such as mime, dance, and theater. Much of his early persona, in fact, was modeled after British musician and stage/film actor Anthony Newley, whom Bowie imitated in regular cabaret performances.

Bowie was a seemingly unremarkable artist in the rock world until the 1969 release of his hit single "Space Oddity," still one of his most memorable recordings and the song that put him on the road to cultish stardom. Timed to coincide with the American lunar landing, "Space Oddity" spoke to the very heart of alienation with the realistic character of Major Tom—an astronaut alone in space, looking down on his home and asking who he was and where he belonged. The song was a major hit in Britain, reaching No. 5 on the charts and giving him enough cachet to continue a career in music that up to that point seemed in danger of disappearing altogether. Although the song was not a hit in the United States until Bowie emerged as a celebrity in 1973, it was released in the States under the Mercury label, giving Americans a taste of what was to come.

As much as "Space Oddity" tickled the public's science-fiction fantasy, it tickled Bowie's interest in alienation. Much like the character of Major Tom, who chose to remain adrift alone in space rather than return to earth, Bowie began to chart his own course, emulating the independence of fringe acts such as the Velvet Underground, Iggy Pop, and T. Rex's Marc Bolan, with whom Bowie briefly played. Emerging rock styles such as punk and heavy metal were already catering to fans who considered themselves "outsiders," but Bowie began to take the theme to a new level, moving beyond the idea of despondent individuals feeling alienated from others and into the realm of individuals celebrating their alienation, and even the human race itself as some sort of alien presence. "David Bowie has never been a conventional anything," read a 1970 article following the release of "Space Oddity." "Certainly he is no run of the mill product of the music business, something rather that was thrown up by accident and never really found its niche."[2]

After "Space Oddity," Bowie was again threatened by the specter of obscurity as follow-up projects failed to sell. Another sci-fi themed hit—1969's "In the Year 2525," an American No. 1 from the duo Zager and Evans—also rode the moon landing hysteria onto the charts, but served only as a one-hit wonder for its writers, a fate that it seemed would befall Bowie as well. But after a series of events in 1970 that could only have fueled his metamorphosis—the death of his father, the confining of his brother to a mental institution, Bowie's firing of his manager, and his marriage to art student Angela Barnett—the reinvented artist emerged from the studio with the ultimate alienation album, *The Man Who Sold the World*.

Affecting a feminine manner that he would soon transform for the stage into poses of homosexuality, bisexuality, and asexuality, Bowie appeared on the now famous cover of *The Man Who Sold the World* wearing a flimsy dress reminiscent of a 1940s Hollywood starlet, lounging in a purposefully effeminate pose with a playing card (the queen of diamonds) dangling from his limp hand. Though a less objectionable animated cover fronted the American version of the record, the songs therein were replete with themes of isolation and disaffection, including perversion ("The Width of a Circle"), insanity ("All the Madmen"), the fallacy of salvation ("Saviour Machine"), and of course out-of-the-mainstream sexuality. "Bowie's music offers an experience that is as intriguing as it is chilling," raved one album review, "but only to the listener sufficiently together to withstand its schizophrenia."[3]

A more commercial and acoustically oriented follow-up—1971's *Hunky Dory*—featured more accessible songs that have since become classics, especially the catchy "Changes," which seemed to encapsulate the transformation Bowie's music and persona were undergoing. *The Man Who Sold the World* and *Hunky Dory* were statements of a work-in-progress, and in retrospect were seen as testimony that Bowie himself was always a work-in-progress, a chameleon-like figure that, as "Changes" suggests, would always be a stranger even to himself.

Though these albums would not chart in the United States for another year, Bowie was making a name for himself in England, capitalizing on press attention with more elaborate costumes and sets in his live shows, taking full advantage of his interest in theater to create a visual production to match his musical persona. In 1972 he finally brought his varying themes of alienation into a cohesive being, a single character that would mark a major advancement in the role of theater in musical performance. On January 29, at the Borough Assembly Hall in Aylesbury, Buckinghamshire, Bowie transformed himself from interesting folk rocker into a sci-fi hero named Ziggy Stardust.

David Bowie, 1973. Courtesy of Photofest.

The performance was a dry run for a major tour, with Bowie sporting a fresh, dyed-orange haircut; a bomber jacket; a conspicuous codpiece; and red plastic boots. Not exactly hurting his enigmatic appeal was his statement the prior week in a *Melody Maker* interview that he was bisexual, a detail not generally announced in public forums at the time. In Bowie's case, his declaration caused a stir in the press and served to further his image as an outsider, too hip to fear public opinion, and much cooler than you. As one critic later noted in an essay on the period, "David Bowie's emergence in the early seventies was perhaps the single most important influence in the development of an explicit and outrageous sexualization of rock. . . . The press coverage given to Bowie and his wife's professed bisexuality and 'open marriage' gave credibility to the singer's musical claim to be a child of the future at a time when 'free sexuality' was being passionately pursued as the most likely candidate to usher western society into a golden age."[4]

After touring England through the spring, revising and enhancing the stage show along the way, Bowie and his band, now dubbed the Spiders from Mars, released the smash album *The Rise and Fall of Ziggy Stardust and the Spiders from Mars*, selling eight thousand copies its first week and jumping to No. 5 on the British charts. With no tour support in the United States, its American sales were noticeably weaker, peaking at No. 75 but spending a full year and a half on the charts and leading to reissues that November of *The Man Who Sold the World* and *Space Oddity*, which rose to No. 16, with its eponymous single reaching No. 15 the following year.

Bowie had generated a buzz. His first four albums were all issued or reissued in the United States in a single seven-month period, and all of them made the charts. They were quickly followed by an album of assorted material from Bowie's 1960s work, aging Bowie in the American mind over an extremely short period. Less than a year after being discovered by American audiences, he was already receiving reissues and a retrospective. Bowie was literally an instant classic.

The character of Ziggy Stardust kept Bowie in the spotlight for a year until he reinvented himself again in 1973 as Aladdin Sane. Ziggy had been a pop star, his ultimately doomed career coinciding with the end of the world. Aladdin was the post-Ziggy, the artist drowned in sex, drugs, and celebrity, portrayed by Bowie in head-to-toe body paint with a lightning bolt across the face. Aladdin Sane—a play on "a lad insane"—was Ziggy in America, suffering the trappings of fame that Bowie would soon face himself. Even more androgynous than Ziggy, Aladdin's skin-tight spandex and heavily airbrushed frame pictured on the album made him look like a randy eunuch, de-gendered and yet very sexual. With 150,000 advance orders, *Aladdin Sane* the album was guaranteed to be a hit. In Britain it shot to No. 1, while in the United States it reached No. 17 and continued bolstering sales of his other albums.

These were the years that would be looked back on and remembered as Bowie's golden period, a time when he was not only combining music, theater, and sexuality as it had never been done, but inspiring others to do the same. The United States was, for the first time, facing its own sexual-identity revolution. On the heels of the civil rights and the women's liberation movements, gay rights were being asserted publicly in the American consciousness. Like psychedelic music of the 1960s, glitter rockers were at least partially influenced by Allen Ginsberg and other openly gay Beat poets, who were undergoing a renaissance at the time. Until the famous Stonewall incident in June 1969— when gays clashed with New York police for three nights of rioting—gay behavior in America was heavily criminalized and a taboo subject. After Stonewall, a major grassroots movement sprang up overnight emphasizing gay pride and fair treatment of non-heterosexuals. By the time Bowie became a major artist, the challenging of established gender roles was rearing its head in American social politics, helping Bowie's career as much as his performances were highlighting the movement. Bowie had become somewhat of a standard-bearer, "responsible for opening up questions of sexual identity which had previously been repressed, ignored, or merely hinted at in rock and roll and youth culture."[5]

Between 1974 and 1976, Bowie placed five straight albums in the American Top 10, as well as resumed an acting career, playing a desperate alien in the 1976 *The Man Who Fell to Earth*. The part was tailor-made for Bowie, as his music, though constantly changing in style, continued to play on the themes of alienation, identity questioning, and dystopian sci-fi. Bowie would go on to make more than twenty films and contribute more than fifty songs to soundtracks over the following decades.

At the height of his popularity, Bowie contributed to the glam movement beyond his own performances by working with other artists who would become stars in their own right. The unsuccessful hard-rock band Mott the Hoople was on their way out when Bowie produced and wrote the song "All the Young Dudes" for them, a hit that revitalized the band's career and became an anthem for gay pride. Both Iggy Pop and the Velvet Underground's Lou Reed had already made names for themselves in the 1960s, but were able to reinvent themselves as glam artists through their work with Bowie in the 1970s. Bowie also engaged in collaborations with established artists like John Lennon (who co-wrote Bowie's first No. 1, 1975's "Fame") and Brian Eno (who founded the seminal group Roxy Music and would become a major producer for other rock artists).

At his peak in the mid-1970s, Bowie was everywhere. His work was more than just "rock 'n' roll with lipstick on," as John Lennon purportedly once told him. Bowie's chameleon-like performances echoed his career; he was an amalgam of different personae: the blues musician, the mime, the modster, the sometimes Buddhist, the folk singer, the gay-pride hero, the Marlon Brando of glam. Though he would tone his act down as he continued to produce quality material through the 1980s and 1990s, it was his influential 1970s work that brought theater and sensuality to rock and that best reveals the mercurial artist as a true original.

GLAM'S SLUMLORDS: THE NEW YORK DOLLS

Although David Bowie is remembered as the man who brought spectacle to rock, that should in no way diminish his status as a talented artist. His crooning voice, his Svengali-like delivery, and his insightful lyrics were worthy of his fame. He was not only a great performer but a great musician as well.

Such praise couldn't be honestly heaped on the barely talented New York Dolls—and they would be the first to admit it. Caught in the crossfire of glam, heavy metal, and early punk, the Dolls were a cross-dressing train wreck of hairspray, spandex, fireworks, and feedback. Fifteen years before hair-metal bands like Poison and Bon Jovi ruled the airwaves, the New York Dolls were setting the New York scene on fire and causing parents of young teens no end of sleepless nights.

Formed in 1971—just as Bowie was reaching the masses—the Dolls featured vocalist David Johansen, guitarist Johnny Thunders, bassist Arthur Kane, guitarist/keyboardist Sylvain Sylvain, and drummer Jerry Nolan (Nolan came into the group a year after it was formed, replacing Billy Murcia, who drowned in a bathtub during their first UK tour). By the late spring of 1972—just before *Ziggy Stardust* began hitting American shelves—the band secured a regular gig at Soho's Mercer Arts Center, one of the more avant-garde performance venues in Manhattan at the time. The Dolls managed to raise eyebrows even in the gutter-hip Mercer, a run-down former hotel that featured underground music, video productions, and whatever alternative arts its regulars could come up with.

The band—a combination of punk rock's angsty ennui and heavy metal's addiction to volume and feedback—counted among its influences punk heroes Iggy Pop and Lou Reed, rock bad boys Mick Jagger and Keith Richards, and 1960s girl groups like the Shangri-Las. Closer in appearance to this latter band than any of the others, the all-male group resembled more than anything a biker gang that crashed through a women's department store. According to author Van M. Cagle in an essay on the band, "In terms of fashion, they dressed (both onstage and off) in all manner of tawdry, gender-bending attire: gold lamé capri pants; tacky polka-dot dresses; fishnets; bouffant wigs; shorty nightgowns; leopard-print tights; football jerseys; feather boas; open-necked shirts; multicolored, "reveal-all" spandex; . . . mod caps and bowlers; oversized plastic bracelets and chokers; bow ties; satin scarves; platform shoes; high heels; and thigh-riding stacked boots."[6] Complemented by an abundance of carelessly applied lipstick, eyeshadow, hairspray, and a mean strut, the band seemed to be enacting all of David Bowie's phases at once.

For three months the Dolls played at the Mercer in relative anonymity, until a British producer, impressed by what he saw as a cross-dressing version of Iggy and the Stooges, booked them for a stint in Europe opening for the Faces. The booking incited label interest and media attention for the band, surprising and often disturbing A&R representatives and rock critics when they actually saw a Dolls performance. The death of drummer Murcia (to which drugs contributed) after their London gig added to the circus, and the band returned to New York the focus of too much attention to ignore. Their excesses worked in their favor, and with the addition of replacement drummer Jerry Nolan, the group worked on parlaying their immoderate behavior into fame and fortune.

Not that they were in it for the money. One key to the Dolls' success was their "everyman" persona. Though they couldn't have looked more different than the average Joe, they were amateur musicians in an age of guitar prodigies, populists in a time of distant celebrities, minimal talents with maximum appetites. The New York Dolls were a garage band in search of a garage. They did not perform for the audience but performed for themselves, doing whatever they wished on stage, and if they weren't getting the sound they wanted, the solution was to turn up the volume. Anyone that desired to be a fan had to pay the price of actually listening to the music.

It was in this way that the Dolls—despite the tendency of some critics to regard them as just another glitter band—differed from artists like Bowie. David Bowie seized upon the use of theater and gender bending to attract audiences. The Dolls sought only to repel them, hence the tagline that appeared in some of their album ads, "The Band You Love to Hate." Perhaps the best evidence was the *Creem* magazine year-end reader's poll from 1973, in which the New York Dolls were voted both "Best New Group of the Year" and "Worst New Group of the Year," a fitting tribute for a band that felt compelled to always be at the extreme. In response to David Bowie's shocking announcement that he was bisexual, Johansen took it one step further with his oft-repeated declaration, "We're trisexual. We'll try anything."[7]

The New York Dolls, 1973. © UPPA/Topham/The Image Works.

By late 1973, the band had played enough gigs outside New York to build a respectable following. Though they generally repulsed most A&R representatives that came to their shows, Mercury took a chance on them and issued *New York Dolls* that August. The album cover featured a black-and-white photo of the band, in drag from their curls to their heels, and beneath the hot-pink, lipstick-inscribed title ran the tagline, "A band you're gonna like whether you like it or not."

Fortunately for the Dolls, the critics did like them, or at least pretended to, hailing their avant-garde minimalism as "post-glitter," "post-Bowie," "authentic," and other words and phrases that attempted to praise the band for their commentary on rock music while making every effort to avoid praising the music itself. Some critics, particularly *Creem*'s Robert Christgau, championed the "careening screech of their music," calling them "the most exciting hard rock band in the country and maybe the world right now."[8]

Their debut album was exciting. Produced by the eclectic musician Todd Rundgren, it was the peak of their career, a landmark in the punk movement that was both hard rock and a critique of hard rock. The raw energy and care-less, full-frontal assault on the senses that drew crowds to their live perfor-mances was deftly captured on vinyl. As printed on the liner notes for a later reissue of the album, "Until the *New York Dolls* a hangover from the sixties had permeated the music scene. That album was where a new decade began, where a contemporary vision of the essence of rock 'n' roll emerged to kick out the tired old men and clear the way for the New Order."[9]

Such an ominous debut that seeks to tear down existing definitions of rock and establish a new way of looking at music would be hard to follow. A band hailed for its adroit critique of their own genre has only two choices once their style catches on: capitalize on their success and go mainstream (i.e., sell out), or attempt to maintain an air of underground rebelliousness with more of the same, only to discover that it's not a revolution the second time you do it, lead-ing to the inevitable implosion. The Dolls, being the Dolls, attempted both.

Less than a year after their debut album, the band released the aptly named *Too Much Too Soon*, which differed little in style from the first record but lacked its adventurous quality. It was generally panned by the critics and disappointing to attention-span-deprived fans, who were finding other punk and metal outfits to frighten their parents with. Eager to salvage their sinking career, the group let go of glam and steered toward the dangerous cliffs of straight-up hard rock, becoming the band they had gotten famous for making fun of. The only thing the Dolls had to start with, the thing that made them popular among the ultra-hip rock connoisseurs, was the specter of authenticity. Failing that, when the band stopped trying to entertain themselves and started trying to entertain the audience, they went overnight from ringmaster to clown.

As the group crumbled under flagging interest, a last-ditch effort at salvation came from none other than British boutique owner Malcolm McLaren, who would later become famous for helping launch the Sex Pistols. McLaren took over as the Doll's manager in 1974 after seeing them perform in England and following them on tour, trying to figure out a direction for the band to take that would allow them to reclaim past glories. In the band's later days, McLaren guided them away from the transvestite image and toward shock gimmicks like swastikas and communist imagery. The transparent attempts to offend audi-ences without any real subtext was itself offensive to the kinds of fans that ap-preciated what the Dolls were doing early in their career. "The fans were content to pay their own dues, and this often carried with it the implicit un-derstanding that the Dolls were not meant to be comprehended beyond the progressive, ironic, and disruptive structures of meaning that they had so clev-erly forwarded as a cult band."[10]

By 1975 the honeymoon was over. Thunders and Nolan left during a U.S. tour, and a lesser Dolls barely held it together until 1976, when the group split up for good. Though several live, compilation, and studio-outtake albums ap-peared over the next fifteen years, there were no reunions, and none of the Dolls alumni went on to spectacular musical careers. But in their time and place, the band was eagerly received by a small New York fandom and an even smaller national following as harbingers of a musical revolution, heavily influencing such groups as KISS, the Ramones, the Sex Pistols, and Talking Heads.

PREDECESSORS AND HEIRS

The themes that separate one musical genre from another are not cut-and-dried. Some genres, especially during certain historical periods, share many common traits, and when several competing genres bloom from the same source, they cannot help but share qualities that make it hard to place one artist squarely in one genre and a not-terribly-dissimilar artist squarely in another. Such is the case with glam, punk, heavy metal, and pop at the dawn of the 1970s. All influenced by, and closely resembling, the psychedelic wave that swept through the United States only a few years before, these genres interplayed as much as they competed, and innovators that changed one genre generally had an effect on them all.

Pre-Glitter Punk: Andy Warhol, Iggy Pop, and Lou Reed

As the hippie forces of the West Coast massed for communal peace and love in the late 1960s, a more guarded and individualistic realism held fast in the poorly lit venues of New York City. A central figure in East Coast avant-garde was the pop artist Andy Warhol—a driving force of experimentation in music, film, and graphic arts whose name conjures up all manner of questions about the value of artistic representation. Running a studio called the Factory in New York City's Union Square, Warhol always sought to be—and usually succeeded—on the cutting edge of the art community, hobnobbing and collaborating with such luminaries as Mick Jagger, Truman Capote, and Lou Reed.

It was with Reed that Warhol made his biggest impact on the New York music scene, adopting the unknown musician and his band the Velvet Underground into his music/film/dance/theater entourage known as the Exploding Plastic Inevitable. At Warhol's suggestion, the Velvet Underground added singer and actress Nico to their lineup to produce their groundbreaking 1967 debut album, *The Velvet Underground & Nico*. Warhol also financed the record and designed the original cover with a peel-off banana sticker. From the packaging to the contents, the album was high art—intricate, conceptual, and postmodern.

Over the next three years, the band produced a string of excellent follow-ups that have become classics of early punk rock—1967's *White Light/White Heat*, 1969's *The Velvet Underground*, and 1970's *Loaded*. Though none of their albums charted higher than No. 85, their murky and cerebral music was enormously influential not only to glam powerhouses David Bowie and the New York Dolls, but to later groundbreaking artists and bands such as Brian Eno, U2, R.E.M., and Nirvana.

Bowie got the opportunity to repay his debt when he met Reed in 1972, two years after Reed had quit the Velvet Underground. Bowie convinced Reed to go solo and helped him become a marginal pop/glam artist with the addition of bleached hair, makeup, and fingernail polish. A resurging Reed was further aided by Bowie in 1972 when the glitter king produced Reed's *Transformer*, featuring the song that relaunched his career, "Walk on the Wild Side." A fond homage to the bizarre crowd that frequented Warhol's side, the song was his first hit, breaking the Top 20 in the United States and the Top 10 in Britain. Reed's success continued with more experimental endeavors through the 1970s that were alternately lauded and panned by critics, but that undoubtedly contributed to the punk, new wave, and grunge movements to come.

Iggy Pop was another figure that alternately influenced and was influenced by David Bowie and the advent of glitter rock. Born James Osterberg near Ann

Lou Reed, 1974. © Bettmann/Corbis.

Arbor, Michigan, the "godfather of punk" founded the Psychedelic Stooges for a Halloween party in 1967. Osterberg had adopted the name Iggy Stooge for a previous incarnation, but his new group quickly became known as Iggy and the Stooges, with Iggy (later adding the Pop) leading them to their excellent 1969 debut *The Stooges*, followed in 1970 by *Fun House* and in 1973 by *Raw Power*. These three releases—their only releases before breaking up shortly after *Raw Power*—are considered seminal albums in any punk-rock collection. Iggy Pop was naturally wild beyond any staged antics delivered by the Rolling Stones or the Who. Like his contemporary Jim Morrison (whom legend has it he was asked to replace in the Doors after Morrison's death), Pop was never sure what he was going to do once the spotlight hit him. Over his performance career—usually aided by copious amounts of drugs—Pop slashed his chest with a broken bottle, knocked some of his teeth out with a microphone, and fell into drug stupors that, on at least one occasion, caused him to throw up on the audience and fall offstage. Even so, his self-destructive behavior was itself part of the show, as it would become a trademark of later punk rock.

Iggy Pop, 1970. Jack Robinson/Hulton Archive/Getty Images.

During the band's declining years, Bowie—who greatly admired Iggy's uncompromising showmanship—became involved with the group by producing *Raw Power*, whose cover featured a lanky, shirtless Iggy with bleached hair, heavy makeup, and skintight, silver lamé pants. Bowie continued his involvement with Pop after the band's demise, eventually encouraging him to go solo after he took a few years off of music. In 1977, Iggy returned to favor with two outstanding albums, *The Idiot* and *Lust for Life*. Bowie produced both albums, played keyboard, and cowrote the song "China Girl," which he later recorded himself.

Iggy Pop was one of rock's more extreme entertainers, the next logical step in a lineage that includes Little Richard, James Brown, Elvis Presley, Jimi Hendrix, and Pete Townshend. He inspired Bowie to bring theater onto the rock stage, and—along with Lou Reed—was subsequently inspired by Bowie to bring sexuality into his theater.

Local Stars and Post-Glammers: Mott the Hoople, T. Rex, Gary Glitter, and Elton John

With competition from numerous developing rock styles, the glam craze was short-lived, and its well-known stars could be counted on two hands, however, its influence carried over into pop, disco, and new wave well into the 1980s. Much of the early glam was British and made little impact in the United States—alongside David Bowie in the *Melody Maker* headlines were local stars Marc Bolan and Gary Glitter, early compatriots of Bowie who missed out on his international stardom.

Bolan had a very successful career in Britain and is remembered as one of the first glam artists. Making a name for himself in a London band called Tyrannosaurus Rex—later shortened to T. Rex—Bolan became known for his quivering voice and Tolkienesque lyrics involving mythical themes and fantastical creatures such as fairies and pixies. During the band's brief tenure, they had a number of Top 20 hits that initially made them more famous than Bowie, with whom Bolan was friends and occasionally performed. Only one song traversed the Atlantic with any success, the 1972 No. 10 hit "Bang a Gong," which might have served as a foothold for a larger U.S. presence had the band not begun disintegrating from internal rivalry shortly thereafter.

Like Bolan, Gary Glitter (born Paul Gadd) had a thriving career in England but only one hit in the United States, the 1972 No. 7 melody "Rock and Roll Part 2." After relatively limited success as a rock and roller in the 1960s, performing under names like Paul Russell and Paul Raven, Glitter reinvented himself in the early seventies in the wake of Bowie's meteoric rise. Complete with thigh boots and sparkly costumes, Glitter rode the glam wave to the top of the British charts with three No. 1 singles and a string of Top 10 hits. By the time the punk revolution commandeered the later 1970s, Glitter was a minor legend, and possibly because his career extended further back than Bowie's, he is mentioned alongside Bowie as a godfather to the glam movement.

Bowie had a more direct influence on the sluggish prog-rock band Mott the Hoople, who were on the verge of breaking up when Bowie offered them his song "All the Young Dudes" in 1972. Though Mott did poorly on the charts, they were a popular live act and were hesitant to accept Bowie's help (which

included producing the single and accompanying album). Fortunately they took the chance and saw *All the Young Dudes* break the Top 20 on the British charts, with the eponymous single reaching No. 3. The song became an anthem for unity among the disenfranchised, particularly for the gay community, and the album—a world apart from the Dylanesque rock of their previous work—gave them an entirely new sound that would deliver several more hits until they broke up in 1974, and established them as respected purveyors of glitter rock.

Of all the artists affected by the glam-rock movement, perhaps none was as successful as Reginald Kenneth Dwight, later to become the ninth all-time album sales leader under the name Elton John. A classical pianist by training, John performed as a blues-revival keyboardist in the late 1960s before teaming up with songwriter Bernie Taupin in 1969 and steering a more pop-oriented course. John's increasingly flamboyant costumes in the early 1970s—including platform soles, boas, spangly outfits, and his famous collection of ornate sunglasses (one

Elton John, 1973. © Neal Preston/Corbis.

of which spelled his name out in flashing lights)—earned him categorization as a glam artist, though his music was decidedly commercial. Between 1971 and 1976, John saw eleven straight albums enter the Top 10, with an incredible thirty-nine weeks at No. 1 between them. Though his highly accessible music has earned him a reputation as a rock star more than a glam artist, his theatrical stage presence and use of gender-bending dress in his performances secure him an honorable place in the annals of glitter rock.

NOTES

1. Charlton 1989, 167.
2. Penny Valentine, "David Bowie: Bowie, Music and Life," *Sounds*, 1970.
3. John Mendelssohn, "David Bowie: *The Man Who Sold the World*," *Rolling Stone*, February 18, 1971.
4. Herman 1982, 71.
5. Bowie 1981, 74.
6. Cagle 1999, 130.
7. Cagle 1999, 145.
8. Robert Christgau, *Creem*, November 1973, 62.
9. *New York Dolls* reissue, 1977, Mercury/Polygram.
10. Cagle 1999, 146.

THE SOUTH RISES AGAIN

The story of southern rock is, by turns, both inspiring and tragic, largely due to the short histories and timeless legacies of its two greatest acts: the Allman Brothers Band and Lynyrd Skynyrd. The parallels that united these groups, as well as the lesser bands that shared their spotlight or later walked in their shadows, form an intriguing—and often heartbreaking—web of highs and lows that would itself make excellent fodder for a southern rock song.

The term "southern rock" is as much cultural as it is geographical. Though some believe it was not southern rock unless it came out of Jacksonville, Florida (origin of the Allman Brothers Band and Lynyrd Skynyrd), or Macon, Georgia (home of Capricorn Records), there were also bands from Mississippi, the Carolinas, and Arkansas. But just as important as the bands' origins were the time—the magic period of the late 1960s and early 1970s as crossover styles were expanding the definition of "rock music"—and the circumstances of the musicians involved, mostly poor kids raised on blues, soul, and gospel, and fiercely loyal to family and the South.

Until the 1960s, it was not terribly difficult to differentiate and classify musicians and their creations. Country artists wrote rural, steel-guitar-driven ballads about luckless loners; folk acts regurgitated populist acoustic standards; and rock and rollers performed blues-based scream-alongs. These are, of course, gross generalizations, and to some degree, artists were influenced by genres outside their own. But in the 1960s, as rock began to take on different forms and divide into more and more subgenres, it gradually became more acceptable to be a crossover artist—to reach beyond the expectations of one's audience and blend genres.

Bob Dylan was one of the most prominent artists of the 1960s to experiment with merging styles. Until 1965, Dylan was claimed by the folk community as one of their brightest stars, the would-be successor to folk legend Woody Guthrie—Dylan's mentor who would die at the peak of Dylan's fame. At the 1965 Newport Folk Festival, Dylan surprised many by plugging in his guitar to play a few songs with the Paul Butterfield Blues Band, violating the unwritten rule that folk artists do not play electric guitars. Only four years later, he befuddled his fans again with his album *Nashville Skyline*, a record that was simpler and more melancholy than his previous releases and a decided move toward country.

Dylan's backing band during the mid-1960s, the Hawks, would also blend musical genres when—under their new name the Band—they premiered their 1968 and 1969 albums *Music from Big Pink* and *The Band*. The group, featuring future stars Robbie Robertson and Levon Helm, mixed traditional folk with rock grooves to influence a generation of Americana. Also in 1968, the Byrds released *Sweetheart of the Rodeo*, seen by many as Americana's foundation album. Although the Byrds were known as folk rockers since their 1965 albums *Mr. Tambourine Man* and *Turn! Turn! Turn!*, personnel changes led them to a more countrified rock that would influence 1970s acts such as Fleetwood Mac and the Eagles (see Chapter 5, "Folk Rock and Its Successors").

The mix of country, folk, and rock took on a regional dialect with the advent of southern rock at the turn of the decade. Roots music in the southeastern United States was saturated with the blues, and southern rock was first and foremost a statement of regional identity. Even though southern-rock audiences were largely self-professed rednecks, they shared a musical tradition with the mainly black gospel, soul, and rhythm and blues of the area. "They lived the life," said Atlantic Records' Jerry Wexler, one of the first in the industry to recognize the southern-rock scene. "They were the low end of America's agrarian society, just like the blacks were. They were some poor boys. . . . They heard the exultation, the frenzy of black church, directly in church, not off records. They eventually related."[1] Much like the original white rockabilly stars of the 1950s, southern rockers counted great boogie-and-blues artists such as B. B. King, Elmore James, and John Lee Hooker among their most potent influences. Southern lyrics were emblematic of these muses, with stories of cheating spouses, loner troubles, and hard luck taking center stage in many of the songs.

The blues were an enormous influence on southern rockers—not just the sound of the blues but the lifestyle. Community was highly valued, and family associations were common within and between groups: the Allman Brothers Band featured siblings Gregg and Duane Allman; the Marshall Tucker Band was founded by brothers Toy and Tommy Caldwell; Wet Willie included brothers Jimmy and Jack Hall; and two of the Van Zant brothers, Ronnie and Johnny, played in Lynyrd Skynyrd (at different times), while a third brother, Donnie, led the later group .38 Special. The various acts that followed the Allman Brothers, including Lynyrd Skynyrd, were dependent on each other and the Allmans for guidance, bookings, and even equipment.

This sense of community spread beyond the acts themselves. Several bands fondly remember the kindness of "Mama Louise" Hudson, owner of a soul-food restaurant called the H&H in Macon, Georgia. The first few years of the southern-rock movement were lean for the young bands, and Hudson built a reputation as a caretaker of struggling musicians. Early in the Allman Brothers' career, they had to pool their money to buy a single plate of food at the H&H, but Hudson brought out full plates for everyone. She became known for her generosity toward Macon musicians, and her bigheartedness was indicative of the southern music culture in which everyone looked out for everyone else like a brother or sister.

In addition to fraternal loyalty, southern musicians exhibited an intense regional pride. Much of 1950s rock had developed out of southern blues, but as rockabilly took a back seat to country, swing, and soul in the 1960s, southern-rock artists felt a need to reclaim what was rightfully theirs—the rock-and-roll throne. Until the Allman Brothers Band reignited the musical south, the best southern artists had to go to Nashville, New York, San Francisco, or Los Angeles to earn a living. The territoriality that possessed southern bands in the early 1970s was evident in some of their biggest hits, such as the Charlie Daniels Band's "The South's Gonna Do It" and "The Devil Went Down to Georgia"; the Atlanta Rhythm Section's "Doraville"; and Lynyrd Skynyrd's smash "Sweet Home Alabama"— a direct rebuttal to Neil Young's slanderous lyrics in "Southern Man."

Southern rockers have even been credited with helping Georgian Jimmy Carter obtain the White House by making southern culture chic. It was described by the *Washington Post* in 1975 (about five years after the Allman Brothers created the

 IMPORTANT PLACES IN SOUTHERN ROCK

Macon, Georgia

Home of Capricorn Records, a studio and label founded in 1969 by Atlantic producer Jerry Wexler and former Otis Redding manager Phil Walden. Capricorn was the premiere label for southern-rock acts, including the Allman Brothers Band, Wet Willie, and the Marshall Tucker Band.

Doraville, Georgia

A suburb of Atlanta that gave rise to the Atlanta Rhythm Section in 1970. The ARS were a group of session musicians at Doraville's Studio One, and the band borrowed the town's name for their debut album.

Mobile, Alabama

Origin of good-time boogie band Wet Willie.

Jacksonville, Florida

For many, the birthplace of southern rock, where the boys from Hour Glass and One Percent grew up and paid their dues before becoming the Allman Brothers Band and Lynyrd Skynyrd. Also the home of later rock giants .38 Special and Molly Hatchet.

Spartanburg, South Carolina

The native soil of the Marshall Tucker Band, as well as its earlier incarnations the Toy Factory and Pax Parachute.

Nashville, Tennessee

Site of Charlie Daniels' first Volunteer Jam in 1974. Although Daniels was born in North Carolina, much of his musical career took place in Nashville.

phenomenon) as "the most popular new rock style to emerge in the last year" and "the hottest sound around."[2] What effect the music of the south actually had on American politics is not much more than "what if" speculation, but the effect it had on the American music scene is self-evident as it vied with heavy metal and progressive rock as the dominant rock form of the early 1970s.

BEGINNINGS: THE ALLMAN BROTHERS AND CAPRICORN RECORDS

Howard Duane Allman and Gregory Lenoir Allman were born in 1946 and 1947, respectively, in Nashville, Tennessee. After their father was killed in a robbery attempt, the boys' mother briefly sent them to military school, but eventually relocated with them to Daytona Beach, Florida, in 1957. On Christmas Day 1959, twelve-year-old Gregg received a guitar as a present, and before long he was teaching his little brother how to play.

Duane took to the guitar immediately, eventually buying his own instrument and dropping out of school to indulge himself in the sound of his fingers dancing up and down the fretboard. Early influences on the duo included Son House, Lightnin' Hopkins, Taj Mahal, B. B. King, and Ray Charles, artists they'd listen to on the local R&B station. The brothers eventually played R&B themselves in a number of local bands, including the House Rockers, the Escorts, and the Allman Joys. In this latest incarnation, the pair developed a small local following, playing everything from area bars to fraternity parties to build a fan base. Their long, blond hair was an anomaly in the conservative south, but the look complemented their electric, charismatic music. By their late teens, Duane was making waves as an exciting guitar player, and Gregg was developing a powerful voice that smacked of his blues influences.

The group extended their touring throughout the south, and during a gig in St. Louis, they met the Nitty Gritty Dirt Band's manager, Bill McEuen, who helped them land a recording deal with Liberty Records. The opportunity would necessitate a move to southern California, and the band decided to adopt a new name to accompany the change—Hour Glass. In 1967 they found themselves in a Los Angeles studio recording covers for a label that did not know what to make of them. The producer recognized their black influences and tried to bring a Motown sound out of them, completely burying Duane's guitar playing, which made their sound unique. The self-titled album was poorly made and poorly received, leaving the band confused, demoralized, and more than 2,000 miles from home.

Despite the botched album attempt, Hour Glass was making waves in the Los Angeles club scene, opening for bands such as the Doors, the Grateful Dead, and Jefferson Airplane before earning a regular gig at the Whisky a Go Go, one of the city's hottest venues. At the Whisky, they developed a reputation for exciting live shows, and their gigs often became jam sessions, with artists like Stephen Stills, Buddy Miles, and Neil Young jumping onstage if they happened to be in the room.

But the band was still contractually committed to their label, Liberty, who gave them more room on their second album attempt, including the freedom to include a few original tracks. The resulting effort, *Power of Love*, was an improvement over *Hour Glass*, but still failed to demonstrate the band's raw and unique qualities. Frustrated, the group left for Fame Studios in Muscle Shoals, Alabama, where great R&B artists such as Wilson Pickett, Aretha Franklin, and Little Richard had recently recorded, and where the band hoped to capture their sound. The group's excitement over the two tracks they laid down at Fame—a B. B. King medley and one of Gregg's originals called "I've Been Gone Too Long"—was short-lived. Upon returning to Los Angeles, the band played the songs for unimpressed Liberty executives, who did not understand the band's sound. After a short, disappointing tour outside of California, Hour Glass decided to call it quits.

The group moved back to Florida, but Duane and Gregg were not willing to give up on their passions. Gregg soon returned to Los Angeles to make a go of recording solo for Liberty. Duane, meanwhile, had impressed producer Rick Hall at Fame Studios, and was invited back to play some session guitar for a new Wilson Pickett album. Duane's unique guitar work made studio execs stand up and take notice, and before long he was playing on tracks for Clarence Carter, John Hammond, Aretha Franklin, and King Curtis.

Duane's work in Muscle Shoals came to the attention of Phil Walden, who was manager for Percy Sledge, Sam and Dave, and the recently deceased Otis Redding. Walden was impressed by Duane's work on Wilson Pickett's most recent recordings, and traveled to Muscle Shoals to meet him. They hit it off immediately, and within minutes Duane had found himself a manager. Duane began recording-session work for Jerry Wexler of Atlantic Records, who was also impressed by the guitarist's obvious talents on Pickett's tracks. Finally Duane was receiving recognition for his guitar skills, but he wanted something more.

Phil Walden was also searching for something more. Since Otis Redding's death in 1967, Walden had felt somewhat alienated in the R&B world, and asked Wexler about getting Atlantic to fund a new studio in the south to handle rock and blues acts. Both men were confident they could create another Motown or Stax, two of the soul hit makers of the 1960s. The duo decided to found Capricorn Records (named after their mutual zodiac sign) and to have Duane Allman be their first act.

Duane was happy with his studio work in Georgia, but enjoyed going home to Jacksonville to play music with his friends. Even though he was under contract with Walden as a solo artist, he eventually decided to move back to Florida with his session drummer, Jai Johanson, and launch a power trio with his old friend Berry Oakley. He soon established a fuller sound by rounding out the act with a group of musicians that would shortly become the Allman

Brothers Band: bassist Oakley, who played in Jacksonville-based cover band Second Coming; guitarist Dickey Betts, also with Second Coming; drummer Johanson, who had played for Otis Redding and Percy Sledge and was introduced to Duane by Phil Walden; and drummer Butch Trucks, who had briefly played with Duane in a short-lived act called 31st of February. Other than Betts, who came into the band through Oakley, all of the musicians had played with Duane before and knew how talented he was. Though Betts was hesitant to leave Second Coming, he clicked with Duane immediately, and from their first jam session, the band knew they were on to something special.

The group was long on instrumental talent but short on vocals. Gregg had been having a rough time playing solo in Los Angeles, so one phone call from Duane and he hitchhiked all the way home to Jacksonville. With Gregg's bluesy voice and songwriting ability added to the mix, the first few sessions were enormously productive. The band wanted to start performing immediately, so they packed all their gear into a van, drove to Atlanta, and set up at the biggest park they could find. Within hours there were 2,000 spectators, and the legend of the Allman Brothers Band was born.

That moment in the spring of 1969 through the fall of 1971 were the golden years for the Allman Brothers Band. Initially they played at every opportunity, touring throughout the east and playing for free at parks on days they did not have a gig. Their unique sound was an amalgam of rock, R&B, gospel, and dixie, touched by the psychedelia that had been pouring out of the West Coast the previous few years. In fact, the band began to indulge in marijuana and psychedelic mushrooms, and adopted the mushroom as their symbol. Though promoters and fans were delighted by this new sound, many did not know what to make of it.

As soon as Phil Walden got his studio up and running in Macon, he began operations at Capricorn, signing the Allman Brothers Band as its first act. Their self-titled debut in late 1969 was a world away from their Liberty recordings, with the band rather than studio executives in control of the production. Because the group was still relatively unknown, the album did not sell very well, but both Walden and the band members knew they were building up to something big, and the group played close to 300 dates their first year to establish themselves in the rock community.

Their relentless touring paid off not only in terms of recognition but also by allowing the members to develop a relationship as a group. Gregg's voice and Duane's mesmerizing guitar work were the stars of the show, but the dual drumming of Jai Johanson and Butch Trucks gave the band a thick percussive layer, and Berry Oakley seemed to always be able to fill in the right place at the right time with his bass. One of the most intimidating places to be in rock music at that time was trying to keep up with Duane Allman's guitar, but Dickey Betts proved himself to be the man for the job. Initially playing in Duane's shadow, Betts began to improvise off of Allman's leads, and the two struck up musical "conversations" as they played—"trading twos" in jazz terms—in which one would play a two-bar phrase and the other would respond with his own improvisation. Many reviews of the band remarked on the interaction between the twin lead guitars as "duels," with some live solos going more than thirty minutes in one key without becoming repetitive. Duane was not possessive of his role as the band's star—he encouraged Betts and gave him due praise for his instrumental and lyrical contributions to the band. Twin lead guitars were unusual at this point in rock, and the resulting effect would not be topped until Lynyrd Skynyrd, heavily influenced by the Allman Brothers, would emerge a few years later with three-guitar leads.

Duane continued to play session guitar at Muscle Shoals as well as adhere to a demanding tour schedule. In 1970 the band returned to the studio to record their sophomore effort, *Idlewild South*, named after Betts' farm in Georgia. The group brought on Atlantic producer Tom Dowd for the album, who had worked with many jazz and blues greats and would prove to be an asset to the band. He appreciated the unique qualities of this new sound and was able to bring it out in the studio. Gregg credits Dowd for teaching him how to play the Hammond organ, which Gregg had been picking up since the group formed and which came to be a recognizable element of the Allman Brothers' sound.

Dowd also introduced Duane to reigning rock-guitar-god Eric Clapton, who had come to Florida that August to record what would be Derek and the Dominos' only album. Duane and Clapton jammed for days; Gregg later remarked that it was some of the best playing of Duane's life. Much to Duane's delight, Clapton asked him to play lead on one of the album's songs, "Tell the Truth." Clapton was so impressed that Duane ended up playing second lead on most of the album, including one of Clapton's all-time greatest hits, "Layla." Clapton had meant "Layla" to be a slow ballad, but Duane created a tense, powerful slide lead that Clapton could not ignore. The song was Clapton's first to reach the Top 10, largely due to Duane's memorable riff.

As word continued to spread about the Allman Brothers' unique sound and Duane's unbelievable guitar abilities, the band became more in demand. During the second annual Atlanta International Pop Festival in 1970—with 250,000 on hand, one of the last major pop music festivals of the period—the Allman Brothers Band received a standing ovation as they tuned up, a bit of local appreciation for an act that was reestablishing a signature sound for the south.

The band's signature sound was not just southern music, it was *live* southern music. The group soon realized that they were far better received on stage than they were on vinyl, and the only solution, they decided, was to record a live album. In December 1970, the group opened for Canned Heat at Bill Graham's Fillmore East in New York City, one of the great rock venues of its time. Although they were the opening act, they were called back for several encores, and it was not until 3:30 in the morning that they gave up the stage to the main attraction.

Graham was understandably impressed by the performance, and offered Fillmore East up for the planned live album. Tom Dowd accompanied the band back to the Fillmore in March 1971 and recorded four shows over two days that came to be one of the seminal live albums in all of rock. *Live at Fillmore East* was both an announcement to the music world that the Allman Brothers Band had arrived and the beginning of stardom for the group. The double album spent forty-seven weeks on the charts, peaking at No. 13 and soon going gold. The summer of 1971 was the group's zenith, playing as tight as they ever would. They were invited back to the Fillmore that June to play the final show at the venue, which Graham was closing down for good. The band played until 7:00 in the morning, a performance that was described by some as a religious experience. After three albums and more than 600 shows in two years, the Allman Brothers Band were stars.

PRIVATE TRAGEDY, PUBLIC TRIUMPH

The death of Duane Allman is as central to the story of southern rock as the plane crash that killed Buddy Holly, Richie Valens, and the Big Bopper in 1959 is to early rock, and the twin overdoses of Jimi Hendrix and Janis Joplin in 1970 are to psychedelic music. In 1971, the Allman Brothers were at the top of their game and poised for superstardom. Each album sold better than the last, with *Live at Fillmore East* the talk of the rock world soon after its release. The band was finally beginning to reap the fruits of their labor.

On October 29, during a much-needed respite from touring, Duane was riding his motorcycle through the streets of Macon, on his way home to change clothes for a birthday party for Berry Oakley's wife, Linda. Traveling in a car behind him were Berry's sister—Candace Oakley—and Duane's girlfriend—Dixie Meadows. As Duane approached an intersection, a tractor trailer that was crossing in front of him suddenly stopped, leaving Duane very little time to react. He tried to skid around it but the truck caught a piece of his motorcycle, causing him and the bike to flip into the air, bounce a few times, and skid about fifty feet. Duane was unconscious when Candace and Dixie reached him. Although the twenty-four-year-old guitarist was rushed into emergency surgery, he succumbed to his injuries within hours.

The band was devastated by Duane's death, particularly his brother Gregg and bassist Berry Oakley, who had grown very close to Duane and who, friends say, was never the same after Duane was gone. Although Duane was modest and did not like to hear it, he was the heart of the Allman Brothers Band and the soul of this new southern-rock sound. "More than anyone else," Johnny Sandlin, drummer for Hour Glass, later told a *Rolling Stone* reporter, "Duane Allman was responsible for the musical revolution in the South."

Duane's death, however, was not the end of the Allman Brothers Band, and some of his more recent recordings survived for the group's fourth album, *Eat a*

The Allman Brothers Band performing, 1972. AP/Wide World Photos.

Peach, released just months after his passing. With the success of their earlier albums, the group was on top. The band knew they could never replace Duane, so Betts took over the guitar lead at performances and the band continued to tour and record, dedicating *Eat a Peach* to Duane, and watching the album climb into the Top 5. They soon added pianist Chuck Leavell to the group, and finally began enjoying the financial rewards of their success.

Despite the band's growing popularity, hit records, and sold-out performances, tension began to brew within the ranks. Gregg was embarking on solo projects, and conflict surfaced between the band and Phil Walden over royalties. In November 1972, just a little more than a year after Duane's death, Berry Oakley was killed in a motorcycle accident chillingly similar to Duane's, crashing into the side of a bus just outside of Macon. The strain was too much for the band, and though their star continued to rise—largely on the strength of their existing recordings—they were never as strong as they were with Duane and Berry. The group continued to give excellent performances and release well-received albums until they broke up under strained circumstances in 1976, after several members, including Gregg, left for solo careers. Some band members reunited off and on over the next few decades, although the later work never held a candle to the golden period in the early-1970s when Duane and Gregg led the band to redefine rock and roll in the south.

But the story of the Allman Brothers is much more than the story of one band. The group inspired other artists, largely from Florida and Georgia, to create their own forms of this musical hybrid. Just as Bob Dylan, the Byrds, and the Flying Burrito Brothers were inspiring country rock in 1970s acts like the Eagles;

Fleetwood Mac; and Crosby, Stills, Nash & Young, the Allman Brothers Band were paving the way for a new generation of southern, roots-rock musicians.

Wet Willie

One of the first southern-rock bands to emerge on the heels of the Allman Brothers was Wet Willie, a good-time, R&B/country group from Mobile,

Alabama. Wet Willie was the third act signed by Capricorn Records, after the Allman Brothers and a short-lived acoustic/jazz combo called Cowboy. Originally named Fox, Wet Willie was founded by brothers Jimmy and Jack Hall and signed to Capricorn in 1971, relocating to Macon, Georgia. With Jimmy on vocals, saxophone, and harmonica, and Jack on bass, the group—including Ricky Hirsch on guitar, John Anthony on keyboards, and Lewis Ross on drums—released their debut *Wet Willie* in 1971 to mediocre sales and began touring in support of other bands like the Grateful Dead and Grand Funk Railroad. Although Wet Willie only had a few songs appear in the Top 40, their fun, uplifting performances made them a popular live attraction.

When the band released their fourth album in 1974, the eponymous single "Keep on Smilin'" made it into the Top 10 and provided the group with a taste of success just as other southern acts were emerging with their own individual styles. The group's use of female backup singers, the "Williettes," inspired Lynyrd Skynyrd to do the same, which contributed to their unique

Wet Willie in concert, 1973. © Henry Diltz/Corbis.

sound. Wet Willie released seven albums with Capricorn until they moved to Epic in 1978, eventually disbanding a few years later.

The Marshall Tucker Band

Another group that Capricorn brought under its wing was the Marshall Tucker Band, a Spartanburg, South Carolina outfit that took its appellation from a piano tuner whose name was found on a key ring in their rehearsal space. Marshall Tucker was a merger between local bands the Toy Factory and Pax Parachute. The Caldwell brothers—guitarist/lyricist Toy and bassist

Tommy—founded the combination rock/jazz/blues/country group with friends Doug Gray on vocals, Paul Riddle on drums, George McCorkle on rhythm guitar, and Jerry Eubanks on saxophone and flute, unusual instruments in a southern-rock band, which helped Marshall Tucker develop a unique sound.

The Toy Factory had already made a name for themselves in the local rock community, opening for the Allman Brothers Band during part of their touring schedule in 1971 and playing at least once with Wet Willie. The members of Wet Willie were stunned by the talent in the group—particularly Toy's guitar playing—and arranged for Phil Walden to attend a show. A week later, Walden offered them a contract with Capricorn, and in 1973 *The Marshall Tucker Band* slowly climbed to No. 29 on the charts and, like most of their later albums, became a gold record.

The group returned to opening for the Allman Brothers Band, which had become a major touring act by late 1973, and were overwhelmed that they were now playing in sold-out arenas. Their extensive exposure, hard-work ethic, and excellent performances made them grow in demand and turned their tour schedule into a constant string of dates. In 1974 the group played more than 300 shows, as well as released their second album, *A New Life*—which peaked at No. 37 and was hailed by the *Washington Post* as one of the year's finest rock albums[3]—and their third album, the double disc *Where We All Belong*. The group was highly respected among other southern rockers for both their discipline and amiability—not to mention their talent—and it wasn't long before they were recognized as one of southern rock's A-list acts, producing memorable tracks such as "Can't You See," "Take the Highway," "Ramblin'," and their highest-charting single at No. 14, 1977's "Heard It in a Love Song." The Marshall Tucker Band continued charting albums until 1980 when Tommy Caldwell was killed in an auto accident. Though he was replaced and the band survived into the 1990s, it wasn't the same group without Tommy, and little success followed them after his death.

Charlie Daniels

One of the Marshall Tucker Band's most notable collaborators was the fiddler Charlie Daniels, who sat in on a number of their albums and would often jump onstage with the band during performances. Daniels had been in the music game since the 1950s, when he formed a high-school band called the Misty Mountain Boys, later changing their name to the Jaguars. His first noteworthy break came when a song he co-wrote with producer Bob Johnston, "It Hurts Me," found its way onto the B-side of Elvis Presley's "Kissin' Cousins" in 1964. At Johnston's suggestion, Daniels left North Carolina for Nashville to find work as a session musician, where he played on several Bob Dylan albums, including his 1969 country-rock landmark *Nashville Skyline*.

After a poor-selling solo album through Capitol Records in 1970, Daniels decided he needed some talent to back him up on a more permanent basis and

The Charlie Daniels Band, 1973. Courtesy of Photofest.

formed the Charlie Daniels Band, releasing two more albums in 1970 and 1973. The latter, *Honey in the Rock*, featured his first hit "Uneasy Rider," the tale of a hippie who gets stranded in a Mississippi bar and has to endure the tense redneck atmosphere around him. The song climbed the charts to No. 9 the following year, and Daniels soon found himself not only labeled a "southern rocker" but also respected as somewhat of a father figure to the other bands because of his age.

Daniels capitalized on the sudden nationwide interest in southern culture by playing to the "good-ol'-boy" theme in his music through hit songs like "Long Haired Country Boy" and "The South's Gonna Do It," both from his 1974 album *Fire on the Mountain*. In the latter song, Daniels goes so far as to call out southern musicians and groups by name, marking their esteemed place in contemporary American music. Daniels was no prima donna—he respected his fellow southerners and gave them credit or jammed with them on stage at every opportunity. During a 1974 show in Nashville, Daniels was joined by the Marshall Tucker Band and the Allman Brothers Band, giving birth to an annual event called the Volunteer Jam (after Tennessee, the Volunteer State). Later Volunteer Jam concerts spawned a series of live albums named after the event.

Daniels reached the height of his popularity in 1979 with his No. 3 pop and No. 1 country hit "Devil Went Down to Georgia," in which he engages the devil in a fictional fiddling contest. The 1980 Iranian hostage crisis and the cold war between Russia and the United States gave Daniels material and ammunition for some overtly political songs like "In America" and "Still in Saigon," in which he panders to hawkish right-wingers, and which solidify his image as a proud southerner and fierce patriot. Daniels continued to perform into the next century, and is seen by many rock and country fans as somewhat of a grandfather in the southern music world.

The Atlanta Rhythm Section

One of the most respected bands to come out of the south in the early 1970s was the Atlanta Rhythm Section, a group of talented session musicians from Studio One in Doraville, just outside Atlanta, Georgia. Organized and managed by producer Buddy Buie, the Studio One session players—including Dean Daughtry, Robert Nix, J. R. Cobb, Rodney Justo, Barry Bailey, and Paul Goddard—spent several days a week working on other artists' albums and the rest of their time recording their own material.

Unlike many 1970s southern acts, the Atlanta Rhythm Section enjoyed a slow, steady climb in popularity and recognition. Though they were celebrated as an excellent live act, they were very focused on songwriting and spent more time in the studio than many bands, averaging an album a year after their first, self-titled release in 1972, with each album taking about three months to record. Though other southern groups were largely performance-oriented bands that saw recording as secondary to being onstage, ARS took to the stage to exercise material bound for the studio.

From 1976 to 1980, the band increased their live appearances to coincide with a series of hits that raised their popularity to the level of a national rock act. Polished, soft-rock staples such as "Imaginary Lover" and "So into You" broke the band into the Top 10 and earned them larger concert venues and a gig at the White House playing a birthday party for President Jimmy Carter's son. However, with the rise of new rock styles like punk and new wave elbowing out existing genres, the Atlanta Rhythm Section declined in popularity at about the same time southern music waned, and their work through the 1980s and 1990s—much of it with replacement players—went mostly unnoticed.

PASSING THE TORCH: LYNYRD SKYNYRD

In 1968, when the little-known Hour Glass was on its way down, the band played a small tour outside California. One of their stops was the Comic Book Club in Jacksonville, Florida. "We're headlining in this little club, and we're sitting in the dressing room," recalls Paul Hornsby, who played keyboards for Hour Glass at the time. "There's an opening band. I heard something very familiar being played. I stuck my head out the door, and there was the opening band, playing one of the songs from our album that we had just finished. . . . And they went from one song, and then played nearly every song off our new album. The few songs that we actually played off the album they did as good or better than we played it. So, we came on. 'What are we going to do? Hey, how are we going to follow this band?' "[4]

Hour Glass, of course, would go on to become the Allman Brothers Band, the first chapter in the history of southern rock. The group that opened for them that night was One Percent, a local band that worshiped Duane Allman and Hour Glass, and would eventually pick up the mantle from the Allman Brothers to take southern rock to new heights under the name Lynyrd Skynyrd.

Affectionately known by fans as simply Skynyrd, the group had been around longer than the Allman Brothers Band, but took years to establish their unique sound and get discovered. Skynyrd was originally composed of vocalist Ronnie Van Zant, guitarists Gary Rossington and Allen Collins, bassist Larry Jungstrom, and drummer Bob Burns. The band members got together in 1964, following a high school baseball game in which Van Zant hit a ball that knocked Burns unconscious. The older Van Zant felt bad for Burns and began hanging out with him and his musician friends. They were soon playing parties and local clubs under names such as the Noble Five and My Backyard before finally settling on One Percent, when they decided that music was what they wanted to do with their lives—they were going to be that one percent of musicians that make a living at it.

The band modeled itself on the earthy, guitar-driven British bands popular at the time, especially Free, the Rolling Stones, the Yardbirds, Cream, and Bad Company. Countless nights were spent at the Comic Book Club watching local and touring bands, absorbing everything they could and eventually playing gigs there themselves. Through the late 1960s, the band developed a fairly loyal local following, even releasing a single through a small Florida label, but little was heard of them outside the Jacksonville area.

One night in 1970, during a show at the local Forrest Inn, Van Zant introduced the band under a false name, as he would occasionally do as a joke. Their local fan base was well aware of a running feud Van Zant, Rossington, and Burns had with their high-school coach Leonard Skinner, who disapproved of their long hair and even suspended them for it more than once. At this particular performance, Van Zant received raucous applause when he introduced the band as Leonard Skinner. Afterward the group decided that their long hair was a point of pride marking their struggle against authority and convention, and decided that the name—with an alternate spelling—would stick.

The band continued to struggle through one-nighters in Florida bars and engage in short southern tours through the turn of the decade, but as they entered their twenties, and several of the members had started families, they knew they had to make it as musicians or move on. Although Capricorn offered them a recording deal, the group did not want to play fourth fiddle to the label's more successful acts—the Allman Brothers Band, Wet Willie, and the Marshall Tucker Band—despite their affinity for the groups and their members. So as the Capricorn artists saw their stars rise, Skynyrd continued playing local bar circuits throughout the south, honing their skills, writing new material, and developing a sound that would differentiate them from other southern musicians.

In the early 1970s, Capricorn was enjoying success as the unofficial label of the south, with the Allman Brothers Band as its flagship. Musicians and industry executives started to take notice, and labels began signing acts whose music revealed deep-south roots. Among the admirers of the new sound was guitarist/organist Al Kooper, who had made a name for himself in the Blues Project and Blood, Sweat & Tears, as well as played for or produced artists such as Bob Dylan, Jimi Hendrix, Stephen Stills, Carlos Santana, and the Rolling Stones. Kooper was intrigued by what Capricorn was doing, and wanted to provide another outlet for southern music, so under the auspices of MCA, Kooper founded the Sounds of the South label in Atlanta in 1972. Skynyrd knew that if they wanted to get anywhere in the music industry, they would have to play the larger cities like Atlanta, and regularly made short trips to the city for gigs in 1972. Soon after starting his label, Kooper saw Lynyrd Skynyrd while they were doing a weeklong stint at Funochio's—a notoriously seedy Atlanta dive—and offered them a contract.

Small lineup changes at this point would later prove to have a major effect on the band's sound. Besides the addition of Skynyrd roadie Billy Powell on keyboards, bassist Jungstrom had decided to leave the group and was replaced by Leon Wilkeson, a childhood friend of several band members. Wilkeson enjoyed playing and touring with the group, but when Kooper was ready to record the band's debut, he decided he wasn't mature enough for success, and returned home to work for a dairy company. Desperately needing a bassist, the group was lucky to find Ed King available, one of the founders of the defunct Strawberry Alarm Clock, for whom One Percent had once opened in Florida. The recording of their first album was a tumultuous event, with Kooper, the experienced producer, constantly butting heads with Van Zant, the band's visionary. In other collaborations this friction might have led to disaster, but Kooper and Van Zant worked out their differences to produce a spectacular debut album, and in 1973, *Pronounced Leh-Nerd Skin-Nerd* hit the shelves.

Pronounced was not an immediate chart success but received a surprising amount of nationwide airplay, and some of its tracks—"Gimme Three Steps," "Simple Man," and "Freebird"—would become southern-rock classics. "Freebird" eventually became a signature song for the band. Although it was originally written by Collins and Van Zant for Collins' wedding in 1970, the group later dedicated it to the late Duane Allman, an association that stuck as the song became one of the most popular offerings of the genre. In producing the tune for *Pronounced*, Kooper had used modern recording techniques to make the famous solo sound like it was being played by two guitarists. After the album was released, Wilkeson returned to the band as bassist, and King was moved to guitarist alongside Collins and Rossington, allowing them to recreate "Freebird"'s double-guitar solo on stage. This triple guitar lineup—later dubbed the "three guitar army"—would become the unique sound Lynyrd Skynyrd had been searching for, and would catapult them to national stardom.

Soon after the release of *Pronounced*, the band was booked to open for the Who on their *Quadrophenia* tour in the fall of 1973, giving them the national exposure they craved. But despite a successful tour and the critical praise of their first album, chart success continued to elude them. Their parent label, MCA, pressured the band to come up with a Top 40 hit. Skynyrd's response was unexpected—a humorous song about the south they had penned in the summer of 1973 right after they established their new guitar trio. "Sweet Home Alabama" was written in response to Neil Young's damning "Southern Man," in which Young berates the south for its racist past. The Skynyrd crew loved Young's music, and even though none of them were from Alabama, they thought it would be funny to write a tune defending the state.

Although MCA was initially hesitant about releasing a regional tune to a national audience, the song was a surprise smash and gave the band their first Top 10 hit in August 1974. Its corresponding album, the sophomore effort

Second Helping, achieved gold status, boosting sales of their debut album, which soon followed with a gold showing of its own. Critics took notice of this simple yet powerful sound emerging over the horizon, deemed by the *Washington Post*, "Good old gut-bucket rock,"[5] and described by the *New York Times* as "a common denominator of Southern rock groups, a little Allman Brothers sound, some Chicago black blues riffs and relentlessly rolling rhythms built around simple phrases."[6]

One of the things that Skynyrd had developed during their tour with the Who was a persona of drunken rowdiness. The Who were one of the loudest and angriest bands in rock, and their opening acts—including Skynyrd—were always intimidated to play with them. The boys from Jacksonville drowned their apprehension in alcohol, and turned their live set into a musical, binge-drinking saloon brawl, going so far as to maintain a wet bar on stage during performances. The persona seemed to fit their party-hardy, southern boogie songs, and the band developed a reputation for knowing how to show their fans a good time.

By 1975, Lynyrd Skynyrd was on top, with songs like "Sweet Home Alabama," "Saturday Night Special," and "Gimme Three Steps" earning airplay all over the country. "Freebird" finally managed to find its way onto the charts in January, and would repeat the feat with a live version two years later. By this time the Allman Brothers Band, though still a top-grossing outfit, had passed their golden years of creativity and were on their way to a breakup in 1976. Skynyrd was the new name in southern music, its trio of lead guitars and slightly more hillbilly brand of rock dominating the genre.

But just as tragedy shortened the career of the Allman Brothers, Skynyrd's ensemble would suffer misfortunes of their own. After their successes in 1974 and 1975, the group embarked on major tours of the United States, Canada, and Europe, grueling expeditions that cost them Ed King and Bob Burns, both of whom left the band due to exhaustion. The group's alcohol-induced rowdiness fueled numerous newspaper and magazine headlines and left battered bars and trashed hotel rooms in its wake.

Burns was replaced by Artimus Pyle on drums, who had played some sets with the Marshall Tucker Band and Charlie Daniels. Pyle debuted with the band on their third album, 1975's *Nuthin' Fancy*, which peaked at No. 9 on the charts and spawned the radio hit "Saturday Night Special," an unusual social commentary on handguns. Political statements were rare in southern rock, but Lynyrd Skynyrd was a rare breed, and would occasionally fuel public debate with their lyrics.

Though *Nuthin' Fancy* was a commercial success, King's absence was noticeable, and after the subsequent *Gimme Back My Bullets*, the group began searching for a replacement for King. Skynyrd had been using gospel-infused backup singers, among them Cassie Gaines, who recommended her younger brother Steve Gaines for the position. Though the band tried out a number of well-known and respected musicians, the unknown Gaines blew the band members away at his audition and was given the job, reestablishing the three-guitar lineup that had become Skynyrd's signature sound.

Gaines was the breath of fresh air the band needed. His peculiar slide style and fret acrobatics complemented Rossington and Collins, and Van Zant even liked him enough to share his singing duties. Lynyrd Skynyrd rode through 1976 and 1977 on top of the world, releasing the live *One More from the Road*, which put "Freebird" back on the charts, and *Street Survivors*, featuring a handful of memorable tunes such as "What's Your Name," "That Smell," "You Got That Right," and the Gaines-penned "I Know a Little." The group backed off their hard-living style a bit, choosing to focus more on their families. Van Zant cut back his drinking and was reportedly even dieting and exercising. The whole band was ready for their world tour in late 1977 to support *Street Survivors*, which had immediately become another gold record for them. But on October 20, only a few dates after their highly anticipated tour began, the group that had become the standard bearer for southern rock would come to a sudden and disastrous end.

The first five performances in Florida, Georgia, and South Carolina went off without a hitch. The band had reduced their alcohol and drug intake and were performing well together. Far from the hellish, overbooked tour just two years earlier, this one seemed like it was going to be an enjoyable experience, dubbed by the band "Tour of the Survivors" in honor of those who had stuck out the previous hardships. This motif was also represented on the *Street Survivors* album by a picture of the band emerging through a wall of flames, an iconic representation of the difficulties they had endured and the triumph that awaited those who carried on.

Unhappily, the "survivor" theme carried a macabre double meaning. The day after a rousing October 19 performance in Greenville, South Carolina, the group left for a show in Baton Rouge, Louisiana, aboard a chartered plane. At approximately 7:00 p.m., the plane ran out of fuel and crashed in a Mississippi swamp, killing Ronnie Van Zant, Steve Gaines, Cassie Gaines, and crewmember Dean Kilpatrick, in addition to the two pilots. The remaining members of the band and many of their road crew were seriously injured, and some would take years to recover. No ensemble could survive such devastation, and even though the group would reform a decade later with Rossington, Powell, Pyle, Wilkeson, King, and the younger Johnny Van Zant on vocals, the Lynyrd Skynyrd of rock legend was dead.

PICKING UP THE PIECES: SOUTHERN ROCK'S LEGACY

The demise of Lynyrd Skynyrd left a major hole in the hearts of the southern music community. *Street Survivors* reached platinum status soon after the accident and spawned several hit singles, quickly followed by the top-selling compilation album *Skynyrd's First and . . . Last*, but other acts would have to fill the musical void Skynyrd left behind. Groups such as the Atlanta Rhythm Section, the Charlie Daniels Band, and the Marshall Tucker Band, already southern rock powerhouses, stepped in to assume the mantle of leadership.

Other performers, heavily influenced by the Allman Brothers Band and other early acts, rode the southern rock wave through the 1970s. Guitarist Elvin Bishop, who made a name for himself in the 1960s with the Paul Butterfield Blues Band, had a string of somewhat popular albums in the 1970s after he joined Capricorn Records at the insistence of the Allman Brothers Band's Dickey Betts. Bishop's mix of country, soul, and R&B were a perfect fit for the Macon label, and with the help of vocalist Mickey Thomas (who would later head Jefferson Starship), Bishop scored a No. 3 single in 1976 with "Fooled Around and Fell in Love."

Another Capricorn act that managed to garner some attention was Grinderswitch, a group of Allman Brothers devotees founded by Allman roadie Joe Dan Petty. The country/blues quartet modeled itself on the Allmans and became known for energetic live performances. Though the group lacked any hits and lived largely in the shadow of their heroes—opening for them regularly and even sometimes borrowing their equipment—they were a popular band on their home turf and known for putting on some of the best live shows in the south.

One of the few southern rock bands that did not originate in Georgia or Florida was the midwest sextet Black Oak Arkansas, a more-rock-than-country band that recorded fourteen albums in their first nine years. Originally known as the Knowbody Else, the group started in 1969 and slowly built a following through the midwest and the south. Like many bands of the genre, their chart success never matched the draw of their live performances, scoring only one Top 40 song with their minor 1974 hit "Jim Dandy." Though a series of replacements left only one original member by 1978, the group continued as a touring band well into the 1980s, after it had ceased its prolific recording career.

If Black Oak Arkansas was more rock than country, then their counterparts, the Outlaws, balanced the equation with their Eagles-like melodies and noticeable twang. Formed in Tampa, Florida, in 1974, the Outlaws got their break opening for Lynyrd Skynyrd, after which they were signed as the first act on the new Arista label. Their self-titled 1975 debut was a critical and chart success, reaching No. 13, while the single "There Goes Another Love Song" became their first Top 40 entry and most memorable tune. Averaging an album a year over their eight-year career, the group only managed one other Top 40 single, 1981's "(Ghost) Riders in the Sky," before disbanding shortly thereafter.

There are, in fact, only a handful of acts one could listen to and immediately identify as belonging to the southern-rock genre. From the first country/rock/soul/R&B hybrid groups in the late 1960s and early 1970s, there developed a string of variations, every band adding their own influences into the mix. To many critics, the tragic demise of Lynyrd Skynyrd marks the beginning of the end of southern rock as a genre, especially as it coincides with the folding of Capricorn Records—which had built itself into the largest independent label in the world[7]—shortly thereafter due to departing acts and financial difficulty. Although groups such as Marshall Tucker and Charlie Daniels had some last-minute hits by the 1980s—Daniels' star actually burned brightest from 1979 to 1982—many successful post-1977 bands claimed by southern rockers lacked a number of the identifiable features of the genre's early form—penniless musicians raised largely around black musical influences; clear indications of blues, country, and soul roots; extended guitar battles between several leads; relatively poor chart success that doesn't measure up to the quality of live performances; and passionate affiliation with the South as a cultural entity.

A very loose definition of southern rock might include acts such as ZZ Top and Hank Williams Jr., and some texts claim them as such. But with the explosion of varying musical styles and cross-pollination through the late 1960s and 1970s, groups that contain a few southern-rock indicators might be better labeled with more specific definitions, such as "gritty Texas rock" (ZZ Top) or simply country (Hank Williams Jr.). Even Molly Hatchet and .38 Special, the last major southern rock bands of the late 1970s and 1980s, could not be more geographically south—both hailing from Jacksonville, Florida, with .38 Special featuring the middle Van Zant brother, Donnie, on lead vocals. But both bands quickly abandoned their bluesy, countrified, southern boogie past for glossy, commercial, hard-rock sounds, a far cry from the soulful rock exemplified by groups such as One Percent and Hour Glass, which created a new genre out of diverse influences and returned the banner of rock to the original home of rockabilly, the South.

NOTES

1. Brant 1999, 23.
2. Larry Rohter, "Southern Boogie," *Washington Post*, June 21, 1975, C8.
3. Alex Ward, "Regrouping the Allman Brothers," *Washington Post*, February 2, 1975, 98.
4. Brant 1999, 37.
5. Alex Ward, "Struttin' the Stuff on the Songs of the South," *Washington Post*, March 3, 1976, E7.
6. "South Rocks Again at Music Academy," *New York Times*, February 2, 1975, 47.
7. Robert Palmer, "Southern Rock is Spreading Around the Country," *New York Times*, July 24, 1977, D18.

FOLK ROCK AND ITS SUCCESSORS

Once upon a time, folk music and rock music could not have been more different. Folk was music for purists who prided themselves on its anticommercial nature. It was the language of the people, a populist genre whose value depended on its being shared—claiming authorship or ownership was frowned on, and many believed that it was not folk music if you knew who wrote it. It was, in fact, the norm to write new lyrics to old melodies, or for each musician to interpret songs to fit their own time and place. Rock, on the other hand, was a corporate endeavor. Someone wrote a rock song, someone else performed it, and many others in between—managers, promoters, engineers—made money off the process. There was, in effect, an essential version of each song. Rock was a one-way street, delivered by the few to the masses for profit. Folk was a two-lane highway, passed between performers and fans as a shared, communal experience. "If someone desires to make money," Joan Baez famously told *Time* magazine, "I don't call it folk music."[1] Folk fans thought rock was a slick enterprise, appealing to the unrefined palate of mass taste. Rock fans thought that folk was an unrefined art of the past, appreciated only by people who feared electricity.

In the 1940s and 1950s, folk underwent a popular upswing as acts like Woody Guthrie, Pete Seeger, and the Weavers (in which both Seeger and Guthrie played) generated rising appeal by revisiting traditional songs in the wake of labor-union tensions and the erosion of civil liberties under McCarthyism. By altering folk standards to address the issues of the day, these artists reinvigorated folk as a vital musical genre, creating what became known as the "great folk music scare," leading to a major folk boom in the early 1960s in which artists were writing new songs in a folk style.

At about this time, the post–World War II baby boom was coming of age, and as this new generation passed through their college years, they were exposed to campus folkies singing about the world around them. The civil rights movement, the youthful energy of J.F.K., and the revolutionary strains of Bob Dylan's music made it clear that change was in the air. Groups like the Limeliters, the New Christy Minstrels, the Kingston Trio, and Peter, Paul and Mary found homes on the pop charts despite their folk sound, creating an excitement about the resurging popularity of folk, but also resentment that these groups were violating one of folk's unwritten rules—they were simply making too much money to be called folk musicians anymore. It was only a matter of time before some visionary combined the newly popular folk with its rock competitor to create the hybrid of folk rock. That visionary was a young Minnesotan name Robert Zimmerman, aka Bob Dylan.

The story of folk rock's chronological origins is told in the Bob Dylan section later on, but there are larger issues that should be mentioned in a thorough discussion of the genre. Those with an overwhelming need for specificity generally agree that folk rock was born when Bob Dylan appeared onstage with an electric guitar at the Newport Folk Festival in July 1965. The emergence of the genre, however, had been a process involving to no small degree the Beatles.

One of the things Bob Dylan and the Beatles brought to rock music was the idea that a musician could both write well and perform well. Until the 1960s, most rock artists had their tunes penned for them, and folkies largely performed traditional works. Even Woody Guthrie, though credited with more than 1,400 songs, gathered most of his melodies and bits of lyrics from migrant camps and hobo jungles. In the early 1960s, Dylan showed that folk could be exciting, and the Beatles showed that rock could be literate. As the Beatles grew increasingly adventurous, the flood gates were slowly pried open for experimentation beyond standard rock setups and cross-pollination between musical genres. It was not long before acts like Dylan and the Byrds were mixing folk themes with rock rhythms, and eventually folk rock incorporated country, bluegrass, honky-tonk, and all manner of sub-subgenres.

It would be difficult to overstate the influence of Dylan and the Beatles on other acts. Stephen Stills once described the influence on him and Neil Young in the early folk-rock act Buffalo Springfield in the simplest of terms: "He [Young] wanted to be Bob Dylan and I wanted to be the Beatles."[2] The Byrds' Jim McGuinn wanted to find "the gap between Dylan and the Beatles,"[3] and based the band's signature 12-string Rickenbacker sound on what he had heard from George Harrison. Many of folk rock's early hits, in fact, were covers of Dylan or Beatles songs, or of traditional songs that Dylan had already resurrected.

One largely ignored aspect of folk rock was its role as a place for women in the music business. Though there were a number of successful female acts in the pop world, very few of them wrote their own songs or were seen as more than the public faces of larger corporate machines. Rock from the mid-1960s on had its occasional Janis Joplin or Grace Slick, but was still largely dominated by men, particularly the more aggressive genres like heavy metal, glam, and progressive. It was at the intersection of folk and rock that women began to be seen as owners of their own image. Though Joan Baez did not write most of her songs in the 1960s, she was an independent artist who tackled material on her own terms, paving the way for musicians like Laura Nyro and Janis Ian in the late 1960s. Nyro was a soulful writer and performer who penned classics like "Stoned Soul Picnic," "Wedding Bell Blues," "And When I Die," and "Eli's Comin'," three of which appeared simultaneously in the Top 10 in late 1969,

 WORDS TO REMEMBER

Even as rock was entering an age of albums gaining popularity over singles, folk rock produced a number of songs that served as anthems for the era. Below is a list of ten of the most important, or at least the most enduring, folk-rock songs from 1967 to 1973, each entry including the artist, the album on which it first appeared, one of its more memorable lyrics and a brief description of its impact.

"For What It's Worth"
Buffalo Springfield
Buffalo Springfield, 1967
"Stop, hey, what's that sound, everybody look what's going down"

Inspired by an incident of police brutality during a protest on L.A.'s Sunset Strip in 1966, "For What It's Worth" was penned by Stephen Stills, later of Crosby, Stills, Nash & Young. Although it was Buffalo Springfield's only hit, it helped galvanize resistance to increasingly violent clashes between authorities and anti-war demonstrators.

"Society's Child (Baby I've Been Thinking)"
Janis Ian
Janis Ian, 1967
"One of these days I'm gonna stop my listening, gonna raise my head up high"

Instantly controversial for its mature subject matter of interracial relationships and virulent attack on hypocrisy, "Society's Child" was all the more remarkable in that Ian was only fifteen years old when she wrote it. The song launched Ian's career as one of the boldest of the new generation of singer-songwriters.

"Both Sides, Now"
Judy Collins
Wildflowers, 1967
"It's love's illusions I recall, I really don't know love at all"

🔊 WORDS TO REMEMBER *(continued)*

After folk-revival singer Judy Collins covered "Both Sides, Now," its chart success introduced songwriter Joni Mitchell to a larger audience, giving her a crucial career boost that made her into one of the biggest folk artists of the 1970s. It has since been recorded more than 300 times by artists including Chet Atkins, Pete Seeger, Bing Crosby, Neil Diamond, the Nitty Gritty Dirt Band, Frank Sinatra, Willie Nelson, and Mr. Spock himself—Leonard Nimoy.

"All Along the Watchtower"

Bob Dylan

John Wesley Harding, 1967

"There must be some way out of here said the joker to the thief"

Though "All Along the Watchtower" might be rock and roll's most covered song, it didn't even reach the charts for Dylan. The tune has been recorded by acts including Neil Young, the Indigo Girls, U2, and the Dave Matthews Band, but for many, the definitive version was recorded by Jimi Hendrix for his 1968 *Electric Ladyland*—the only song Hendrix brought into the Top 20.

"Alice's Restaurant Massacree"

Arlo Guthrie

Alice's Restaurant, 1967

"You can get anything you want at Alice's Restaurant"

One of music's most entertaining sing-alongs, the eighteen-plus-minute track took up an entire side of Guthrie's first long-play album. A true story of the trouble Guthrie got into when he tried to help a neighbor dump her garbage, the song demonstrates Arlo's worth as storytelling heir to his father—the great folk singer Woody Guthrie, who died soon after Arlo's album debut.

"Mrs. Robinson"

Simon and Garfunkel

The Graduate (soundtrack), 1968

"And here's to you, Mrs. Robinson, Jesus loves you more than you will know"

Director Mike Nichols asked Simon and Garfunkel to write an entire soundtrack for his 1967 film *The Graduate*, but decided he liked their existing material so much that only one new song—"Mrs. Robinson"—made it into the movie. The song spent three weeks on top of the charts, with its accompanying soundtrack spending nine weeks in the No. 1 spot.

"Fire and Rain"

James Taylor

Sweet Baby James, 1970

"Sweet dreams and flying machines in pieces on the ground"

Although rock myth proclaims that Taylor wrote "Fire and Rain" about a girl-friend who died in a plane crash, it was actually an amalgam of experiences involving Taylor's depression, heroin addiction, and the breakup of his band. The tune reached No. 3 on the charts, bringing Taylor to national attention and serving as his signature song for decades.

"Woodstock"

Crosby, Stills, Nash & Young

Déjà vu, 1970

"We are stardust, we are golden"

One of Crosby, Stills, Nash & Young's biggest hits, this Joni Mitchell composition captures the sense of celebration and dawning possibilities of the 1969 Woodstock festival in upstate New York. The song's great irony is that its author missed the event due to traffic, but wrote the tune after hearing her good friends Crosby and Nash talk about it.

"Ohio"

Crosby, Stills, Nash & Young

4 Way Street, 1971

"Tin soldiers and Nixon coming"

A chilling recounting of the May 4, 1970, shooting of four Kent State students by National Guardsmen, "Ohio" was written, recorded, and released within two weeks of the incident. Legend has it that Neil Young wrote the song within hours of Crosby showing him news pictures of the event, and its quick release, while nerves were still raw, made it an instant rallying point for opponents of Vietnam and the Nixon presidency.

"American Pie"

Don McLean

American Pie, 1971

"Something touched me deep inside, the day the music died"

One of rock music's most deconstructed songs, the 8 minute 27 second paean to Buddy Holly was so long it took up both sides of a single, but still reached No. 1 in the United States and No. 3 in the United Kingdom. The No. 1 hit for Roberta Flack in 1973, "Killing Me Softly with His Song," was originally written about a live performance of "American Pie" by McLean.

covered by other artists. Like Nyro, Janis Ian found success at a young age with "Society's Child (Baby I've Been Thinking)," a song she wrote when she was fifteen years old (see Words to Remember). As women found greater equality as all-around artists in folk rock, the singer-songwriter movement of the early 1970s garnered fame for some of rock's greatest women, including Carole King, Joni Mitchell, and Carly Simon. But we are getting ahead of ourselves; first, of course, there was Dylan.

BOB DYLAN

Barring the great folk hero Woody Guthrie and the famed musicologist Alan Lomax, there has arguably been no figure that has made more of an impact on American music than Bob Dylan. From the beginning, when he journeyed from Duluth, Minnesota, to New York City in 1961 to meet the ailing Guthrie, Dylan set himself up as heir to Guthrie's legacy as a popularizer of folk music. Within two years, the folk world had come to agree with him. Partially through the help of folk's reigning queen, Joan Baez—who adored Dylan—and partially through the large number of artists that covered his songs, he became the voice of the new folk, a position he enjoyed for only a short time before it grew to be an albatross around his neck.

Many of Dylan's important accomplishments are outside the chronological scope of this book—namely his emergence as a folk icon in the early 1960s, his blending of folk and rock in the mid-1960s, and his excellent albums in the mid-1970s. But no chapter on folk rock would be complete without at least a cursory recounting of the controversial period when folk's biggest hero became, in the minds of some, its bitterest enemy.

Dylan wore his mantle only briefly before making waves in the folk world. Initially his protest songs sparked a revolution in the popularization of folk but as the weight on his shoulders became burdensome, he moved toward more vague and personal works on his 1964 release, the aptly named *Another Side of Bob Dylan*.

It was his next album, however, that would put the folk world on its ear. With the early 1965 release of *Bringing It All Back Home*, including the free-form single "Subterranean Homesick Blues," Dylan began to violate the sacred rules of folk by incorporating electric guitar, drums, and rock rhythms into his music. Only months later, at the 1965 Newport Folk Festival, Dylan was practically booed off the stage when he came out backed by the electric Paul Butterfield Blues Band—an event generally marked in the American consciousness as the moment that folk rock was born.

Dylan had actually been looking to incorporate rock rhythms and instruments into his music for years. As early as 1962, he was recording electric instruments in songs that were never released, largely because of his manager's belief that a sudden divergence to rock was not the way to go, with his folk career skyrocketing the way it was. Folk purists looked down on rock (and indeed some still do) as simple and hollow entertainment that did not carry the weight of generations like folk did.

Dylan, with his gifted and literate songwriting, changed all of that. Bob Dylan and the Beatles had built a mutual admiration society of sorts. Dylan gave the Beatles independence and poetic license, while the Beatles showed Dylan that rock could be art instead of mere entertainment. Much of the creativity of this era of rock music, from the mid-1960s to the early 1970s, was directly or indirectly born from the influence Bob Dylan and the Beatles had on each other.

It is at this point that our story really begins. Dylan had broken the barrier, bringing rock's literal and metaphorical electricity into folk's literary and meta-generational breathing space. Though other artists scored major hits with his material, *Bringing It All Back Home* was Dylan's first Top 10 album. His follow-up releases, 1965's *Highway 61 Revisited* and 1966's *Blonde on Blonde* (believed to be rock's first double album), were also Top 10 hits and among his finest work, with songs like "I Want You," "Just Like a Woman," "Rainy Day Women #12 and 35," and "Like a Rolling Stone" establishing him solid footing in the folk and rock worlds and making him into a major commercial attraction in the United States and overseas.

In 1966, an exhausted Dylan was stretched to the limit with his fame, recording, touring, acting, and his attempt to write a novel. His commitments looming and his relationship with Grossman deteriorating, Dylan was seriously injured in a motorcycle accident in July, causing him to disappear from the scene for almost two years. The rest seemed to be just what he needed, and the reclusive Dylan became somewhat of a Salingeresque myth, rumored to have quit music altogether. In fact, after a brief respite, he began recording with his backing band the Hawks in a pink house near Woodstock, New York. The house, nicknamed Big Pink, became another object of Dylan myth for the many songs he composed there. The Hawks would eventually become known as the Band, and their album *Music from Big Pink* would reach the Top 30 as their debut in 1968, spawning a renewed interest in traditional sounds and helping establish the genre of Americana. Other artists would record songs Dylan wrote during this period, but Dylan himself would not release the material until 1975 on *The Basement Tapes*.

Dylan emerged from his solitude in early 1968 to participate in a memorial concert for his mentor Woody Guthrie, who had died the previous fall from Huntington's chorea. Only a month before the concert, he had released the excellent *John Wesley Harding*, once again a departure from the expected—the new, mellower Dylan cooing surreal, but not displeasing, lyrics. The most recognizable single from the album, "All Along the Watchtower," did not even chart, but became Jimi Hendrix's highest charting single that same year and eventually one of the most covered songs in rock (see Words to Remember).

Never one to sit still for stereotyping, Dylan's next album, 1969's *Nashville Skyline*, was an even greater departure from expectations. After turning folk into rock, Dylan helped turn rock into country with this straightforward,

Bob Dylan, 1973. Courtesy of Photofest.

unpretentious collection of gems recorded in Nashville with the likes of Charlie Daniels and Johnny Cash. As rock's other offshoots—progressive, heavy metal, glam—were building on more complex studio technology and larger stages, *Nashville Skyline* enflamed a budding new subgenre that would find mass popularity in the 1970s: country rock. "*Nashville Skyline* continues Dylan's rediscovered romance with rural music," claimed the *Rolling Stone* album review. "Although the symbolism is hobo-traditional, the *mise-en-scene* of melody, lyrics, and performance overpowers and explodes any genre limitation in a glorious flow of every sort of imaginable triumph. . . . It could well be what Dylan thinks it is, his best album."[4]

Dylan's recordings from this point until the mid-1970s continued to sell well but are not remembered as his best. Already dragging a complex and storied career behind him, he reemerged in peak form with several top-selling albums in 1974 and 1975, particularly the brilliant *Blood on the Tracks*. Dylan continued to produce quality material for decades, occasionally altering his style as he saw fit, perplexing fans and adding to the growing cadre of "Dylanologists" that would cull his garbage to find the hidden meanings behind his songs. Perpetually celebrated as one of America's greatest songwriters and most influential figures, Dylan's place in rock history may have best been captured by the closing lines Johnny Cash wrote in a poem for the *Nashville Skyline* liner notes: "here-in is a hell of a poet, and lots of other things, and lots of other things."

THE BYRDS AND THEIR OFFSPRING

Bob Dylan was certainly not alone in charting folk's musical frontier in the 1960s. With the first wave of the British invasion, America's musical troops scrambled to return fire in answer to the Beatles' unprecedented assault. Although many bands (though more often their record companies) claimed to be the American response, it was a Los Angeles quintet, the Byrds, that most rightfully held the title.

Formed in 1964 (after one failed incarnation), the Byrds featured vocalist/ guitarist Jim McGuinn (who later changed his name to Roger), vocalist/

guitarist David Crosby, bassist Chris Hillman, drummer Michael Clarke, and vocalist/guitarist/percussionist Gene Clark. Their first album featured no less than four Bob Dylan songs, including "Mr. Tambourine Man," which the band took to the top of the charts soon after its release in April 1965. Dylan had released his folk-rock debut *Bringing It All Back Home* in March, and between the two, the new subgenre was born.

The Byrds scored another No. 1 hit only six months later with their classic single "Turn! Turn! Turn!" a bible verse originally put to music by Pete Seeger, now interpreted by a rock band. McGuinn created a signature sound with his 12-string Rickenbacker guitar, creating a bright, warm tone that served as a centerpiece in many of the band's songs. The group suffered a setback when they lost radio play over their next hit, "Eight Miles High"—a song about flying that was believed by conservative forces to be a drug ditty. By coincidence, it was flying that led the band to lose their first member, Gene Clark, who left because his fear of flying made it difficult to tour. Rather than replacing Clark, the group carried on as a quartet for two more excellent albums and their memorable single "So You Want to Be a Rock 'N' Roll Star" before growing rivalries reduced the foursome to a trio.

The Byrds, 1968. Courtesy of Photofest.

In late 1967, David Crosby struck out on his own due to personal conflicts with his bandmates, soon to be followed by Michael Clarke. The remaining members—Hillman and McGuinn—took on studio musicians for their next outing, utilizing new recording technology to produce the highly sophisticated *The Notorious Byrd Brothers*, a skillful spattering of rock, folk, protest, electronica, and country that would serve as warning for their next album, 1968's landmark *Sweetheart of the Rodeo*. Before recording the album, the group brought in the talented Gram Parsons, who quickly changed the band's direction with his country influences. Bob Dylan may have beat the Byrds to the punch with the creation of folk rock, but the Byrds had their day when *Sweetheart of the Rodeo* founded the new subgenre of country rock one year before Dylan's *Nashville Skyline*.

Some critics have suggested that the Byrds could have been as productive and as famous as the Beatles if they had only been able to maintain a steady roster. "Rock history is striated by the influence of The Byrds," wrote a later critic. "Theirs is one of the great stylistic lineages, forever shadowing those of the Fabs and the Stones. Without them we would never have had Big Star, Tom Petty & the Heartbreakers, R.E.M., The Stone Roses or Teenage

Fanclub—that blissed-out, churningly harmonic, quintessentially white sound which continues to thrive in the age of Britpop. Come to that, we would never have had Dillard And Clark, Crosby, Stills And Nash, The Flying Burrito Brothers and a dozen other folk-country-rock aggregations of the late '60s. 'Influential' is the understatement of the epoch."[5]

We'll never know how high their star may have risen, since Parsons and Hillman both departed the group in 1968, leaving McGuinn by himself. As the group's frontman, McGuinn carried on with replacement players for several moderately successful albums until the band voted to dissolve in 1972. Ironically, all five of the original Byrds reunited in 1973 for the one-off album *Byrds*, after which they parted ways for good.

But the influence of the band carried on in the significant groups that its members formed after exiting the Byrds. After Parsons and Hillman left McGuinn's side in 1968, they formed their own alterative country band, the Flying Burrito Brothers, with Michael Clarke soon joining them. Unfortunately, just like the Byrds, the band was plagued with constant personnel changes, resulting in a short run. Their brief appearance, however, managed to produce some fine albums—notably 1969's *The Gilded Palace of Sin*—which established them as one of the first full-on country-rock bands, along with Dylan, influencing 1970s acts like Poco, Fleetwood Mac, the Eagles, Jackson Browne, and the Band.

Crosby, Stills & Nash, 1970. Courtesy of Photofest.

David Crosby had one of the most successful post-Byrds careers after joining Stephen Stills and Graham Nash in 1969 to form the supergroup Crosby, Stills & Nash. An enormously talented band that often played both acoustic and electric sets (most memorably at Woodstock), the trio became instantly recognizable for their perfect three-part harmony and complex guitar work—compliments of master composer Stills, who also played bass and keyboards in the band. Their first album, 1969's *Crosby, Stills & Nash*, rose to No. 6 on the charts with stunning tunes like "Long Time Gone," "Wooden Ships," and the remarkable "Suite: Judy Blue Eyes," which Stills wrote for the popular folk singer Judy Collins.

Overwhelmed by their success as a touring act, the group decided to add Neil Young to the lineup just before Woodstock, forming the even more successful Crosby, Stills, Nash & Young. Young had played with Stills in Buffalo Springfield, a moderately successful folk-rock group that had made a name for itself in

1967 with the anthemic song "For What It's Worth" in response to a police brutality incident in Los Angeles (see Words to Remember). With CSN&Y, the tremendously gifted Young would contribute some of the band's most memorable tunes.

The group released their first album as CSN&Y in 1970, the excellent *Déjà vu* that is now remembered as one of the finest recordings of the decade. The album demonstrates the amazing versatility of the foursome, from the driving harmonies of Stills' "Carry On," to the country-rock pedal steel (played by Dead frontman Jerry Garcia) of Nash's "Teach Your Children," to the lyrical acrobatics of Crosby's "Déjà vu," to Young's soft but powerful "Helpless." The album was the first of three in a row to reach the top of the charts, followed by the double live album *4 Way Street* in 1971 and, after they broke up, their greatest hits release *So Far* in 1974.

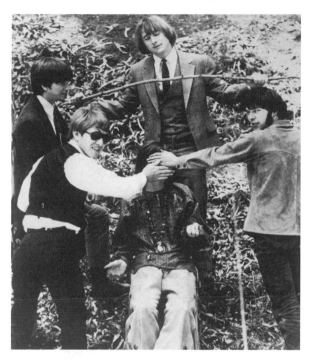

Buffalo Springfield, 1967. Authenticated News/Getty Images.

Internal ego wars led to the band's demise in 1971, as the four went separate ways to pursue solo projects, reuniting in different permutations well through the next three decades. Though they lasted less than two years as CSN&Y, their impact on later groups is measurable, demonstrating how acoustic and electric instruments could be seamlessly blended to astonishing effect. The majority of their songs remain staples of classic-rock radio decades later, and two stand out as memorable anthems to a particular point in history to which the band was ideally suited.

The first captured the hippies' moment in the sun with an unforgettable harmonic reading of Joni Mitchell's "Woodstock" (see Words to Remember). The second captured the country at a time of mourning and confusion as the war in Vietnam led to increasingly violent demonstrations and jadedness among the left, causing uncertainty about America's future. In 1970, four unarmed students were killed by National Guardsmen at Kent State University in Ohio, prompting Neil Young to pen his most famous song, "Ohio"—a powerful indictment of the government's heavy-handedness in dealing with its own citizens (see Words to Remember). The song functions as somewhat of a second bookend for the tumultuous period that started with "For What It's Worth," recorded in 1967 by Young and Stills' pre-CSN&Y group, Buffalo Springfield.

SONGS OF PROTEST: JOAN BAEZ, TOM PAXTON, AND PHIL OCHS

Crosby, Stills, Nash & Young were not afraid of wearing their politics on their sleeve, a quality inherited from a long line of folk singers who used music to voice their opinions on the American political and social machines. Woody Guthrie and Pete Seeger were the undisputed kings of early political songwriting, credited with the "great folk music scare" of the 1950s that brought about a resurgence in interest in traditional music and an awareness of the power of music as a force for social change, summed up eloquently in print on the front of Guthrie's guitar: "This Machine Kills Fascists."

Joan Baez, 1967. Courtesy of the Library of Congress.

With the 1960s came a swell of civil unrest in the United States over issues like civil rights, women's rights, drug laws, police brutality, and the war in Vietnam, and always on the front lines of the battle was folk music's reigning queen, Joan Baez. Though we owe Baez a debt for taking Bob Dylan under her wing and launching him to folk stardom, her greater legacy is her own music, which from the late 1950s inspired a generation of activists to use music to bring people together and empower them to create a better world.

Baez was already a legend by the late 1960s for her anthemic interpretation of the classic "We Shall Overcome" and other traditional songs, as well as highly regarded covers of tunes by Dylan, Phil Ochs, Tim Hardin, and Donovan. Her music made her a star in the folk world, but her political leanings were always a visible force, garnering her popular attention—such as the cover of *Time* in 1962—that motivated others to pick up their guitars and spread the word. Between 1967 and 1974, Baez's album sales faltered a bit as rock bands took over the charts, but she remained a popular live attraction and a constant advocate for social justice, founding the Institute for the Study of Nonviolence in 1965, and participating in numerous protests that landed her in jail on more than one occasion. Though it was the mid-1970s before she became a full-fledged songwriter, Baez is remembered for popularizing protest music and bringing to life some of America's most enduring traditional tunes.

As the list of social problems that required political demonstration grew in the 1960s, topical songs about specific events became its own subgenre in folk, and nobody did it better than Phil Ochs. For a brief time Ochs even rivaled

Dylan, his poignant, tangible lyrics peppered with sharp wit tackling issues such as the Bay of Pigs invasion, draft dodging, political prisoners, and safe working conditions for Kentucky miners. As politically active as Baez, Ochs engaged all social causes within reach, often long before they were popular among the protest cognoscenti (e.g., writing dissent songs about Vietnam as early as 1962). Although Ochs was a highly respected and influential figure in the Dylan and Baez crowds, his star shown only briefly, as his attempts to convert to electric were less than fruitful and occasionally disastrous. Eventually succumbing to schizophrenia, Ochs hung himself in 1976, but left behind a legacy of folk artists and folk rockers who continued to address society's ills through song.

A close associate of Ochs in 1960s Greenwich Village was the clever songwriter Tom Paxton. When most of the folkies left for sunny Los Angeles after the Byrds hit it big, Paxton and Ochs remained in New York to play the clubs and cafes that had made them folk powerhouses. Paxton, a Chicagoan by way of Oklahoma, was a versatile and erudite lyricist, capable of composing children's songs like "Goin' to the Zoo" with the same sophistication as his more political material. Though not as acerbic as some of his politically charged contemporaries, he railed about the themes of the day, such as America's involvement in Vietnam in "Lyndon Johnson Told the Nation" and the heroic mythologizing of the working class in "I'm the Man That Built the Bridges." Like Ochs, Paxton never saw the financial rewards of Dylan or Baez, but he cultivated a loyal following that grew through the years, as he steadily released quality material into the next century.

The proselytizing power of music started with folk, but with the advent of folk rock and other mixed genres, musicians utilized heavier forms of rock to spread predominantly antiestablishment messages. The psychedelic movement, largely built on "power of the people" themes by bands with folk and bluegrass influences (such as the Grateful Dead and Big Brother and the Holding Company), was particularly prone to insinuating political messages into their songs. The most outspoken of these acts, the talented San Francisco jug band Country Joe and the Fish, eschewed national fame to maintain an air of authenticity with their constant politically charged material, creating an anti-Vietnam anthem with their famous "I Feel Like I'm Fixin' to Die Rag" (see Chapter 1, "The Psychedelic Experience").

MAKING FOLK POPULAR

While the big names in 1960s folk and folk rock made waves in certain circles, few of them beyond Bob Dylan, the Byrds, and Crosby, Stills, Nash & Young attained large-scale commercial popularity. Those who did helped establish a blend of folk and rock that would aim for the heart the way rockabilly aimed for the feet and progressive rock targeted the head, bringing about a surge in soft rock, country rock, and the singer-songwriter movement that would dominate the airwaves for the next decade.

The Mamas and the Papas and the Lovin' Spoonful

In 1965's New York folk scene, an unsuccessful jug band called the Mugwumps decided to call it quits (the group's name means "politically neutral," an odd statement for a folk act in mid-1960s Greenwich Village). The band's members, weaned on the artistic energy of Dylan's New York, relocated to Los Angeles, where the Byrds had recently launched a West Coast folk-rock movement with their two No. 1 singles, Dylan's "Mr. Tambourine Man" and Pete Seeger's "Turn! Turn! Turn!" From the ashes of the Mugwumps—John Sebastian, Zalman Yanovsky, Cass Elliot, and Denny Doherty—Sebastian and Yanovsky formed the pop-oriented Lovin' Spoonful and Elliot and Doherty teamed up with the talented duo John and Michelle Phillips to create the more folk rock the Mamas and the Papas.

Though the Lovin' Spoonful lies at the outer edges of rock with its simplistic bubble-gum sound, Sebastian was a respected folk artist and talented lyricist. Following in Dylan's footsteps of recording his own material, Sebastian racked up nine Top 20 hits for his band in their short career spanning 1965 to 1968, including feel-good pop ditties like "Do You Believe in Magic" and "Did You Ever Have to Make Up Your Mind" and the surprisingly edgy No. 1 "Summer in the City." Sebastian also penned tunes for Woody Allen and Francis Ford Coppola soundtracks, again helping to bring folk leanings into the mainstream. Folk rock, soon after its birth, turned into rock more than folk, and the Lovin' Spoonful's poppy sound became quickly dated, facilitating the band's demise.

Less than six months after the first Lovin' Spoonful album debuted on the charts in December 1965, the Mamas and the Papas reached No. 1 with their first release *If You Can Believe Your Eyes and Ears*. Their blend of folk and rock more genuine than the Lovin' Spoonful, the band soon held major commercial appeal, rivaling the Byrds as the rulers of the new California sound. Powerful harmonies and excellent songwriting from John Phillips gave the band four albums and six singles in the Top 5 in their first two years, including enduring tunes like "California Dreamin'," "Dedi-

The Mamas and the Papas, 1967. Courtesy of Photofest.

cated to the One I Love," and their No. 1 "Monday, Monday." "Their vocals, rooted in post-Seeger hootenanny took on a lush, subtropical splendour," wrote a later critic. "They soared in a usually rising cadence, as harmony was laid on harmony laid on harmony. It was like Wagner with white walls and a candy paint job."[6] Phillips quickly became a leader in the California rock community as one of the main organizers of the pivotal 1967 Monterey Pop Festival. By 1968 the group had disbanded, following John and Michelle's divorce and legal problems on a European tour, but their success as harbingers of a softer hippie sound helped bring folkies into California's rock fold.

Simon and Garfunkel

Unique among the mid-1960s New York–based acts was the acoustic duo of Paul Simon and Art Garfunkel, who found stardom as a direct result of rock's new influence on folk. After the Byrds hit No. 1 with "Mr. Tambourine Man" in June 1965, a producer at Columbia Records decided to add drums and electric backing instruments to an unsuccessful Simon and Garfunkel single, "The Sounds of Silence." The producer, Tom Wilson, had recently finished work on Bob Dylan's electric-folk *Bringing It All Back Home* and saw the potential for this new trend. Simon and Garfunkel had released several poor-performing singles and the album *Wednesday Morning, 3AM*, but weak sales led them to part company and return to school in 1964. When the reworked "The Sounds of Silence" suddenly rose to No. 1 in the United States in January 1966, the twosome hastily reunited for what became an enviable folk-rock career.

With a softer, more intimate sound than many folkies and folk rockers of their time, Simon and Garfunkel quickly carved out a niche with the Top 5 singles "I Am a Rock" and "Homeward Bound," as well as other tunes that would become radio standards for decades, such as "The 59th Street Bridge Song (Feelin' Groovy)" and "For Emily, Whenever I May Find Her." The pair's big break came when they were asked to record material for a 1968 film called *The Graduate*, one of the first major films of the era to use a rock soundtrack. The film used several existing Simon and Garfunkel songs, but the one new tune they wrote—titled "Mrs. Robinson" after one of the movie's characters—spent three weeks at No. 1 (see Words to Remember), helping the soundtrack itself camp at the top of the charts for

Simon and Garfunkel, 1967. Courtesy of Photofest.

nine weeks. The duo's sudden popularity propelled their next two albums to the top as well, 1968's *Bookends* spending seven weeks at No. 1, and 1970's *Bridge over Troubled Water* holding the lead spot for ten weeks, producing the three Top 10 singles "Cecilia," "The Boxer," and "Bridge over Troubled Water," the song often said to be the favorite of the duo as well as of their fans. Large-scale success took its toll, and the pair parted ways again in 1970, reuniting occasionally over the next few decades for one-off performances or short tours.

The Band

Most successful folk-rock acts of the 1960s and 1970s were influenced or helped in some way by Bob Dylan, but none more directly than the popular 1970s country-rock group the Band. Known as the Hawks when they backed up Dylan in his 1966 rocker phase, the group reunited with the enigmatic folk singer during his reclusive period in 1967 and 1968, recording originals and Dylan-penned tunes for their 1968 debut *Music from Big Pink*. A blend of folk, rock, soul, blues, and country, the traditionally inclined *Music from Big Pink* and its 1969 follow-up *The Band* were enormously influential, leading to another resurgence of interest in traditional American sounds and helping establish country rock as its own subgenre of folk rock. Reviewing *Music from Big Pink*, veteran rocker and critic Al Kooper claimed, "Every year since 1962 we have all singled out one album to sum up what happened that year. It was usually the Beatles with their double barrels of rubber souls, revolvers and peppers. Dylan has sometimes contended with his frontrunning electric albums. Six months are left in this proselytizing year of music; we can expect a new Beatles, Stones, Hendrix, perhaps even a mate for JW Harding; but I have chosen my album for 1968. *Music from Big Pink* is an event and should be treated as one. . . . This album was recorded in approximately two weeks. There are people who will work their lives away in vain and not touch it."[7]

It is one of rock's more curious ironies that perhaps the most influential Americana band was composed of only one American (the future solo star Levon Helm) and four Canadians (including another future soloist, Robbie Robertson). Nonetheless, the group managed to evoke a strong sense of history and place circa late-1800s rural America with songs like the Civil War saga "The Night They Drove Old Dixie Down"; the folksy, back-porch tune "Up on Cripple Creek"; and Robertson's masterpiece, the semibiblical tale "The Weight." The Band's chart success was admirable, placing six albums in the Top 10 between 1969 and 1975 (three of them with Dylan), but they were better known for their emotive live performances that saw four of the group's five members weaving complex vocal arrangements around seemingly simple melodies. Lacking the high-ranging harmonies of Crosby, Stills, Nash & Young, the Band maintained the warm and energetic presence of a talented family singing at a backyard barbecue.

After a very successful run, the group decided to call it quits in 1976 with a memorable farewell performance on Thanksgiving Day in San Francisco, which included guest performers Van Morrison, Muddy Waters, Bob Dylan, Eric Clapton, Ringo Starr, Joni Mitchell, Paul Butterfield, and Neil Young. The concert was captured on film by a young Martin Scorsese, who released it in 1978 as the classic rockumentary *The Last Waltz*.

THE SINGER-SONGWRITER MOVEMENT

The success of acts like the Beatles, Bob Dylan, and Simon and Garfunkel opened the door for more artists who wrote and performed their own material. The 1970s saw a swelling in the ranks of singer-songwriters—artists who performed mostly original material, usually performed on acoustic instruments without a backing band. Some of these artists were inspired by the likes of Dylan, Ochs, and Paxton to just get onstage and play what they wrote. Others were established songwriters who parlayed their writing talents into a performing career.

Carole King, Joni Mitchell, and James Taylor

Perhaps most successful among the latter group was the gifted Brill Building composer Carole King. King was one of the industry's great songwriters of the 1960s, collaborating with husband Gerry Goffin to produce soul classics like the Shirelles' No. 1 "Will You Love Me Tomorrow," Bobby Vee's No. 1 "Take Good Care of My Baby," the Drifters' "Up on the Roof," Little Eva's "Loco-Motion," and Aretha Franklin's "(You Make Me Feel Like) a Natural Woman." After divorcing Goffin in 1968, King concentrated on her own recording career, striking gold with her third album *Tapestry* in 1971. *Tapestry* spent an incredible 15 weeks in the No. 1 spot and 302 weeks in the Top 200—making it the fifth most successful album of all time, in any genre, in terms of chart longevity. With songs like "So Far Away," "It's Too Late," and "You've Got a Friend," *Tapestry* made one of music's most respected female composers into one of its most respected artists. King's next four albums also made the Top 10, with two of them reaching the No. 1 spot.

Joni Mitchell, 1972. Courtesy of Photofest.

Only six weeks after King reached No. 1 with the two-sided single "It's Too Late/I Feel the Earth Move," a recovering heroin addict named James Taylor had his first No. 1 with King's "You've Got a Friend." Taylor was an overnight sensation when his sophomore release *Sweet Baby James* rose to the Top 5 in 1970, and his picture on the cover of *Time* in March 1971 summed up the exploding singer-songwriter movement with the subtitle "The New Rock: Bittersweet and Low."[8] Though "You've Got a Friend" would be Taylor's only visit to the top of the charts, he produced a string of self-penned singles in the early 1970s—"Carolina in My Mind," "Fire and Rain," "Country Road," "Don't Let Me Be Lonely Tonight"—that have endured the test of time and remain emblematic of the softer side of the 1970s (see Words to Remember).

By the time King's *Tapestry* was released, Canadian singer-songwriter Joni Mitchell had already produced her finest work. While King was the New York insider writing inspiring Jane Everywoman hits with mass commercial appeal, Mitchell was the lost outsider penning personal ballads of former and current loves in unusual guitar tunings. After paying her dues in New York's coffeehouses, Mitchell caught a break when Judy Collins took her song "Both Sides, Now" to the Top 10 in 1967 (see Words to Remember). Shortly afterward, Mitchell debuted with her own *Song to a Seagull* (aka *Joni Mitchell*), an excellent work that nonetheless performed poorly on the charts. Producing an album a year afterward, Mitchell finally found critical acclaim with her 1970 *Ladies of the Canyon* and her 1971 masterpiece *Blue*, leaving a legacy of songs including "Big Yellow Taxi," "The Last Time I Saw Richard," and "Woodstock," which Crosby, Stills, Nash & Young took to No. 11 (several members of CSN&Y had helped Mitchell produce her albums). After 1974, Mitchell distanced herself from the folk world, achieving noteworthy success as a jazz artist.

Jim Croce, Cat Stevens, Carly Simon, and Don McLean

Because of the relatively cheaper costs of touring as a solo artist and the widening availability of venues on school campuses opened up by popular college attractions Simon and Garfunkel, individual performers could make a living playing their material before small crowds like plugged-in rock stars never could. From this environment of independence sprang numerous singer-songwriters like Jim Croce, Cat Stevens, Carly Simon, and Don McLean, who would endure through the 1970s and inspire even more solo artists to take the stage.

Croce began his career as a university disc jockey before hitting the New York coffeehouses and making a name for himself with his 1972 sophomore album, *You Don't Mess Around with Jim*, which spent five weeks at No. 1. After his first No. 1 single the following year, "Bad, Bad Leroy Brown," Croce's promising career ended tragically when he was killed in an airplane crash, though his singles continued to sell, and the two albums released after his death both reached No. 2 on the charts. A contemporary of Croce, Cat Stevens emerged in 1971 when his fourth album, *Tea for the Tillerman*, broke into the Top 10 with the hit single "Wild World." Only months later came *Teaser and the Firecat*, featuring many of his best-remembered songs, including "Moon Shadow," "Morning Has Broken," and "Peace Train." Stevens remained one of the favorite singer-songwriters of the 1970s, placing five more albums in the Top 10 before 1978.

Though Carly Simon began recording several years before Croce and Stevens, it was not until her minor 1971 hits "That's the Way I've Always Heard It Should Be" and "Anticipation" rose into the Top 20 that she began to receive critical notice. More of a rocker than an independent folkie, Simon employed Rolling Stone Mick Jagger to sing backup on her biggest hit "You're So Vain," which rose to No. 1 in January 1973. (Despite the rock legend that Jagger, Warren Beatty, or Simon's husband, James Taylor, was the song's subject, Simon insisted that the tune refers to no specific person.) The accompanying album *No Secrets* spent five weeks at No. 1, launching Simon's career as one of the ranking singer-songwriters of the 1970s.

Don McLean did not start his recording career until 1970, suffering a number of rejections and setbacks before the unknown New Yorker won the lottery with his 1971 smash "American Pie," one of folk rock's all-time greatest hits (see Words to Remember). The song's album of the same title also contained the painfully beautiful tribute to Van Gogh, "Vincent," and McLean was instantly pegged to be one of the most promising singer-songwriters of the age. His follow-up albums, unfortunately, sold poorly; however, McLean was a talented cover artist as well as a writer and continued to perform and release originals and covers into the 1980s.

NOTES

1. "Sibyl With Guitar," *Time*, November 23, 1962.
2. Friedlander 1996, 150.
3. Friedlander 1996, 149.
4. "Bob Dylan: *Nashville Skyline*," *Rolling Stone*, May 31, 1969.
5. Barney Hoskyns, "The Byrds: *Mr Tambourine Man, Turn! Turn! Turn!, Fifth Dimension, Younger Than Yesterday*," *Mojo*, June 1996.
6. Mick Farren, "Fossils Exhumed: Back into the Lost World of Prehistoric California," *NME*, July 23, 1977.
7. Al Kooper, "The Band: *Music from Big Pink*," *Rolling Stone*, August 10, 1968.
8. *Time*, March 1, 1971, cover.

ROCK GOES PROGRESSIVE

Of all the new genres emerging from the diversification of rock music in the mid to late 1960s, progressive rock is the most enigmatic and difficult to define. The label "progressive" has been applied to a number of musical genres over the course of the twentieth century—mostly centering on a certain musical style's ability to break barriers and create something truly original—but here we will be focusing on the progressive rock (also known as prog rock, classical rock, symphonic rock, and art rock) of the period between 1967 and the mid-1970s.

Originating almost exclusively in Britain, progressive rock was born of English blues bands seeking to break away from traditional and oft-imitated molds of guitar-based rock. To this end, the musicians reached back to the piano-based forms of nineteenth- and twentieth-century classical composers. In the simplest of terms, progressive was a blending of rock music and classical ideas. As shall be discussed further when we cover specific bands and artists, the extent to which prog rockers borrowed from classical traditions ranged from insinuating non-rock instruments into an established rock style to creating multimovement works and truly original, avant-garde productions.

Much has been made—and rightfully so—of the changes in rock format in the 1960s, particularly the expansion of the three-minute pop song and the advent of FM radio stations that were willing to play these longer tracks. Such bravery inspired bands that may have been previously limited (for their career's sake) to curt, catchy jingles to experiment with longer, more developed forms, which allowed for more profound musical statements. Longer tracks meant more developed topics and more complex ideas to carry out these topics, resulting in new creations like theme albums (the Beach Boys' 1966 *Pet Sounds*) and rock operas (the Who's 1969 *Tommy*).

In the grand scheme of things, progressive music was rock and roll's chance to gain respectability as a legitimate art form, something more than music to drink and dance to. It was music for the head as much as for the feet or the heart. Once the more experimental acts of the 1960s—the Beatles, Miles Davis, John Coltrane, the Beach Boys, Dave Brubeck, Jimi Hendrix—had propped open the doors of possibility, rock progressed beyond a steady beat and catchy melody to open its audience's eyes and see what could be. And once the technology of the age caught up to the talents of rock's more curious innovators, how could they resist the urge to tinker?

It was with this license that nascent British bands of the mid-1960s set to work. Heavily influenced by San Francisco's psychedelic movement; American jazz; and experimental classical artists such as Varèse, Stravinski, and Stockhausen, young art-school students set out to re-create rock into a form of high art. Some groups, such as Yes and King Crimson, reached back to the romantic period to draw on pastoral themes, or into the works of author J.R.R. Tolkien to create fantasy worlds between their album jackets. Others, such as Pink Floyd and Frank Zappa, reached forward to develop space rock and postmodern sounds as their own vision of rock's possible future.

Many artists used instruments or technology that had rarely or never been used in rock before. Jethro Tull led a standard blues-rock outfit with a lead flute instead of a guitar. The Moody Blues initially hired an entire orchestra to back them before taking on the mellotron to synthesize orchestral sounds. Keith Emerson of Emerson, Lake & Palmer created a keyboard setup so elaborate—a system of Moog synthesizers, organs, and a revolving grand piano—that he required three roadies to maintain it. Pink Floyd and Frank Zappa borrowed from Edgard Varèse's ideas for incorporating nonmusical instruments into musical pieces and Karlheinz Stockhausen's pioneering work in electronic composition. It also became fashionable to reinterpret respected composers in a rock style; Bach, Tchaikovsky, Bernstein, Copland, Bartók, Mussorgsky—none of them were safe.

The groundbreaking work was not without its detractors, who felt rock should maintain its assigned place in the cultural strata. "If earlier attempts to expand rock and roll's horizons by means of blending it with folk, gospel, or jazz styles had created storms of criticism, the attempts to combine rock with classical music brought on a virtual monsoon. . . . The critics assumed the worst motives on the part of the new musical explorers, accusing them of 'lame affectations of a cultured sensibility' and of seeking 'to dignify their work, to make it acceptable for upper-class approbation.'"[1]

Nevertheless, progressive rock became enormously successful, emerging out of the London dance clubs in the late 1960s to become a staple in stadiums and on the airwaves in the 1970s. Much like glam rock, progressive rock was as focused on presentation as it was on the music (see Chapter 3, "Glamour Kings: The Birth of Glitter Rock"). Rock became theater, with lasers, smoke, light shows, moving stages, and elaborate costumes. Much of the visual elements came out of London's club scene—particularly the UFO Club, where Pink Floyd turned a short residency into the beginning of a visual feast. "The club names said it all—the Middle Earth, Gandalf's Garden, the Perfumed Garden—so long as it sounded exotic and looked preposterous, a scene could coalesce around it in London in 1968."[2]

Though it is beyond the scope of this book, it should be mentioned that progressive music did not only consist of rock musicians reaching across the aisle to classical traditions. Respected composers such as Leonard Bernstein, Lalo Schifrin, and Stanley Silverman poked their heads out of the orchestra pit and, seeing the explosion of innovative rock surrounding them, chose to engage it head on instead of ducking for cover under the conductor's stand. But that is a story for another text.

Nearly every scholar of progressive rock has attempted to create his or her own classification system to categorize the genre's acts according to what elements of classical music each band brings to the table. Some of these systems have been unnecessarily complex, others woefully inadequate. None of them hold the final word on the subject, and each in its way contributes to the multilevel prism through which such an unusual musical style should be viewed.

Given the nature of this text, it seems most appropriate to organize progressive acts as they were classified by Katherine Charlton in her 1990 book *Rock Music Styles*—along a three-part scale that measures to what extent each band borrowed from classical traditions. This system ranges from the simple use of classical instruments by rock bands, to the borrowing of more involved classical elements to create multimovement works, to the nonderivative experimentation of avant-garde artists. As stated elsewhere in this book, there is always a gray area when trying to categorize artists along such specific lines. Some bands could fit into several of these categories depending on how rigidly one interpreted the groupings and which of their compositions one was looking at. Suffice it to say that although these assignments are flexible, they are hardly random.

 BLASTS FROM THE PAST

Progressive rock artists owe a large debt to the classical figures from which they borrowed so extensively. Below is a short list of the individuals who helped create a new style of rock in the 1970s—for some, many years after they had died.

Edgard Varèse (1883–1965). Called by some "the father of electronic music," Varèse was one of music's first electronic experimenters and champions of the theremin. Frank Zappa and Pink Floyd both adopted the composer's ideas of incorporating nonmusical instruments into musical compositions.

Karlheinz Stockhausen (b. 1928). Another early electronic composer, Stockhausen's imaginative creations included one that was required to be performed by four instrumentalists flying overhead in four helicopters. His unusual composing practices—such as giving the performer wide latitude in interpreting his material—was imitated by rock's most avant-garde.

Modest Mussorgsky (1839–1881). Mussorgsky's "Pictures at an Exhibition" is one of the more famous examples of program music (compositions based on a nonmusical theme)—in this

BLASTS FROM THE PAST
(continued)

instance, the feeling of walking through a museum looking at different works of art. Emerson, Lake & Palmer released their own interpretation of this classical piece with jazz and rock elements in 1972.

Pyotr Tchaikovsky (1840–1893). A Russian composer from the romantic period, Tchaikovsky was best known for his ballets, such as "Swan Lake," "Sleeping Beauty," and "The Nutcracker." Keith Emerson interpreted several of the composer's works during his tenure with the Nice and later with Emerson, Lake & Palmer.

Igor Stravinski (1882–1971). One of the most influential composers of the twentieth century, Stravinski pioneered the use of widely varying ensemble combinations and the incorporation of folk themes into classical music. His diverse instrumentalization and severe compositions made him fodder for serious progressive acts such as Yes, whose "rock chamber ensemble" sound owes a debt to him.

Johann Sebastian Bach (1685–1750). One of music's all-time great geniuses, Bach has inspired musicians in almost every genre, including rock, jazz, folk, and the blues. His work has been interpreted by a number of progressive artists, including Jethro Tull, Procol Harum, and Keith Emerson.

J.R.R. Tolkien (1892–1973). While a professor of Anglo-Saxon at Oxford University, Tolkien achieved widespread fame for his book *The Hobbit* and the *Lord of the Rings* trilogy. His high-fantasy writings became very influential to London's psychedelic scene in the late 1960s, lyrically influencing progressive acts that played at Tolkien-named clubs such as the Middle Earth and Gandalf's Garden.

CLASSICAL INSTRUMENTATION IN A ROCK SETTING

The most basic blending of rock and classical music in the new progressive movement was simply the use of non-rock instruments—and sometimes entire orchestras—in established rock formats. The word "basic" here should not be taken to mean "unsophisticated" or "lacking in complexity"—some of the artists mentioned in this section were enormously talented and their works critically praised. But there is a difference between rock musicians using traditionally classical instruments in a rock setting and rock musicians converting that rock setting into a classical space, as shall be discussed in the next section.

The Moody Blues

One of the first popular efforts to combine rock and classical music was attempted by the Moody Blues, a mid-sixties R&B outfit known—as many British rock groups were—for covering American blues standards by artists such as Sonny Boy Williamson, James Brown, and Bessie Banks. Though the band met critical and commercial success in the United Kingdom with their 1965 debut *The Magnificent Moodies*, they altered their sound in 1966 when they brought in guitarist Justin Hayward and singer/bassist John Lodge.

Lodge and Hayward took the group in a classical direction the following year with the band's tremendously successful *Days of Future Passed*, a solid rock album featuring lush accompaniment from the London Festival Orchestra. The record rose to No. 3 in America and spawned their best-remembered single, "Nights in White Satin" (though the song didn't break the American charts until released as a single in 1972, when it rose to No. 2).

The band trod a path many others would soon follow, establishing a sound so unique they could do little else but stick with it. Orchestral conductor Peter Knight and producer Tony Clarke, both of whom helped the Moody Blues establish their classical sound on *Days of Future Passed*, stuck with the group for several more albums, helping to create a cottage industry with their studio-oriented sound that wandered between thick violins and melodic guitar lines. "The Moodies have become the first breed of artist who see the recording studio as their platform," read one *Days* review. "Their intricate sound is the result of hours of work laid down in the studio. Producer Tony Clarke is considered a sixth member of the group. [If] they had mixing equipment on stage Tony would be up there playing it."[3]

The downside to such complicated musical arrangements was the prohibitive expense of touring with an entire orchestra. This problem was solved soon after *Days of Future Passed* with the introduction of the mellotron, a rudimentary electronic sampling device that allowed the band to mimic orchestral instruments using keyboards. Though the Beach Boys had introduced the mellotron to rock a year earlier to create individual alternative sounds, the Moody Blues used it to simulate an orchestra, and soon every British band with progressive ambitions wanted one.

The band continued to hover in the American Top 40 over their next few albums until again entering the Top 5 in 1970 with *A Question of Balance*, followed by their No. 2 album *Every Good Boy Deserves Favour* a year later, and their biggest American hit the year after that, *Seventh Sojourn*, which spent five weeks in the top spot. Though by then enormously popular in the United

The Moody Blues, 1970. Courtesy of Photofest.

Kingdom, the band suffered ridicule throughout their career from those who did not believe a rock band deserved "high-art" status. Despite their great success, the band parted ways in 1974 to pursue solo projects, reuniting in the late 1970s for several more well-received albums.

Procol Harum

Rising from the tattered remains of the popular early-1960s R&B group the Paramounts (remembered largely as the Rolling Stones' favorite band), Procol Harum became overnight successes in 1967 with their debut single "Whiter Shade of Pale." The song spent six weeks at No. 1 in the United Kingdom, and reached the No. 5 spot in the United States. A large part of its appeal was the haunting Hammond organ intro, featuring a memorable sequence borrowed from several of Johann Sebastian Bach's melodies, thus the band's entrance into the progressive set.

Few of today's rock fans would not recognize the classic song, but even fewer could name any other Procol Harum tunes; in the words of one former band member, the group "fired the gun and burnt the mast."[4] Experiencing continuous lineup changes—mostly consisting of ex-Paramounts entering and exiting the band—Procol released several more well-appreciated albums over the turn of the decade, all popular in the United Kingdom and moderately successful in America. In 1972, the band dove headlong into the classical arena with their biggest U.S. hit *Procol Harum Live in Concert with the Edmonton Symphony Orchestra*, a Top 5 record in America that featured some of their better-known songs reworked for symphony. Modest success followed the band through several more albums before they parted ways in 1977, but it was the surreal opening to "Whiter Shade of Pale" that would be remembered by later generations, and that the band would never again live up to.

Jethro Tull

Though Jethro Tull was the moniker of a popular blues- and jazz-rooted rock band, many mistakenly thought it was the name of the group's frontman, Ian Anderson, an exciting performer whose distinctive voice, murky lyrics, and disheveled look all added to the peculiar persona of the man who played the group's lead instrument—not a guitar, but a flute. There's no telling how accomplished Jethro Tull might have been had Anderson been a guitarist, but his pied-piper-like fluting—standing stage front, bedraggled in appearance, one knee cocked in the air—gave the band a distinctive look and sound that certainly contributed to their success. The use of flute in a rock band was not unheard of—the Beatles included the instrument in some of their more exploratory works—but as the lead instrument around which the band was centered, it initially placed Jethro Tull among the more basic forms of collusion between rock and classical music.

The group did not long remain a "blues band with a flute lead." After their derivative, though excellent, 1968 debut *This Was*, Anderson expanded Tull's repertoire on their quick follow-up *Stand Up*, which featured a jazzy reworking of Bach's "Bourée." It was their fourth release in 1971, however, that gained the band critical and commercial success in the United States and saw Anderson fully engage his potential for cross-genre experimentation. *Aqualung*, their multiplatinum record that introduced them to the American Top 10, was Anderson's attempt at a concept album, in which the songs all tend toward the same subject—in this case an indictment of organized religion seen through the eyes of a wandering tramp. Featuring the memorable songs "Aqualung," "Cross-Eyed Mary," and "Locomotive Breath," the album highlighted Anderson's penchant for obscure lyrics and ability to make a flute lead sound as exciting as any electric guitar.

Capitalizing on *Aqualung*'s success, the band released two fine records the following year: *Thick as a Brick*—another concept album that would reach No. 5 in the United Kingdom and be their first U.S. No. 1—and *Living in the Past*—an album of their earlier British material that made it to the No. 3 spot on the American charts. Now a massive concert draw in both countries, the band began to concentrate on their U.S. audience after receiving some criticism in their home country for producing pretentious and egotistical music. The band would continue to sell very well in the United States, with two more Top 5 albums—1973's *Passion Play* and 1974's *War Child*—as well as a string of Top 40 releases over the next two decades.

BORROWING MORE SOPHISTICATED CLASSICAL IDEAS

Introducing traditionally classical instruments into a rock-and-roll setting was only the first step in the development of progressive rock. The initial practitioners of the burgeoning genre proved immensely popular, but the style took on a new direction when bands moved from using classical instruments to restructuring their albums and bands to incorporate larger classical ideas. The pioneering heavy-metal band Deep Purple deserves mention as one of the first groups to attempt a full-on merging of rock and orchestra with their 1970 *Concerto for Group and Orchestra*, an album orchestrated by their classically trained organist Jon Lord before the band switched gears to found a harder rock sound (see Chapter 2, "Hard-Rock Lightning, Heavy-Metal Thunder"). Along with Yes and King Crimson, these progenitors of a more fully developed progressive style picked up where the Moody Blues left off—abandoning orchestral accompaniment to rock songs to create complementary, multimovement compositions.

The Who

The first attempts at penning "theme albums"—records on which the songs are tied together by a common theme—are generally credited to the Beach

Boys in America for their 1966 *Pet Sounds*, and to the Beatles in the United Kingdom for their 1967 *Sgt. Pepper's Lonely Hearts Club Band*. Both albums are considered essential landmarks in rock, but the songs are only loosely linked by a common idea: *Pet Sounds* by teen angst and isolation, and *Sgt. Pepper's* by the idea of a mythical touring band.

It was the Who, through its art-school genius Pete Townshend, that created the first album to be dubbed a "rock opera" with their 1969 milestone *Tommy*. Instead of a loose idea linking songs together, Townshend created a narrative that tells the story of a boy struck deaf, dumb, and blind by emotional tragedy, and his struggle and eventual recovery to become something of a messiah. Each song is a chapter in the boy's life, tracing his experiences from birth to eventual freedom from his fears. Though Townshend had penned a mini-opera entitled "A Quick One While He's Away" on their 1967 album *Happy Jack*, it is *Tommy* that's remembered as the first full-length rock opera.

Tommy was unique in the annals of progressive rock in that the Who maintained their power-trio format of guitar, drums, and bass, managing to create a mesmerizing theatrical work with the instruments of a basic garage band, described by one critic as "the finest extended thematic structure any rock group ever pulled off."[5] The album was a major hit, leading to a film version, a ballet, a Tony-winning Broadway play, and an orchestral version by the London Symphony Orchestra that reached No. 5 on the American charts (the original album reached No. 4). In 1973, the band returned to the rock-opera format for *Quadrophenia*, a less-tightly woven set of songs exploring the four distinct personalities within the band. Though the Who are more properly placed in the genres of hard rock and early metal (see Chapter 2, "Hard-Rock Lightning, Heavy-Metal Thunder"), their contribution of the rock opera to progressive music—later imitated in successful rock musicals like *Jesus Christ Superstar*, *Godspell*, and *Grease*—cannot be overlooked (see Chapter 8, "Rock and the Media").

King Crimson

Some critics and fans of the progressive movement believe that progressive rock definitively begins as a distinct genre with King Crimson's 1969 debut *In the Court of the Crimson King*. Lauded by British and American critics as well as by the Who's Pete Townshend, the mellotron-infused album echoed the Moody Blues but with frontman Robert Fripp's complex classical guitar work and a much wider range of effects, styles, meters, and volume, from heavy-metal loud to whisper quiet—a cocktail Fripp described as "the sound of 170 guitarists almost hitting the same chord at the same time."[6]

The band followed with their sophomore *In the Wake of Poseidon*, which was nearly as stirring as their debut but contained nothing particularly new. Robert Fripp remained the leader of the group, as an impressive array of musicians joined and then went on to fame with other bands, including original lineup members Greg Lake (Emerson, Lake & Palmer) and Ian McDonald (Foreigner), and later Bill Bruford (Yes), John Wetton (Roxy Music, Uriah Heep), Boz Burrell (Bad Company), and Adrian Belew (David Bowie, Frank Zappa).

It was Fripp, however, who maintained the band's sound through his avant-garde compositions and electronic experimentation. Beyond innovative use of the still novel mellotron, Fripp did pioneering work with Brian Eno on tape-delay technology to add even more unworldly sounds to his repertoire. Though Fripp dissolved the band in 1974 (to be reborn in the 1980s), King Crimson remained one of the most influential sounds of the decade through the prominence of its alumni and the groundbreaking work of Fripp.

Yes

With their soaring three-part harmonies and virtuosic instrumentals, the British supergroup Yes were probably the most popular progressive rock band of the 1970s, placing nine albums in a row in the American Top 20 between 1972 and 1980. Despite such success, the group had only one single in all that time reach the Top 30—1972's "Roundabout"—an example of how progressive albums as interwoven collections were valued more highly than their individual songs.

Yes used the classical concept of the suite—instrumental movements consisting of a succession of related pieces—to tie their albums together. The band's early works—after their debut in 1968—brought them to the attention of an eager British public but failed to make a splash overseas. After the addition of

Yes in concert, 1973. © Neal Preston/Corbis.

guitarist Steve Howe in 1970 and keyboardist Rick Wakeman in 1971, the group developed more sophisticated classical leanings, utilizing Wakeman's keyboard prowess to synthesize multilayered orchestral instruments and introducing the suite to rock audiences.

Both of their 1972 albums struck gold in the United States—*Fragile* peaking at No. 4 and *Close to the Edge* at No. 3—ushering in the short-lived heyday of progressive rock in the United States, with Yes, the Moody Blues, and Emerson, Lake & Palmer leading the caravan. Yes albums became less collections of songs and more long-winded instrumental works with occasional, abstract lyrics thrown in now and again, sometimes bordering on the pretentious according to the critics of the day. "[Vocalist Jon] Anderson's lyrics probably draw more fire than any other single commodity in Progressive, described as they are in almost unanimously negative terms ranging from incomprehension to hostility, but they are none the less of enormous contemporary interest. Music papers once ran small ads from people offering to 'explain' Yes lyrics (for a fee)."[7] The band's albums since *Fragile* were often made up of suites or very long songs (sometimes one tune taking up an entire side), featuring lengthy instrumentals and minimal vocals that gave listeners the impression that they were listening to a symphonic work, were it not for the band's ability to keep the music aligned to rock rhythms that allowed one to groove to its beat while enjoying its heady sophistication.

Yes continued to push the envelope through the 1970s with the triple-live album *Yessongs* in 1973, the double album *Tales from Topographic Oceans* the same year, and several more heavy-selling studio works through the decade. Their live performances became emblematic of progressive's pomp and pretension: elaborate light shows, fog machines, and overdressed musicians incorporating a great deal of style into their substantive compositions. Such brazen pageantry would also fuel progressive's detractors, as the more populist punk and new wave caught hold in the late 1970s, relegating bands like Yes to the dinosaur bin of rock. But most members of the band went on to lucrative solo careers, and a surprise reunion in the 1980s led to another string of well-received albums and tours into the 1990s, demonstrating the survivability of remarkable talent in any age.

Emerson, Lake & Palmer

Perhaps no progressive band drew more on classical influences than the talented trio Emerson, Lake & Palmer—particularly in the keyboards of Keith Emerson, an avant-garde impresario who was celebrated as always on the cutting edge of musical possibility. A classically trained pianist, Emerson made his name in England with the early art-rock band the Nice. Emerson met Greg Lake, then bassist for King Crimson, when the two bands split a bill in San Francisco in 1970.

After picking up R&B drummer Carl Palmer, the group made a smashing large-scale debut at the Isle of Wight Festival later that year. In one of rock music's greatest "might have been" stories, the group seriously considered asking Jimi Hendrix to join the band after auditioning Hendrix's drummer, Mitch Mitchell, and getting positive feedback from Hendrix himself. The British press got wind of the story and announced the possibility of the supergroup "HELP" (Hendrix, Emerson, Lake & Palmer). Because of his technical virtuosity and his obsession for sonic experimentation, Emerson had been dubbed the Jimi Hendrix of the organ, and to have the two performing in the same group would have been like Napoleon and Patton coordinating efforts on the battlefield. Alas, Hendrix tragically retired his axe too early, and despite the Jimi-sized hole in the rock scene, ELP went on to become a major progressive act on their own.

After causing a stir on stage, the band released a self-titled first album that cracked the U.S. Top 20, where the band would remain for six more albums until 1977. Emerson had already shown his range of talents with the Nice by reworking compositions by Sibelius, Tchaikovsky, Tim Hardin, and Bob Dylan in his own style. With ELP, he continued creating brilliant interpretations by classic and modern composers such as Mussorgsky's "Pictures at an Exhibition" (which comprised their entire third album, ending with an interpretation of Tchaikovsky's "The Nutcracker"); Copland's "Fanfare for the Common Man"; Bach's "Toccata"; and Bartók's "Allegro Barbaro" (though he did come under some criticism for not always giving credit to the original composers).

By the mid-1970s, ELP was one of rock's top-grossing acts, transporting thirty-six tons of equipment from stage to stage for their elaborate performances—limiting their touring ability but magnifying their stage appeal with Yes-like lasers, explosions, and light shows. Though more thoroughly immersed in progressive's experimental and classical sides, ELP shared Yes's penchant for high-selling albums and low-selling singles, placing no song higher than No. 39 on the American charts (1972's "From the Beginning," from their No. 5 album *Trilogy*). Fortuitously disbanding in the late 1970s before being forced out by punk, the group made a surprisingly successful return as Emerson, Lake & Powell in the late 1980s, featuring drummer Cozy Powell to replace Palmer, who at the time was playing in the hit band Asia.

THE "ÜBER-ORIGINAL" AVANT-GARDE

No music, no matter how new and exciting, develops in a vacuum. All artists are influenced by their predecessors and their environment, and the new sound of progressive rock was no exception. But in every genre there are those that go farther out on the limb than their contemporaries, the more creative and experimental artists that extend the music more forward (or some might say sideways) than others of their generation.

In progressive rock, there are two essential names associated with the farthest reaches of experimentation: in Britain, there is the legendary Pink Floyd, and in the United States, the immortal Frank Zappa. Other artists certainly deserve mention, but in other contexts. In the early 1970s, Brian Eno began his experiments in electronica, but his major work did not come until after the period being discussed in this text. Jazz greats like Miles Davis and John Coltrane were years ahead of their time, and despite their contributions to the rock world, they deserve to be profiled in a manuscript that can afford them respectable room. Keith Emerson—profiled earlier with Emerson, Lake & Palmer—was certainly on the cutting edge, but much of his work involved new ways of combining and restructuring old styles, whereas Floyd and Zappa were largely nonderivative, truly setting footprints in virgin snow. Sharing the spotlight with these two powerhouses is Captain Beefheart, who, as a confederate of Zappa and a hero of the 1970s avant-garde underground, deserves his place in the sun.

Pink Floyd

The story of Pink Floyd is long and complicated, spanning a period of more than thirty years. Taking a critical look at their music helps to break down the band's life into four distinct phases: 1965 to 1968, when Syd Barrett led the group; 1968 to 1973, when the band continued to live under Barrett's shadow; 1973 to 1983, when David Gilmour and Roger Waters led the group to superstardom; and post-1983, when Gilmour assumed control upon Waters' departure. As this text is temporally specific, we'll concern ourselves with the first two stages of the group until their 1973 album *Dark Side of the Moon* turned a small Cambridge psychedelic band into a worldwide phenomenon.

When critics refer to progressive music as "art rock," it is Pink Floyd, or bands that wanted to be Pink Floyd, that they are talking about. In 1965, art-school dropout Syd Barrett and his high school friend and bassist Roger Waters (an architecture student) salvaged what they could from an earlier group gone defunct to found the Pink Floyd Sound, with Nick Mason on drums and Rick Wright on keyboards. The group soon shortened the name to Pink Floyd (from Georgia bluesmen Pink Anderson and Floyd Council, who were influential to Barrett). Barrett—as singer, guitarist, and lyricist—was the clear principal of the band, and soon led them to respectable status among the counterculture cognoscenti in hip, flower-power London.

Pink Floyd invented in London their own San Francisco sound, with long, wandering improvisations, recycled feedback, electronic experimentation, and some of England's first rock-and-roll light shows. The difference between Floyd and the Bay Area bands was largely in the way they were interpreted by the listeners. San Francisco psychedelic groups were jam bands, out to bring the community together for a good time and possibly a political message or two. Pink Floyd, however, was Art. Barrett was believed to be somewhat of an avant-garde genius, and the band's music absorbed classical, jazz, blues, and psychedelic influences to create a respectable art form that drew on visual, aural, and behavioral aesthetics. During one of their breakout gigs—a 1967 Games for

May festival on London's South Bank—they were billed as "a musical and visual exploration—not only for themselves, but for the audience too." In the process of making art, not only was music played and a light show performed, but "Waters hurled potatoes at a gong, Mason sawed wood, eggs were fried onstage."[8]

Pink Floyd became enormously popular on the club scene, especially during a residency at London's UFO club in 1966, where the group led the nascent psychedelic revolution in Britain with their unearthly sounds and intense light shows, which have become synonymous with the band. Their first release, 1967's *The Piper at the Gates of Dawn*, was limited to the short, pop-song format but nonetheless contained creative sonic experiments and intriguing sound effects, such as the illusion of sound traveling from speaker to speaker on "Interstellar Overdrive." Floyd was deemed by some to be "space rock," an otherworldly sound with ethereal lyrics that gave listeners the impression that they were on a musical rocket ship destined for parts unknown. Opined a critic during Floyd's nascent stages, "As thousands in ballrooms and assorted hell-holes across the country are deafened and blinded nightly by the Pink Floyd, the well-known psychedelic group, thousands might be forgiven for thinking: 'What the 'ell's it all about?'"[9]

The honeymoon was short-lived. Like the clichéd eccentric genius, Barrett was emotionally fragile and could not hold up under the stress of a particularly grueling American tour after *Piper* was released. His behavior was erratic and, sinking into the quicksand of drug abuse, he became undependable, putting additional strain on the rest of the band. Waters brought in another high school friend, David Gilmour, to play Barrett's parts when Barrett was unavailable—mentally or otherwise—and by the summer of 1968, Barrett was asked to leave the group.

The remodeled Pink Floyd entered their second stage without their founder and creative leader, and fans held out little hope that they would survive. However, Waters was a talented lyricist and arranger, and Gilmour an inventive guitarist, making the band's 1968 album *Saucerful of Secrets* a surprisingly high-quality affair, followed by 1969's *Ummagumma*, defying expectations and making the group into a major concert draw.

Pink Floyd, 1972. Courtesy of Photofest.

Clever promotion—including a free concert in London's Hyde Park for one hundred thousand fans, and a performance in a meteor crater in Pompeii—helped the band's image. Although the band peeked into the American Top 100 with 1970's *Atom Heart Mother* and 1971's *Meddle*, it could not crack the U.S. market on a large scale; and despite their growing success, they seemed to be continually living in the shadow of Barrett's talent, even as their music was finding a wider audience.

In 1973, the band somehow managed to put their ghosts to rest and realize their potential on the extraordinary album *Dark Side of the Moon*. A major leap forward from their previous work, *Dark Side* is the ultimate space-rock album, a musical journey of madness, alienation, and age that includes powerful minimalist uses of space and pauses interrupted by ticking clocks and maniacal laughter. The album opens and ends with a lone heartbeat, and between the two, the universe is splayed out before the listener in long, slow beats; snippets of conversation; odd tempos and measures; Waters' brilliant songwriting; and Gilmour's captivating guitar work. "*The Dark Side of the Moon* is a fine album with a textural and conceptual richness that not only invites, but demands involvement," wrote *Rolling Stone* of the album. "There is a certain grandeur here that exceeds mere musical melodramatics and is rarely attempted in rock."[10]

Not only did the album move the band onto a higher level of play, but it opened up the American market by shooting to No. 1 on the U.S. charts, its accompanying single "Money" reaching No. 13. More impressive, the album immortalized the band in a very real sense by remaining on the *Billboard* Top 200 for an incredible 741 weeks (more than fourteen years). By comparison, the next longest-ranking album of the rock era was Carole King's *Tapestry* at 302 weeks, followed by *Led Zeppelin IV* at 259 weeks.

Dark Side of the Moon launched the band into the highest strata of rock stardom, beginning a series of now classic 1970s albums like *Wish You Were Here*, *Animals*, and 1979's *The Wall*, which would become the third highest-selling album in music history (*Dark Side of the Moon* would rank at twenty-first). The 1970s would also make Pink Floyd the seventh best-selling musical act in twentieth-century rock. The group's experimental sounds would become benchmarks of classic rock, and Pink Floyd would be known as the ultimate art-rock band.

Frank Zappa

"If it were possible to get whiplash just listening to music, Zappa would be the one to give it to us."[11]

Within the United States, there were very few bands that successfully toyed with rock music as rock commentary. To some extent, an important aspect of genres like progressive rock and glam rock were their functions as vehicles for analysis of their own medium. In progressive music, this took the form of a reevaluation of the guitar-centered rock band that failed as a form of high art. In glam, this medium was the testosterone-fueled hard rock that had taken over the charts and airwaves, and the commentary was explicitly gender-oriented. If one were to dismiss the use of gender bending to critique rock's status quo and replace it with satire and honed-razor wit, one would find oneself in the awe-some presence of rock music's most prolific cult figure, Frank Zappa.

Though Zappa lacked the overtly sexual underpinnings of glam rock and the pretentious nature of progressive, he more than made up for it in his dramatic use of rock as theater and social commentary. More accessible than the New York Dolls yet more underground than the Moody Blues, Zappa was an unstoppable champion of authenticity and ruthless adversary of conformity. His bizarre music and over-the-top performances were simultaneously derided as the work of a madman and celebrated as brilliant modern extensions of classical, jazz, blues, and rock genres. Denigrated as a hippie, lauded as a genius, castigated as a troublemaker, honored as a patriot, Zappa had as many sides as there were people to hear his music. Whether one liked him or hated him, his pointed wit and tremendous musical talent made it simply impossible to ignore him. Over a career that spanned more than thirty years, Zappa ran up a list of achievements that would seem to have taken several lifetimes: almost sixty original albums; more than a dozen films as writer, director, producer, actor, or composer; cultural liaison to the Czech Republic; opponent of censorship before the U.S. Congress; Grammy winner; and collaborator with some of the great artists of his time, including Tina Turner, Steve Vai, Cream bassist Jack Bruce, violinist Jean-Luc Ponty, pianist George Duke, composer Pierre Boulez, talk-show host Steve Allen, Who drummer Keith Moon, the Beatles' John Lennon and Ringo Starr, the Kronos Quartet, and the London Symphony Orchestra.

Born in Baltimore, Maryland, in 1940, Zappa moved out to California at a young age to hone early talents as a writer, drummer, and rhythm and blues guitarist. His wide-ranging musical influences—which reached from blues greats Howlin' Wolf and Muddy Waters to modern classical figures Stravinsky, Stockhausen, and Varèse—made him stand out among other rock figures. He spent his early twenties working odd jobs, scoring films, releasing minor singles, and eventually buying a small recording studio outside Los Angeles, which he named Studio Z.

In 1964, Zappa began writing for local band the Soul Giants, which evolved into the Mothers before their first release in 1966. Under pressure from their label, the band called itself the Mothers of Invention, a less controversial name that would be one of the few concessions Zappa would ever make to the increasingly corporate music industry. The band's 1966 debut album, *Freak Out*, was a mammoth release—a double LP (one of the first) with wild drumming, scathing social satire, extensive musical experimentation, and song titles—"Who Are the Brain Police?" "Help, I'm a Rock," "The Return of the Son of Monster Magnet"—that should have alerted listeners that trouble was on the horizon.

Even more bizarre than the music were the performances. From early on, the band incorporated stage gimmicks ranging from catapulting rotten vegetables to a giant faux giraffe that sprayed whip cream at the audience. Mothers shows were not concerts, they were Events, with a capital *E*. Zappa soon found himself the center of cult appreciation, his fans drooling over the extensive depth of his satire from which no one—not even Zappa himself—was safe.

The band released an incredible eleven albums over the next four years—all of them worth a listen, some regarded by critics as simply brilliant. Among them was 1968's shot across the bow of hippie idealism *We're Only in It for the Money*, whose cover parodied the Beatles' *Sgt. Pepper's Lonely Hearts Club Band*. Zappa and his crew stand in front of a mob of influences, much like the *Sgt. Pepper's* cover, but the band is wearing dresses, and several of the cutout figures are plastered with black rectangles across their eyes and mouths, a comment on censorship that Zappa would rail against—and suffer from—throughout his career. Ironically, Paul McCartney claimed that the Mothers' *Freak Out* was one of the albums that influenced *Sgt. Pepper's* in the first place. But Zappa was always the first to lampoon conformity, taking potshots at whatever was being unquestionably swallowed by the mass gullet. Though often mistaken as just another acid-dropping California hippie, Zappa claimed to be drug-free and ridiculed the droves of come-lately hipsters that descended on the West Coast, releasing his satire on single-minded peaceniks as venomously as he mocked politicians, racists, rock stars, consumers, disco, Californians, prudes, censors, and, most viciously, rock journalists, whom he described as "people who can't write interviewing people who can't talk for people who can't read."[12]

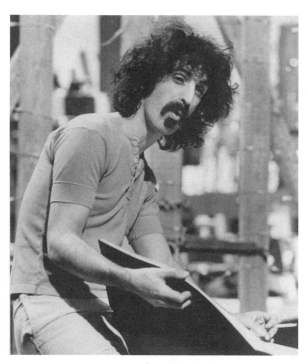

Frank Zappa, 1971. Courtesy of Photofest.

By 1970, the original Mothers had broken up, but Zappa would continue a prolific recording career as a solo artist and with a constantly changing lineup of new Mothers. Fed up with constant censorship, he began recording and distributing through his Bizarre and Straight labels, also releasing material for Captain Beefheart, Tim Buckley, and Alice Cooper. Zappa would continue his fight against censorship throughout his career, making headlines in the mid-1980s when he battled the PMRC (Parents Music Resource Center), a powerful interest group that lobbied to have warning labels printed on albums that they found obscene. Referring to the PMRC's plan as "the equivalent of treating dandruff by decapitation,"[13] Zappa began to issue a warning label on his own albums, which neatly illustrated his ability to combine witty satire and serious social activism—the hallmarks of his music: "WARNING GUARANTEE This album contains material which a truly free society would neither fear nor suppress. . . . The language and concepts contained herein are GUARANTEED NOT TO CAUSE ETERNAL TORMENT IN THE PLACE WHERE THE GUY WITH THE HORNS AND POINTED STICK CONDUCTS HIS BUSINESS. This guarantee is as real as the threats of the video fundamentalists who use attacks on rock music in their attempt to transform America into a nation of check-mailing nincompoops (in the name of Jesus Christ). If there is a hell, its fires wait for them, not us."[14]

Zappa's growing catalogue into the 1970s contained surprise after surprise—a doo-wop tribute on 1968's *Cruising with Ruben and the Jets*; a highly skilled instrumental album *Hot Rats* in 1969; the big-band sounds of *The Grand Wazoo* in 1972; the surreal, jazz-infused *One Size Fits All* in 1975; and Zappa's attempts at xenochronicity (overlaying unrelated tracks to create nonsynchronous music) on 1976's *Zoot Allures*. Later releases and performances would find a more respected Zappa mastering the synclavier, collaborating with renowned classical conductors and musicians, and becoming more directly involved in politics, even considering a run for U.S. president in the early 1990s (though his failing health kept him from going through with it).

In addition to his music, Zappa's side projects increased his fame as an avant-garde artist and his cache as an underground cult figure. His 1971 film *200 Motels*, a most undocumentary-like representation of a rock band's life on the road, features Ringo Starr as the Zappa-inspired character Larry the Dwarf. Though only loosely threaded with Mothers performances (with the aid of the Royal Philharmonic Orchestra), the film was a predecessor to modern music videos. In typically unpredictable Zappa fashion, one of the characters is played by the completely unknown Martin Lickert. Legend has it that the actor who was scheduled to play the part quit days before production began, and his replacement quit at the last minute, so Zappa said he would hire the next person who walked in the room. Lickert, who was Ringo's chauffeur, had gone out to retrieve a pack of cigarettes for Starr and, as timing would have it, returned an actor.

Zappa also suffered some setbacks in the early 1970s. During a December 1971 performance at Montreux Casino in Switzerland, the band lost all of its equipment in a fire that burned down the venue—an event immortalized in the hit song "Smoke on the Water" by Deep Purple, who were performing at the casino with Zappa. Not long afterward, Zappa was pushed off the stage by an overzealous fan at London's Rainbow Theatre, injuring Zappa seriously enough to confine him to a wheelchair for months.

Zappa rebounded in the mid-1970s with some of his most popular material. Though he only broke the Top 20 once—with 1974's *Apostrophe* climbing to No. 10—his albums of this period have endured as classics. Most artists mellow with age, but Zappa only got weirder and more adventurous. His songs through the 1970s and beyond spoofed valley girls, yuppies, evangelists, aliens, furniture, dental floss, truck drivers, B-movie cowboys, and a pet echidna his family had adopted at the local zoo. His song titles reflected this breadth of subject matter as well as his sense of humor: "Aerobics in Bondage," "Don't Eat the Yellow Snow," "Wet T-Shirt Nite," "Chrome Plated Megaphone of Destiny," and "What's the Ugliest Part of Your Body" are only a few of the three hundred-plus songs Zappa recorded over his career. There seemed to be no end to the list of his potential victims, and no limit to Zappa's whimsical depth. In 1993, Zappa succumbed to prostate cancer, and the rock world lost one of its most unique and versatile artists.

Captain Beefheart

An early compatriot of Zappa was school friend and kindred spirit Don Van Vliet, a talented sculptor and painter who later renamed himself Captain Beefheart. After the two played together for a short time in their teens, Beefheart formed Captain Beefheart and the Magic Band, a popular local R&B group in southern California. Although signed to A&M Records, several unsuccessful singles got them dropped from the label, and their 1967 debut album *Safe as Milk* was released on the independent label Buddah. *Safe as Milk*, a complicated mix of soul, jazz, and R&B, was not as groundbreaking as Zappa's debut *Freak Out*, but nonetheless revealed Beefheart's flair for heavily coded lyrics and the unmistakable sound of a young Ry Cooder, who would go on to become a session-guitar legend with such acts as Little Feat, Randy Newman, and the Rolling Stones.

The band followed *Safe as Milk* the following year with *Strictly Personal*, furthering Beefheart's status as a golden underground find. The album is almost unbearable, a postmodern free-for-all that features Beefheart's trademark non-sequitur style but that is marred by spacey, psychedelic production done without his knowledge, causing him to disown the record and almost leave music for good. Appropriately, it was Zappa that convinced Beefheart to stick it out, and signed him to his own Straight Records, giving him all the recording freedom he wanted.

The result was the 1969 Zappa-produced *Trout Mask Replica*, Beefheart's most celebrated album. Seen by some as one of psychedelia's greatest achievements and by others as one of the greatest practical jokes in rock, *Trout Mask Replica* was the height of anti-harmony, anti-rhythm, and anti-lyrical sense. The twenty-eight-track double album features songs that would make even Zappa fans raise an eyebrow—"My Human Gets Me Blues," "Neon Meate Dream of a Octafish," "Hobo Chang Ba"—and the lyrics echo their titles. Whether work of art or work of nonsense, *Trout Mask Replica* earned Captain Beefheart an exalted place in the underground music hall of fame.

The band's subsequent releases, 1970's *Lick My Decals Off, Baby* and 1972's *The Spotlight Kid*, increased Beefheart's status as a creator of alternative music, though the latter indicated a more structured direction, which led to increasingly commercial albums in the mid-1970s that Beefheart regarded as his worst. Another stab at musical greatness came in 1975 when he re-paired with Zappa for a tour, captured on the album *Bongo Fury*—an intense live performance in Austin, Texas. Despite his small but devoted fan base, Captain Beefheart tired of the music industry and in 1982 once again became Don Van Vliet, retiring to the Mojave Desert to become a very successful painter. But much like Zappa, he lives on in legend as a true rock innovator, inspiring later acts such as the Replacements, the B-52s, the Talking Heads, the Meat Puppets, and Soundgarden.

NOTES

1. Stuessy 1994, 275.
2. Stump 1997, 49–50.
3. Steve Turner, "The Moody Blues: Justin Time for the Moodies," *Beat Instrumental*, June 1971.
4. Larkin 1997, 980.
5. Dalton and Kaye 1977.
6. Sylvie Simmons, "King Crimson," *Rolling Stone*, 1995.
7. Stump 1997, 162.
8. Stump 1997, 31.
9. Chris Welch, "The Great Pink Floyd Mystery," *Melody Maker*, August 5, 1967.
10. Loyd Grossman, "Pink Floyd: *The Dark Side of the Moon*," *Rolling Stone*, May 24, 1973.
11. Campbell and Brody 1999, 195.
12. Rock and Roll Hall of Fame biography.
13. United States Senate Hearing Before the Committee on Commerce, Science, and Transportation, September 19, 1985.
14. Warning label, *Frank Zappa Meets the Mothers of Prevention*, 1985.

7

THE FESTIVAL IS BORN

> With the advent of pop festivals, kids could trek into the countryside to hear the music, because, well, it was more "natural" there, wasn't it? The Man hadn't got his hands on the countryside, had he? Rock wanted the wind in its hair and the sun on its back.[1]

At some point over the weekend of June 16, 1967, John Phillips flipped a coin. Phillips, one of the main producers of the Monterey Pop Festival, had to decide who would go on first for Sunday night's lineup—the Who or the Jimi Hendrix Experience. Neither wanted to follow the other, since they were two of the wildest and most energetic acts anywhere. The Who won the toss, prompting Hendrix to stand up on a chair and state that if he had to follow the Who, he was going to pull out all the stops.

Hendrix did as he promised, setting his guitar on fire, smashing it, and throwing the pieces into the audience after a raucous set in an attempt to upstage the Who, who destroyed their instruments onstage as a matter of course. Both bands had built loyal followings in England, but were relatively unknown in the United States. Their over-the-top performances at Monterey would earn them major tours in America and celebrity worldwide.

Before the Monterey Pop Festival, rock performances were fairly simple. There was a headliner, whom audiences came to see, and sometimes an opener to warm up the crowds for the main attraction. For the most part, fans came to see one performer, and they pretty much knew what they were going to get. The rock festival, following in the footsteps of jazz and folk festivals, changed this formula. In 1958, the Monterey Jazz Festival was born, a three-day event that raised money for music education for children. Though not the first jazz festival, it did lead to the creation of the Monterey Folk Festival in 1963, which in turn brought about Monterey Pop in 1967, considered by many to be America's first major rock festival.

Unlike folk and jazz festivals, which tended toward fairly narrow tastes, pop/rock festivals often incorporated a wide range of musical styles. Monterey, for instance, saw performances from Brit-pop, soul, folk, Indian, jazz, blues, and psychedelic artists, one after the other, spread out over a three-day period. The mixed lineup was a positive force for artists and audiences alike. Audience members who came to see a few of their favorite bands would be exposed not only to other acts but to entirely different musical styles. It was obvious that few Monterey festival-goers had experienced much Indian music when the crowd gave a polite round of applause to Ravi Shankar after his first song, which, it turned out, was just an extensive tuning of his sitar.

Performers benefited tremendously from the festival format by virtue of acquiring new fan bases. Jimi Hendrix and the Who were popular bands in Britain, but they could never have been exposed to the large crowds that Monterey provided if they were performing solo. By arranging for a number of performers to come together in one place and share audiences, festivals brought fame to musicians who were, essentially, piggybacking on larger and more popular acts. Who knows how long it would have taken the relatively anonymous Janis Joplin to achieve the fame she did if not for her spectacular performance at Monterey?

Monterey Pop, and by extension the rock-music festival, was one of the most important cultural productions to come out of late-1960s San Francisco, a tremendously bountiful place and time that also brought about psychedelic rock, poster art, underground radio, and the idea of community-driven musical events (see Chapter 1, "The Psychedelic Experience"). Monterey was not the first large musical gathering, and its place in the history books has been unjustly overshadowed by the Woodstock Music and Arts Fair of 1969, but it was a pivotal moment in rock history, and it would not be a stretch to divide the phenomenon of "performance" in rock history into two periods: pre-Monterey and post-Monterey.

THE GATHERING OF THE TRIBES

San Francisco at the dawn of 1967 was exploding with musical possibility. The psychedelic movement was barely more than a year old, and musicians from all over the country—and some from other countries—were converging on the city to expose themselves to what was justly regarded as a wild new musical frontier. The confluence of diverse musical tastes in the Bay Area created a maelstrom of improvisation and cross-pollination between styles. San Francisco was poised to be a centrifugal force in music, mixing folk, blues, jazz, country, raga, and electronica, and spinning the resulting hybrids across the globe.

Beyond the musical element, there was a social element to the ever-expanding San Francisco scene. Music was more than a cultural production created by individuals and dispensed to the masses; it was a social force, a means by which the community could come together and share in a cultural experience. From the earliest days of the psychedelic scene in 1965, when bands like Jefferson Airplane, the Warlocks, and the Great Society would get together to jam in the basements of Haight-Ashbury communes; to the growth of music halls and acid tests in 1966, where microphones were dangled above audiences to incorporate their noise into the music; to the first large music festivals in 1967, where performers would join the audiences to listen to other musicians, music in the San Francisco area was, at heart, an exercise in community (see Chapter 1, "The Psychedelic Experience").

The first indication of what was to come was a small event in the fall of 1966, organized by artist Michael Bowen and writer Allen Cohen. LSD, the social lubricant of the psychedelic machine, was scheduled to be outlawed on October 6, fueling the ire of San Francisco's counterculture community over continuing crackdowns on marijuana and other psychotropics. After repeated incidents of rioting and brutal police responses to protests of the government's heavy-handed antidrug campaign, Cohen thought it would be more productive to demonstrate how unnecessary the drug laws were. "Without confrontation, we wanted to create a celebration of innocence," said Cohen in a later interview with Radio Netherlands. "We were not guilty of using illegal substances. We were celebrating transcendental consciousness. The beauty of the universe. The beauty of being."[2]

Cohen was the founder of the *San Francisco Oracle*, a popular psychedelic arts-and-literature-oriented publication. Using his ability to reach large numbers of the counterculture crowd, Cohen managed to draw 3,000 people to Panhandle Park for what was termed the Love Pageant Rally, featuring Janis Joplin and the Grateful Dead performing on the back of a flatbed truck. By the standards of subsequent music festivals, the small turnout makes it barely worth mentioning. But the Love Pageant Rally was an important step from the *communitas* of the 1966 San Francisco ballroom scene to the large outdoor festivals of 1967 and beyond. Part concert, part town meeting, part block party, the Love Pageant Rally was one of the events that redefined the social potential of rock music.

In attendance at the rally was Richard Alpert, a former Harvard psychologist who collaborated with Timothy Leary on early LSD experiments and who would soon become a counterculture guru under his adopted spiritual name, Ram Dass. In a conversation with Cohen and Bowen, Alpert remarked, "It's a hell of a gathering. It's just being. Humans being." "Yeah," responded Bowen, "It's a Human Be-In."[3]

This idea of bringing a group of people together to just "be," making the entertainment and political causes secondary to the actual assembly, was inspired and inspiring. It was decided after this conversation to hold another, much

THE HUMAN BE-IN PRESS RELEASE

A union of love and activism previously separated by categorical dogma and label mongering will finally occur ecstatically when Berkley political activists and hip community and San Francisco's spiritual generation and contingents from the emerging revolutionary generation all over California meet for a Gathering of the Tribes for a Human Be-In at the Polo Fields in Golden Gate Park.

Twenty to fifty thousand people are expected to gather for a joyful Pow Wow and Peace Dance to be celebrated with leaders, guides and heroes of our generation: Timothy Leary will make the first Bay area public appearance; Alan Ginsberg will chant and read with Gary Snyder, Michael McClure, and Lenore Kandel; Dick Alpert, Jerry Rubin, Dick Gregory, and Jack Weinberg will speak.

Music will be played by all the Bay area rock bands, including the Grateful Dead, Big Brother and the Holding Company, Quicksilver Messenger Service, and many others. Everyone is invited to bring costumes, blankets, bells, flags, symbols, cymbals, drums, beads, feathers, flowers.

Now is the evolving generation of American young the humanization of the American man and woman can begin in joy and embrace without fear, dogma, suspicion or dialectical righteousness. A new concert of human relations being developed within the youthful underground must emerge, become conscious, and be shared so that a revolution of form can be filled with a Renaissance of compassion, awareness, and love in the revelation of the unity of all mankind. The Human Be-In is the joyful, face-to-face beginning of the new epoch.[4]

larger event in the near future, bringing thousands of people together to celebrate the spiritual delight of mere existence.

The event, proclaimed on the cover of the *Oracle* as "A Gathering of the Tribes for a Human Be-In," was a spiritual jamboree planned to coincide with the winter solstice on January 14, 1967. Between twenty and thirty thousand people gathered on the polo fields of San Francisco's Golden Gate Park near the psychedelic ground zero of Haight-Ashbury, not so much to focus on war, politics, or protest, but to simply be. There were, of course, discussions of the current political issues such as the Vietnam War, the environment, and civil rights, but the emphasis was less on rallying for and against these issues and more on empowering the assembled masses to take responsibility for their own enlightenment, to expand their consciousness with meditation, spiritual guidance, and LSD.

To facilitate this enlightenment, Cohen and the other organizers managed to round up all of counterculture's heavy hitters for this one event, including Richard Alpert, beat poets Allen Ginsberg and Lawrence Ferlinghetti, activist comedian Dick Gregory, Youth International Party founder Jerry Rubin, controversial poet Lenore Kandel, environmentalist and beat figure Gary Snyder, and LSD-guru Timothy Leary, who chose the Be-In to unveil his famous pro-enlightenment mantra, "Turn on, tune in, and drop out," reflecting three of the central tenets of the hippie revolution: sexual freedom, chemical experimentation, and escape from the conformist dogma of centralized authority.

This was the first major enlightenment assembly, and a crucial phase in the birth of the rock festival. Top San Francisco bands—including Jefferson Airplane, the Grateful Dead, and Quicksilver Messenger

Service—provided entertainment, but in the communal spirit of 1967 San Francisco, they were, like everyone else, just along for the ride. The Be-In holds a place in the collective memory of the hippie community as possibly the most perfect crystallization of its ideals and goals. By all published accounts, there were no arrests or fights at the event, the Hell's Angels brought on board for security whiled away their time reuniting lost children with their parents, and as the warm sunny afternoon slipped into a mild evening, the remaining congregation cleaned up the entire park, leaving no trace of the event.

The Gathering of the Tribes demonstrated what was possible when music met social activism. According to Cohen, the event was a "meeting of the minds" between the politically active radicals at the University of California–Berkeley and the psychedelic dropouts that made up the Haight-Ashbury hippie community (thus, a gathering of tribes). By combining social cause and self-enlightenment, particularly through the medium of music, Be-In attendees discovered in each other powerful allies, and found themselves on the front of a new battle for personal empowerment against the centralization of authority. "The predominant feeling among the Hippies from about 1965 through the summer of '67 was that they were agents and witnesses of a dawning of a new age," Cohen later remarked.[5] The early incarnations of this new age were represented largely in the period's rock music and most visible—both its beauty (Woodstock) and its beast (Altamont)—in its festivals. It has been argued by many that the battle against centralized authority—the banner under which the hippie troops marched—eventually brought about the personal computer in the 1970s. It is no coincidence that this modern means of decentralized power (itself a revolution against the mainframes owned only by businesses and government) was invented in the very same small corner of the country that produced the psychedelic revolution and the first rock festival.

THERE'S SOMETHING HAPPENING HERE: MONTEREY POP

The increasingly widespread disregard for conservative conformity in the Bay Area brought about an extraordinary summer in 1967, named in advance and remembered fondly as the summer of love. Although it is believed that the moniker was created by local businesses to capitalize on the recent flood of hippie refugees from around the country and the tourists attracted to the new, exotic Haight culture, the summer lived up to its name. The Haight-Ashbury district was buzzing with energy as locally produced psychedelic music began taking a front seat in the American musical tradition.

Since the Be-In, a number of important changes had taken place in the alternative consciousness of the San Francisco identity. In February, local rockers Jefferson Airplane were catapulted toward stardom with their psychedelic cornerstone album *Surrealistic Pillow*. In April, local FM station KMPX launched underground radio with Tom Donahue's rock music show. In May, New York folkie Scott McKenzie scored a worldwide smash with the single "San Francisco (Be Sure to Wear Flowers in Your Hair)." And on June 1, the Beatles released their psychedelic masterpiece *Sgt. Pepper's Lonely Hearts Club Band*, partly inspired by the new wave of experimental and community-driven music in San Francisco.

Rock music, particularly the new and exciting styles that were sweeping the country in the late 1960s, was a very visceral experience. The genre's greatest heroes—the Grateful Dead, Janis Joplin, Eric Clapton, the Doors, Jimi Hendrix, to name a few—were renowned for their live performances. It is the ultimate comeback to one who brags about owning a classic album to be able to say "I saw them live."

On the weekend of June 16, 1967, a group of California musicians and record executives put on an event that would fall into this category, and it would take no further explanation if one were to brag decades later to a friend, "I was at Monterey." Only two weeks earlier, on June 2, the KFRC Fantasy Faire and Magic Mountain Music Festival brought 15,000 people to nearby Mount Tamalpais to benefit the Hunters Point Child Care Center. Top acts such as the Doors, the Byrds, Smokey Robinson, Country Joe and the Fish, and the ubiquitous Jefferson Airplane greeted festival-goers who rode the free "Trans-Love Buslines" shuttles from the parking area at the bottom of the mountain. Though not organizationally related to the Monterey Pop Festival, historically Fantasy Faire has often been described as a warm-up for Monterey.

The Monterey International Pop Festival was the brainchild of Ode Records president Lou Adler and frontman for the Mamas and the Papas, John Phillips. Adler had supervised production of the recent Scott McKenzie hit "San Francisco (Be Sure to Wear Flowers in Your Hair)," which was written by Phillips and released at just the right time to build anticipation for the festival (the "love-in" McKenzie croons about is Monterey). Adler and Phillips enlisted the help of luminaries such as Paul Simon, Paul McCartney, and Derek Taylor, once the press officer for the Byrds and the Beatles. Through skillful organization and careful attention to both the artist lineup and music-industry needs, Monterey was a tremendous success.

Though official accounts vary widely, Monterey reportedly drew close to four times the expected crowd of 50,000 over the course of the weekend. Straight-laced music lover and freestyling bohemian alike enjoyed one of the greatest three-day lineups of all time, including Jimi Hendrix, Big Brother and the Holding Company, Otis Redding, the Who, Paul Butterfield, the Grateful Dead, Simon and Garfunkel, and the Mamas and the Papas (see Performer Lineups for the Major Musical Events of the Late-1960s). Though the festival spent about $80,000 more than it made in ticket prices, ABC paid nearly $290,000 for the television rights, leaving approximately $200,000 for the earmarked charities—free clinics and music programs for underprivileged communities. Because it was a nonprofit event, the bands played for expense money only. For the lesser-known acts, the festival paid off a hundredfold, as the large audience and heavy media exposure—including D. A. Pennebaker's celebrated documentary of the event—were major boosts to their careers.

Although the Beatles had all but broken up, having performed their last public concert the previous year, the British invasion was well represented by the Who in an instrument-smashing spectacle that brought them a sudden increase in popularity in the United States. Not to be outdone, the newcomer Jimi Hendrix gave a raw, sexually explicit performance, playing the guitar behind his head, behind his back, between his legs, and with his teeth and other body parts, after which he doused the instrument in lighter fluid and set it on fire, garnering him enough national attention for a string of Top 5 albums over the next few years (as well as a major U.S. tour with, inappropriately, the Monkees).

Big Brother and the Holding Company were considered a local and relatively unmarketable band, and given an early Saturday afternoon spot. But Janis Joplin's performance with the group was so electrifying that they were scheduled for another set on Sunday evening so that they could be captured on film. Joplin's astonishing performance earned the band a $250,000 recording contract with Columbia Records, resulting in the classic album *Cheap Thrills*. The band also signed with Bob Dylan's manager, Albert Grossman.

Otis Redding, who tragically died only months later, had a brief taste of major success when his powerful Saturday night performance put him on the fast track to international stardom. Indian musician Ravi Shankar—mentor to Beatle George Harrison and musical influence to the Yardbirds, the Byrds, and the Rolling Stones—mesmerized audiences with his blinding speed and creativity on the sitar on Sunday afternoon, the first close-up exposure many of the listeners had ever had to Indian music.

It is a sad postscript to the Monterey legend that the second festival in 1968 was prevented by local taxpayers, who claimed the 1967 event brought "sale of pornographic literature, trafficking in narcotics, an invasion of 'undesirables' and 'open fornication.' "[6] Though the protesters did not dissuade the local government from granting permission for the second festival, they were influential enough to require extraordinary measures be taken by the festival organizers, including campgrounds segregated by gender, massive insurance policies to protect the city, an antinarcotics campaign, and restrictive curfews. That, coupled with a continuing investigation of $52,000 in missing funds from the previous year's event (it was later found that a bookkeeper had embezzled the money), was enough to cause promoters Adler and Phillips to cancel the 1968 event.

Just the same, the 1967 Monterey Pop Festival was a watershed moment for music festivals. The Gathering of the Tribes opened the door for large assemblies of the peace-and-love crowd with its more than 20,000-strong flock, but Monterey's 200,000 listeners (though not all in attendance at the same time) demonstrated that a thirst was out there for a sense of musical community, and that this thirst could be quenched on a grand scale.

Another insight was just as obvious but far less noble—that there was money to be made off this new phenomenon, and lots of it. For promoters inclined toward this way of thinking, putting on a good festival was a secondary goal to putting on a profitable festival. As soon as the news of Monterey's record crowds and critical and financial success got out, promoters all over the country started renting land and booking acts. Only two years later Adler would say, "The music industry has prostituted Monterey. Monterey was a climax of a fantastic time of our music. And now it's a hype. It's become a promoter's tool."[7]

Over the next few years, a number of festivals managed to top 100,000 attendees, but poor planning or downright dishonest management earned these events the dubious media title "bummers in the summers." A host of problems plagued the new rock festival phenomenon: organizers advertised acts before they were signed; necessities such as parking and toilets were woefully underplanned or ignored altogether; stages were too small for large audiences to view, or visibility was blocked by filming equipment; helicopters, hawkers, and poor PA systems made hearing the music a chore or an impossibility for all but the closest fans; acts used to being the main attraction became unreliable, knowing that the show would go on without them; and, largely as a result of these other factors, crowds often turned violent and destructive, taking their angst out on the festival grounds and surrounding community.

It was mostly this last side effect that tarnished the image of the rock festival and saw the passage of many local "mass gathering" ordinances preventing them—much as the good citizens of Monterey had instituted—usually after the damage had already been done. Shoddy organizing and the prevalence of harder drugs that were not as "enlightening" as LSD and marijuana made festivals in 1968 and 1969 more problematic. Legions of fans would show up to concerts without tickets, hoping to sneak in (a much easier feat at large, outdoor festivals than at indoor concerts), only to be met by overeager policemen who spent the previous weekend battling similarly grungy youth at a civil rights march or a war protest rally.

By 1969, festivals were more or less out of control; the organizers were little more than scam artists out for a buck, and the crowds were disenfranchised youth showing up with barbiturates and alcohol for a free show. "You may find many of the 40 or so festivals planned for this warmest of seasons a joyous event," claimed a *Rolling Stone* article on the eve of the 1969 summer, "but you also may be the prey of a shuck-and-jive man, one of the inept and/or greedy promoters who've been leaping for the festival bandwagon the past year or so."[8] The dishonesty and ineptitude of promoters became such a problem that the American Federation of Musicians began publishing a "Do Not Play for or With" list, naming promoters, clubs, and production companies that had earned dubious reputations. In the Los Angeles area alone, the list included more than 200 names.

The *Rolling Stone* prediction was fairly accurate. Despite a number of decent events during the summer of 1969, the ones that captured the national headlines were the disasters. Over Easter weekend in April, 2 people were wounded by gunfire and 250 arrested at a Palm Springs festival featuring Procol Harum and Ike and Tina Turner. Organizers had crammed 25,000 people into a drive-in theater to watch the show, after which concertgoers tore apart fencing behind the screen and set it on fire. Police helicopters inspired rioting when they attempted to disperse the fans, which led the mob to destroy a nearby gas station.

Two months later, over the weekend of June 20, the Los Angeles Newport Pop Festival (not affiliated with the famous jazz and folk festivals in Newport, Rhode Island) was so poorly executed that the city banned large outdoor rock concerts altogether. Between 150,000 and 200,000 fans gathered at a horse-racing track in the residential suburb of Northridge to see Jimi Hendrix, Joe Cocker, Creedence Clearwater Revival, and thirty other acts over a sweltering three-day period. Because of a poorly designed stage and an inadequate sound system, the vast majority of concertgoers could not see or hear the music (which was reported to be, for the most part, amazing). When coupled with inadequate food, water, and toilets, and the brutality of both local law enforcement and the concert's private security force (several hundred members of a local bike gang called the Street Racers), the weekend was a recipe for chaos. Tens of thousands crashed the festival without tickets, knocking hurricane fencing down onto the already cramped crowds and inciting numerous fights that turned into one large riot on Sunday. Approximately 300 people were injured—fifteen of them police officers—and seventy-five placed under arrest for assault and property damage. When the smoke cleared Monday morning, as much as $50,000 worth of damage had been done to a local shopping mall, a grocery store, two gas stations, and a nearby apartment building. Much of the track had been burned or torn down, and three members of the Don Ellis Orchestra were injured by kids throwing rocks at them as they prepared for their set backstage. Details are sketchy as to what extent the promoter was held accountable for the fracas, but records show that he made close to $200,000 more than his expenses.

The scene was eerily repeated the very next weekend at Mile High Stadium in Denver, as many of the same acts (including Hendrix, CCR, and Joe Cocker) presented a reportedly excellent weekend of music marred by crowd violence and police brutality. A small number of gate crashers on Saturday and Sunday evening led to several clashes with a battalion of heavily armed police in full riot gear. Dozens were arrested and several injured in the scuffles. On Saturday, thousands in the stands fled plumes of tear gas as police responded to groups in the crowd that were hurling bottles and fruit at the officers. Unlike the Los Angeles event, the Denver Pop Festival was fairly well-planned, and much of the blame for the violence was placed on overzealous police who claimed to be combating antiwar protesters who had provoked them.

Not all of the year's events made such infamous headlines. The first weekend of August saw two large festivals in Atlantic City and Seattle—with somewhere near 100,000 fans at each—go over with little incident, largely due to a relaxed police presence and nonconfrontational security measures. Proper organizing meant good music that everyone could hear and well-planned amenities that kept the crowds relatively sated. Throughout the course of 1968 and 1969, the occasional well-executed festival showed that when audience members were treated like invested members of the musical community rather than profit-generating consumers, the spirit of Monterey and the Gathering of the Tribes could be salvaged. Unfortunately, the majority of promoters cared more about Monterey's profit margin than its spirit, and the large rock festival earned an unsavory reputation. In this atmosphere, the massive and peaceful Woodstock festival was a minor miracle.

GETTING BACK TO THE GARDEN: WOODSTOCK

> The baffling history of mankind is full of obvious turning points and significant events: battles won, treaties signed, rulers elected or disposed, and now seemingly, planets conquered. Equally popular are the great groundswells of popular movements that affect the minds and values of a generation or more, not all of which can be neatly tied to a time or place. Looking back upon America of the '60s, future historians may well search for the meaning of one such movement. It drew the public's notice on the days and nights of Aug. 15 through 17, 1969, on the 600-acre farm of Max Yasgur in Bethel, NY.[9]

This excerpt from a *Time* magazine article, written only days after Woodstock, was truly prophetic. Historians of music and American culture have, indeed, dwelled on the significance of Woodstock and its place among cultural movements in twentieth-century America. Entire acres of forest have bravely given their lives to debate whether Woodstock was the end of an era of innocence, the beginning of a generational movement, or just a bunch of stoned hippies grooving to some really amazing music. It was, of course, all these things, and so much more.

The festival bearing the unwieldy name of the Woodstock Music and Art Fair and Aquarian Exposition was the pet project of four friends—Michael Lang, Arthur Kornfeld, John Roberts, and Joel Rosenman—all between the ages of twenty-four and twenty-six years old. At first it seemed like just another in a string of rock festivals that swept the country after Monterey, and that's all the organizers were expecting it to be. But three factors made it stand out from comparable events, and as a result it has become the "über-festival," unsurpassed and unsurpassable in popular imagination and, though it was attempted in 1994 and 1999, incapable of being repeated.

The first differentiating factor was location. Woodstock was held on 600 acres of a 2,000-acre dairy farm in Bethel, New York, several hours' drive from the nearest major metropolitan area. Unlike most similar events up to that point, the crowds were not sardined into a small space surrounded by easily ignitable urban environs like gas stations and apartment buildings. Though

Woodstock was certainly crowded, with as many as 400,000 attendees over the three-day event, there were pastures to roll in, corn fields to hide in, and a small lake to swim and bathe in. There was little consumer culture for angst-ridden youths to rebel against, and plenty of nature to get in touch with. It was an ideal setting for an audience that delighted in its identity as rebels against corporate conformity. The trip to Woodstock was not just a long drive but a pilgrimage, a crossing over into a sacred place, as Canned Heat's "Going Up the Country"—a favorite Woodstock anthem—attests: "I'm goin' up the country, babe don't you wanna go/I'm goin' to some place where I've never been before."

Secondly, Woodstock's unorthodox security measures gave its attendees a wide berth and made them feel like they were in a "safe" place. The organizers had initially interviewed 800 off-duty New York City police officers to work as traffic and crowd control. Among the sample questions asked: "What would you do if a kid walked up and blew marijuana smoke in your face?" Correct answer: "Inhale deeply and smile."[10] Of these 800 interviewees, 300 were selected. Unfortunately—or, in retrospect, possibly a stroke of good luck—the New York police chief chose the day before the festival to remind his force that moonlighting was against department policy, and in one stroke, Woodstock lost most of its security force. Bethel police and state troopers were left, vastly outnumbered, to do what they could to simply handle emergencies outside the festival, giving them little presence within the festival grounds.

Much of the responsibility for keeping order fell to a well-respected commune from New Mexico called the Hog Farm, who were brought in specifically to set the example as counterculture heroes. Members of the group defused potentially explosive situations—usually groups such as the SDS (Students for a Democratic Society) trying to turn the festival into a political rally. "Hip beyond any doubt," read a later *Rolling Stone* feature, "[the Hog Farm] spread the love/groove ethic throughout the farm, breaking up incipient actions against 'the system' with cool, low-key hippie talk about making love not war, the mystical integrity of earth, and the importance of doing your own thing, preferably alone."[11] When supplies and workers ran short, the Hog Farm ran a free-food operation and took over the medical system. The few state troopers and off-duty police officers from twelve surrounding counties who worked within the sacred gates were issued red T-shirts emblazoned with a peace sign, reinforcing the goal of the festival as "three days of peace and music." It was also a smart move for the organizers to declare the festival a free event the first night, when it was clear that they did not have the manpower to control the overwhelming crowds assembling at the gates. Had a large security presence allowed for restricting admission to paid entrants only and for large-scale arrests of marijuana smokers—two of the main tipping points for violence at other festivals—demonstrations and riots would almost certainly have ensued, and Woodstock might be remembered as one of the great tragedies of the era rather than one of the great successes.

A poster for the Woodstock Music and Art Fair, 1969. Courtesy of the Library of Congress.

The third, and certainly not the least important, characteristic of Woodstock that made it stand out from other festivals was the sheer assemblage of talent (see Performer Lineups for the Major Musical Events of the Late-1960s). It would almost be easier to list which top acts were not present that weekend. In rock's short fifty-year history, only a handful of events—1967's Monterey Pop, 1985's Live-Aid—come close to the star power generated by Woodstock. The performances—as countless media reports and later interviews with festival-goers agreed—were beyond par and generated some of the great moments in rock lore: Country Joe getting the crowd to repeat his famous "F-I-S-H" cheer so that it could be heard, literally, for miles; Santana introducing himself

PERFORMER LINEUPS FOR THE MAJOR MUSICAL EVENTS OF THE LATE-1960s *(continued)*

The Butterfield Blues Band
Quicksilver Messenger Service
The Steve Miller Band
The Electric Flag
Moby Grape
Hugh Masekela
The Byrds
The Butterfield Blues Band
Laura Nyro
Jefferson Airplane
Booker T and the MG's (with the Mar-Keys)
Otis Redding

Sunday, June 18

Ravi Shankar
The Blues Project
Big Brother and the Holding Company
The Group with No Name
Buffalo Springfield
The Who
The Grateful Dead
The Jimi Hendrix Experience
Scott McKenzie
The Mamas and the Papas

Woodstock Music and Art Fair and Aquarian Exposition August 15–17, 1969

Friday, August 15

Richie Havens
Sweetwater
Bert Sommer
Tim Hardin
Ravi Shankar

Initially 60,000 fans were expected. By noon on Thursday, 25,000 had already arrived and made themselves at home in the surrounding fields. Within hours of the first act on Friday evening, the grounds had swelled to 200,000 fans, with more than a hundred thousand more on the way. The press picked up on the story, and after the announcement Friday night—carried by the media—that the concert was now free, thousands more converged on the area. By late Friday night, the food concessions were sold out, the 600 portable toilets on site were overflowing, the above-ground water lines were crushed by the crowd, and the chief medical officer had declared a "medical crisis" from the large number of drug trips gone awry. One radio station erroneously declared that New York governor Nelson Rockefeller had deemed the site a disaster area, but the announcement could not have been far from the truth. At about midnight, lightning parted the skies, and the rain began to fall.

Incredibly, according to even the more negative accounts of the event, the audience just didn't seem to mind, and even treated the situation—as participants in pilgrimages and rituals do—as a bonding experience. The logistical circumstances improved little over the weekend, but the mood moved beyond one of cooperation into the realm of true community. When food and water were scarce, people walked around handing out what they had. When folks were injured or suffering bad trips, strangers took them to the medical tent where volunteers patched them up or brought them down. And whenever the rain temporarily stopped the music and turned the fields into mud pits, people got naked and danced to their own music. During a second rainstorm on Sunday afternoon, the orgiastic crowd so inspired to the rock world with a performance so renowned that it launched this relative unknown's first album into the Top 5 when it debuted only weeks later; the Who's Pete Townshend knocking Abbie Hoffman off-stage with his guitar after the Yippie leader hijacked the microphone to make a political statement; and, of course, Woodstock's great musical tragedy—that only a few thousand stragglers remained to see Jimi Hendrix ending the show on Monday morning with a blistering electric-guitar rendition of "The Star-Spangled Banner."

Despite the overall success of the festival, it was by no means perfect, and early on it looked like it was going to be a disaster. Woodstock was initially planned for the town of Woodstock—about an hour from Bethel—home of the mythical Bob Dylan, who had all but disappeared from public view in the late 1960s. After the town managed to get the festival barred, the promoters moved it to Wallkill, about fifteen miles from Bethel. With only a month to go before curtain, a zoning challenge by the Wallkill Concerned Citizens Committee forced the promoters to move to Max Yasgur's farm, for which they paid $50,000 in rent. Some local property owners tried to get an injunction against the event, but grudgingly gave their consent after a court hearing at which the promoters agreed to hire the New York City police officers for security.

When the 300 officers failed to show, traffic control was the first casualty. Vehicles were backed up for miles, choking all of the supply routes so that food, water, medical supplies, and even some entertainers could not get through. Helicopters were hired to bring in as many emergency supplies as possible, and the scheduled opening act, Sweetwater, had to be plucked by chopper, along with their equipment, from their bus three miles away.

 PERFORMER LINEUPS FOR THE MAJOR MUSICAL EVENTS OF THE LATE-1960s

**Gathering of the Tribes
January 14, 1967**

Timothy Leary

Richard Alpert

Allen Ginsberg

Lawrence Ferlinghetti

Gary Snyder

Michael McClure

Robert Baker

Jerry Rubin

Lenore Kandel

Dick Gregory

Jefferson Airplane

The Grateful Dead

Quicksilver Messenger Service

Big Brother and the Holding Company

The Sir Douglas Quintet

**Monterey International Pop Festival
June 16–18, 1967**

Friday, June 16

The Association

The Paupers

Lou Rawls

Beverly

Johnny Rivers

Eric Burdon and the Animals

Simon and Garfunkel

Saturday, June 17

Canned Heat

Big Brother and the Holding Company

Country Joe and the Fish

Al Kooper

the musicians that Country Joe and the Fish played without electricity just to be part of it all, the guitarists miming the tunes and bounding around on stage as the drummer pounded out a steady rhythm that kept thousands on their feet, dancing in the muck.

Woodstock, for that weekend the third largest city in New York, had come to resemble a third-world country but a first-rate community. Despite the weekend's setbacks, which ranged from the trivial (hungry concertgoers raiding nearby crops for food) to the tragic (two deaths—one from a drug overdose, the other a sleeping attendee run over by a tractor), numerous testimonials confirm the overwhelming sense of togetherness the festival inspired. According to the event's chief medical officer, Dr. William Abruzzi, "there has been no violence whatsoever, which is really remarkable for a crowd of this size."[12] Of the 5,000 medical cases over the weekend—most for cut feet and bad acid trips—"We didn't treat one single knife wound or a black eye or a laceration that was inflicted by another human being."[13] Similar descriptions of cooperative spirit came from the nearby townsfolk and even law enforcement. "I never met a nicer bunch of kids in my life," said Sullivan County Sheriff Louis Ratner.[14] Another officer, Lou Yank, told a reporter, "Notwithstanding their personality, their dress, and their ideas, they are the most courteous, considerate, and well-behaved group of kids I have ever been in contact with in my 24 years of police work."[15]

Lest the beatniks get all the credit for the remarkable cooperation over the weekend, it should be noted that many outsiders from the surrounding areas pitched in as well; as one *Rolling Stone* reporter put it, "dirty hippies are one thing, but hungry children are another."[16] The nearby town of Monticello,

PERFORMER LINEUPS FOR THE MAJOR MUSICAL EVENTS OF THE LATE-1960s *(continued)*

Melanie
Arlo Guthrie
Joan Baez

Saturday, August 16

Quill
Country Joe McDonald
John B. Sebastian
Keef Hartley Band
Santana
Incredible String Band
Canned Heat
The Grateful Dead
Creedence Clearwater Revival
Janis Joplin
Sly and the Family Stone
The Who
Jefferson Airplane

Sunday, August 17

Joe Cocker
Country Joe and the Fish
Mountain
Ten Years After
The Band
Johnny Winter
Blood, Sweat & Tears
Crosby, Stills, Nash & Young

Monday, August 18

Paul Butterfield Blues Band
Sha-Na-Na
Jimi Hendrix

fourteen miles from the site, opened its parks for camping and set up emergency medical clinics and food drives at its schools. The local women's group of the Jewish Community Center made 30,000 sandwiches over the weekend, distributed by the sisters of the Convent of St. Thomas to underfed concertgoers. And in what may be the greatest irony of the weekend, the Air Force diverted two assault helicopters from training missions to carry in food and medical supplies and carry out injured fans.

Media reports of the festival over the following week called it, by turns, a nightmare, a financial disaster, and a success. There were two deaths, but there were also two births. By throwing open the gates on Friday night, the organizers ended the weekend almost $2 million in the red, but made it up when the documentary of the event grossed more than $20 million over the following six months. The *New York Times* called the festival in a Monday editorial an "outrageous episode," asking "What kind of culture is it that can produce such a mess?"[17] But another editorial the next day summed up the event nicely: "They came, it seems, to enjoy their own society, free to exult in a life style that is its own declaration of independence. To such a purpose a little hardship could only be an added attraction. . . . For comrades-in-rock, like comrades-in-arms, need great days to remember and embroider."[18]

Much like the Gathering of the Tribes, Woodstock made progress toward the thinning of the generation gap by demonstrating what was possible when youth were allowed to revel in their chosen lifestyle without outside interference. The violence and destruction at concert festivals over the previous two years had given the rock community a black eye and made locals more than a little weary of such events in their community. The host of Woodstock, forty-nine-year-old Max Yasgur, nervously took the microphone Sunday afternoon and, with the adoration of a proud parent, addressed the hundreds of thousands assembled with whom he had only this weekend in common: "You have proven something to the world," he said. "That half a million kids can get together for fun and music and have nothing but fun and music."[19]

SYMPATHY FOR THE DEVIL: THE ALTAMONT DISASTER

It would have been nice, to say the least, if the cooperative essence of Woodstock could have lasted more than a weekend. Certainly its spirit survived in some respects, and much has been written about "the Woodstock Generation," as if the tens of millions of American youths had all been there and were all capable of exulting "in a life style that is its own declaration of independence" while simultaneously asserting their interdependence. The myth was born almost immediately and has survived to this day, but the innocence regained at Woodstock held its place in reality for only a few short months, until the concert at California's Altamont Speedway on December 6, 1969.

A number of peaceful and even profitable events were held between August and December 1969. The word "Woodstock" was invoked at other festivals with both admiration and a sense of foreboding: it would be great to have Woodstock the spirit, but we want to avoid Woodstock the logistical disaster. Several festivals in other parts of the country were nearly canceled by local governments fearful of a humanitarian nightmare in their own backyard, and promoters took the lessons of Woodstock to heart, planning for the worst of circumstances, hoping for the best of hippie spirit. As it happened, nothing on Woodstock's scale occurred again that year, and the festivals that were carried out—35,000 fans in Dallas, Texas, over Labor Day weekend; 30,000 in Jackson, California, on October 4; 40,000 in West Palm Beach, Florida, on November 30—generally occurred with little incident.

Throughout that fall, the Rolling Stones were on the road in America for their first U.S. tour since 1966. By this time they were monsters of rock, having placed twelve Top 10 albums on the American charts in the previous five years, and had no problem filling seats at large venues anywhere in the country. Just the previous week, the band played three shows in two days at New York's voluminous Madison Square Garden. It should have been no surprise, then, that when the group ended their tour in northern California on December 6 with a free concert at Altamont Speedway—accompanied by extant California giants the Grateful Dead, Jefferson Airplane, Santana, and Crosby, Stills, Nash & Young—there might have been a bit of a crowd problem.

More than 300,000 fans descended on the ill-prepared site, an eighty-acre oval infield whose record crowd up to that point had been 6,500 attendees of a demolition derby. Organizers of the event were concerned with sheer numbers—get enough fans together and we have got ourselves a West Coast Woodstock. San Francisco newspapers printed over the weekend hailed the event in those very terms before the concert was even over, painting portraits of happy hippies holding hands in a landscape of peace, love, and brotherhood.

The truth was not only bleaker but downright tragic, later deemed by *Rolling Stone* "perhaps rock and roll's all-time worst day."[20] The Rolling Stones' manager, Sam Cutler, had hired at least 100 Hell's Angels to work as security for $500 worth of beer. The Stones had previously used a British chapter of Hell's Angels for a concert in London's Hyde Park, but were not fully aware of the much more violent nature of the original California chapters. The Hell's Angels were to maintain crowd control, particularly near the stage, and they took their job very seriously, wielding sawed-off pool cues and bashing anyone who got too near. This was a far cry from the "we're all in this together, man" attitude that commune personnel used to defuse situations at Woodstock. By the time the weekend was over, 850 people were injured and 4 were dead—one drowned in an irrigation canal adjacent to the speedway, two crushed when a hit-and-run driver plowed through their campsite on the grounds, and one man, eighteen-year-old Meredith Hunter, knifed to death by Hell's Angels right in front of the stage as the Rolling Stones performed.

Contrary to early news reports—obviously prefashioned in anticipation of the large peacenik crowd—Altamont was the anti-Woodstock, a poorly planned money grab concerned only with the number of fans in attendance, and not whether those fans would enjoy the experience. The racetrack was reminiscent of a Mad Max film, a bleak, treeless dirt bowl bordering a highway, where fans kept warm at night by burning giant piles of trash. The event was moved from another venue only twenty hours before show time, leaving logistics more or less up in the air; sanitation, toilet facilities, and medical care were woefully inadequate. The Hell's Angels, many fans later said, were worse than the police, who at least had some sense of organization and relative fairness when they provided security at earlier concerts. The biker group, many of whom were taking acid and drinking through the show, essentially hijacked the festival—standing on stage during performances, picking fights with anyone who got too close, and even riding their bikes through the audience. "Altamont was the product of diabolical egotism, hype, ineptitude, money manipulation, and, at base, a fundamental lack of concern for humanity,"[21] railed a twenty-page *Rolling Stone* story the following month, generally considered the authoritative account of the event.

No one was willing to accept responsibility for the catastrophe. The fans blamed the Hell's Angels, the Hell's Angels blamed the Rolling Stones (particularly manager Sam Cutler), and the Rolling Stones tended to shy away from

Music fans gather for the Rolling Stones concert at Altamont Speedway near Livermore, California on December 6, 1969. AP/Wide World Photo.

comment, except for an extremely naive statement by guitarist Keith Richards that since they had used Hell's Angels successfully in London, American fans are just more violent than the British.

Many fingers initially pointed to Mick Jagger, who continued performing as Meredith Hunter was murdered at his feet, and who, many felt, should have been less indifferent to the chaos since he was the main attraction of the event. However, journalists close to the stage report that Jagger tried to suppress the violence throughout his set, begging the crowd to calm down. Ultimately it was clear that all of the performers were aware of the violence around them and tried their best to quell it. Marty Balin, guitarist for Jefferson Airplane, even interceded in a brawl during his band's set, and was knocked unconscious as he tried to come between six Hell's Angels and a hapless fan. After the Stones' set and Hunter's death, the Grateful Dead—who were to close the show—decided to end the concert early to prevent further disaster.

As it turned out, cameramen filming the festival captured Hunter's death in gruesome detail. Just as the Rolling Stones had wanted Altamont to be another Woodstock, they were intrigued by recent rock films such as *Dont Look Back* (D. A. Pennebaker's documentary on Bob Dylan) and the Beatles' *A Hard Day's Night*, and had tried to recruit Pennebaker and Haskell Wexler (director of *Medium Cool*) to make a documentary of their American tour before eventually settling on David and Albert Maysles and Charlotte Zwerin. The film team had followed the band through their American trip and were hoping to capture Altamont as a massive, peaceful exclamation point to the tour.

The cinematographers—among them future *Star Wars* director George Lucas—got more than they bargained for when Altamont turned tragic, and what was to be a simple tour documentary became a hotly debated chronicle of Hunter's death. *Gimme Shelter* was a visual record of one of rock's saddest days, ingrained in music's institutional memory alongside other tragic events like the Who concert in Cincinnati in 1979 and the Pearl Jam show in Roskilde, Denmark, in 2000.

AFTER THE FALL

When the smoke cleared and the truth surfaced, Altamont was mourned by many as the end of the sixties—not just the decade, but the remarkable mobilization of a disenfranchised counterculture. By this time, the psychedelic reserves of San Francisco's Haight community were all but drained, with most of its founding groups disbanded and the Beatles on their way out. Although some promoters still clung to the dream of creating another Woodstock (claiming it was possible to be prepared for all contingencies), many of the groups at Altamont, who formed the backbone of the festival circuit, vowed publicly to never play a large festival again.

The rock festival did survive, though in smaller form and with lesser bands. Three months after Altamont, organizers of a festival in Lubbock, Texas, faced obstacle after obstacle trying to get a show past locals who feared the kind of hippie hordes that put Altamont in the national headlines. Originally seventeen bands were planned for about 65,000 attendees, but after much-publicized battles for space and legal authority, the concert wound up with five bands performing for about 7,500 folks. The police took no chances, enlisting local, state, and private officers to the point that they made up about 10 percent of the audience. Facing no violent outbreaks, they switched their focus to apprehending drug users in the crowd. Though the concert was a complete loss, local authorities bragged that they broke all of the arrest records for Lubbock County the Saturday of the event.

Promoters in Orlando, Florida, held a larger event several weeks later over Easter weekend. Facing even more injunctions and legal challenges than the festival in Lubbock, the event was called off and called back on again several times. Even though it was unclear at the last minute whether the festival would continue, 80,000 fans showed up to see a notable roster, including the Grateful Dead, Canned Heat, Johnny Winter, Ike and Tina Turner, Mountain, and the Allman Brothers. The festival was technically illegal, and the promoters were arrested for violating a local antifestival ordinance, introducing "a new kind of criminal—the first promoters ever to be charged with conspiracy to rock and roll."[22] Despite such obstacles, dozens of volunteers carried out the festival anyway, reported to be, although a financial disaster, a good and essentially peaceful weekend of music, at which "[o]nly a Woodstockian endurance on the part of the crowd prevented this one from being an out-and-out disaster."[23]

The closest thing to another Woodstock was the Second Annual Atlanta International Pop Festival, held over Fourth of July weekend, which drew close to 250,000 fans and mirrored, in a smaller fashion, both the pros and cons of the Woodstock festival. On the plus side was the music; several festival greats—including Jimi Hendrix, the Allman Brothers, Ravi Shankar, and Ten Years After—gave excellent performances, including a memorable execution of "Here Comes the Sun" by Richie Havens as the sun rose Sunday morning, and Hendrix's repeat of his "Star-Spangled Banner" rendition from Woodstock, only this time played on July 4 as fireworks blazed all around him.

The logistics, unfortunately, mirrored Woodstock as well, with inadequate food, water, toilets, medical care, and traffic control to accommodate the large crowd. It was fortunate that the promoters decided to withdraw the biker security gangs as thousands lined the fences demanding to be let in for free. There were numerous medical emergencies from bad drug trips but little violence, as the temperature soared near 100 degrees and concertgoers sought shelter instead of confrontation. Despite the well-behaved crowds and the excellent music, the festival was another financial mess, as only 40,000 of the fans actually paid admission. The promoters pleaded with attendees for donations at the gates via a quickly typed flyer: "Woodstock was beautiful, but there are fewer large festivals this summer due to fears of other huge financial losses. If you do not help, this may be one of the last big festivals ever. Think about how hard the establishment everywhere is trying to stop festivals. They are afraid of us when we are together. If we kill the festival, we play right into the establishment hands. We destroy our own scene."[24]

Few attendees answered the call to pay up, and the event was a financial debacle as well as, as the promoters predicted, one of the last large festivals for many years. Local authorities began preventing or at least becoming more closely involved with rock events—a hassle for promoters and fans, but ultimately a positive step toward averting another Altamont. In the year after Woodstock, approximately forty-eight major festivals were planned in the United States but only eighteen of them carried out.[25] It was becoming obvious that the rock festival, while occasionally a memorable event, was rarely a sound financial investment. The thirst for more free entertainment had repercussions beyond the rock world; lacking another Woodstock in the northeast, hundreds of young hippies crashed the fences at the venerable and well-mannered Newport Jazz Festival, forcing police to shut down the event two days early out of concern for public safety.

"Free" seemed to become the buzzword for festivals. Fans began to feel they had a right to the music—that rock was about fighting the system, and that if you are paying for your music, then you are no more than a consumer of goods. But how (and why) would promoters put on festivals to lose money? How could festivals survive? Many did not, of course, and many a promoter went bankrupt. Some festivals became government-sanctioned events, such as the annual Sunshine Festival in Waikiki, efficiently run by a Hawaiian radio station and supported by the city and state governments as well as U.S. Army units in the area. And there were still the occasional mid-to-large gatherings (between 100,000 and 200,000 fans) that did their best to make a profit.

During 1972 and 1973, there were two minor shifts in festival tactics that would bring changes to the concert game. One was the idea to better control crowds (and thus ensure everyone pays to get in) by holding festivals in stadiums. The Beatles had essentially held the first stadium-rock concert in 1965 at Shea Stadium in New York. However, few bands could sell enough tickets to book an entire stadium, and the stunt was rarely repeated.

In 1972 KROQ, a new AM station in Los Angeles, booked the L.A. Memorial Coliseum for a November 25 rock festival. Like a dozen other festivals over the previous three years, it billed itself as a "West Coast Woodstock." Like all of them, it was a promotional gimmick with no basis in fact. The promoters hoped to fill the 100,000-seat sports arena to capacity, but largely due to a heavy and discouraging police presence at the gates, the crowd topped off at less than 33,000. The police arrested approximately one percent of the attendees for drug possession, including some of the members of the band Crazy Horse who were to perform at the concert. Despite the poor turnout of the event, it was clear that a festival held in a seated arena was much easier to manage than an outdoor event held on a farm. Sports arenas were built specifically for large crowds, with adequate food, water, medical care, and egress points. With the poor reputation rock festivals had garnered up to that point, arena owners were understandably hesitant to allow the events. But as it became clear that rock festivals could be properly managed with the right facilities, and as the continuously varying rock genres began producing more superstars, festivals started using arenas more often, and top acts of the 1970s—such as the Grateful Dead, Queen, Pink Floyd, Peter Frampton, and the Rolling Stones—proved that they could draw enough crowds by themselves to become purveyors of "stadium rock."

Another historical event that had a large impact on rock festivals was the 1971 Concert for Bangladesh, held on August 1 at Madison Square Garden in New York City. The concert was actually two shows—one in the afternoon and one later in the evening—put together by ex-Beatle George Harrison to raise money for relief in the war-torn country of Pakistan. Rock concerts and festivals had donated proceeds to charities before, but this was the first time a major rock event was created specifically for the purpose of raising money for a single humanitarian cause. Harrison founded the concert at the request of his yogi, master sitar player Ravi Shankar, who performed at the show for free, along with Harrison, Eric Clapton, Bob Dylan, Ringo Starr, Billy Preston, and several others.

Although the show was more a multiartist concert than a festival, it reintroduced on a grand scale the possibilities of using rock music to address social causes—a theme largely lost since rock festivals became money-making scams after Monterey. A film and album quickly followed the event, raising more money and awareness. The success of the Concert for Bangladesh generated more large-scale "cause" events over the following decades, such as Concerts for the People of Kampuchea in 1979; Live Aid in 1985, which was broadcast to more than a billion people around the world; and Farm Aid in 1985, which raised $7 million for struggling American farmers and became an annual event.

Rock festivals came a long way in a short time, from local bands playing on the back of a flatbed truck in 1966 to the largest rock gathering to date: 600,000 fans assembled in Watkins Glen, New York, on July 28, 1973, to hear the Allman Brothers, the Band, and the Grateful Dead, three of the supergroups of the period. The Dead seem to tie the picture together nicely, not only for having appeared at the original Love Pageant Rally, the Gathering of the Tribes, Monterey, Woodstock, Altamont, and Watkins Glen, but because the large-scale concert would not have been possible without increasingly powerful and sophisticated sound equipment, and from the beginning, the Dead were pioneers of loud, high-quality sound systems. When the Beatles played Shea Stadium in 1965, much of the crowd could not even hear them. Less than ten years later, a single voice could reach more than half a million people, announcing to the world that the large-scale rock festival was here to stay.

NOTES

1. Stump 1997, 41.

2. Neville Powis, Radio Netherlands, January 22, 2003.

3. Neville Powis, Radio Netherlands, January 22, 2003.

4. Radio Netherlands, www.rnw.nl/special/en/html/030122be-in_press.html. All spelling errors in original press release. 4. Allen Cohen, www.be-in.com.

5. Allen Cohen, www.be-in.com.

6. *Rolling Stone*, April 6, 1968.

7. Jerry Hopkins, "Festival Shucks," *Rolling Stone*, June 28, 1969, 11.

8. *Rolling Stone*, June 28, 1969, 11.

9. "The Message of History's Biggest Happening," *Time*, August 29, 1969, 32–33.

10. "It Was Like Balling for the First Time," *Rolling Stone*, September 20, 1969, 30.

11. *Rolling Stone*, September 20, 1969, 30.

12. *Rolling Stone*, September 20, 1969, 20.

13. William E. Farrell, "19-House Concert Ends Bethel Fair," *New York Times*, August 19, 1969, 34.

14. *New York Times*, August 19, 1969, 34.

15. *Rolling Stone*, September 20, 1969, 20.

16. *Rolling Stone*, September 20, 1969, 24.

17. "Nightmare in the Catskills," *New York Times*, August 18, 1969, 34.

18. "Morning After Bethel," *New York Times*, August 19, 1969, 42.

19. *Rolling Stone*, September 20, 1969, 1.

20. John Burks, "In the Aftermath of Altamont," *Rolling Stone*, February 7, 1970, 7.

21. "Let It Bleed," *Rolling Stone*, January 21, 1970, 20.

22. "Nearly Everybody Got Burned," *Rolling Stone*, May 14, 1970, 16.

23. *Rolling Stone*, May 14, 1970, 14.

24. "Atlanta: The Biggest—And Maybe Last?" *Rolling Stone*, August 6, 1970, 14.

25. "The View From the Mud," *Rolling Stone*, August 6, 1970, 12.

ROCK AND THE MEDIA

The previous chapters have extensively covered the emergence of various subgenres of rock through the late 1960s and early 1970s, each genre spawning its own superstars and hit songs, and each achieving a respectable degree of success as an independent art form. The creation of music, however, is only half the equation. These new forms of rock had to reach the masses somehow; there had to be some sort of delivery system for a small act playing a San Francisco ballroom to reach potential rock fans in San Antonio, Texas.

Pop music already had such a system in place. AM radio played the top hits, the *Billboard* charts publicized the successful acts, and the mainstream press carried articles and pictures about the hottest sounds. It was through the manipulation of these media outlets that underground rock—in this chapter referring to the newer strains of rock such as psychedelia, folk rock, and progressive—increased its exposure to the outside world and eventually came to dominate airplay and album sales. Between 1967 and 1973, the explosion of rock styles helped the record industry double its sales from $1 billion to $2 billion (much of this was due to the Beatles, whose success led record companies in the mid-1960s to sign more experimental acts).[1] Before 1964, the only rock artist who could find a place on the top of the charts was Elvis Presley. Only six years later, every single No. 1 was by an artist or group that would have once been considered "underground" rock.

Once again, San Francisco gets much of the credit. In addition to the folk rock of Greenwich Village and Los Angeles, the Bay Area's psychedelic scene launched a number of highly successful groups in 1966 and 1967—most prominently the Grateful Dead and Jefferson Airplane—largely through the help of the emerging FM radio at San Francisco's KMPX. This led FM radio to move away from the singles format and into AOR, or album-oriented rock. It was also San Francisco that saw the country's first major rock magazine when *Rolling Stone* debuted there in the fall of 1967, to be followed by a number of other publications that heralded a new, politically charged style of rock journalism. Outside of San Francisco, rock music began seeping into the film and theater outlets with movies like *Easy Rider, The Graduate*, and a number of music documentaries, followed by the enormously successful runs of *Hair* and *Jesus Christ Superstar* on Broadway.

This chapter will trace the reasons for rock's eruption as a highly commercial genre that would quickly dominate the music industry, including the advent of FM radio as a home for underground rock, the use of rock music in film and theater, and the creation of national magazines that exclusively covered the rock world. By the time most of these changes took place, rock was already well on its way to becoming a major force in music—again, largely thanks to the Beatles. These changes in the media, however, significantly sped up the process and helped countless acts achieve stardom as well as influence future generations of rock and rollers.

KMPX AND THE FM REVOLUTION

Since much of America's rock movement in the 1960s was antiestablishment in nature, it is ironic that one of the most important boons to rock music was precipitated not by guitar-wielding rockers or banner-waving hippies, but by the federal government, in the guise of the Federal Communications Commission (FCC). For most of the 1960s, FM radio was a fairly useless patch of space in the ether between 88 and 108 megahertz. FM stations were generally owned by media corporations who used them to rebroadcast their AM programming or, occasionally, to broadcast classical music. AM stations had greater range and could thus reach a larger audience, but FM stations had better sound quality. Before the mid-1960s, sound quality was not a major concern with regard to radio, so few homes and almost no automobiles sported FM receivers. With little audience and almost no original programming, FM radio had no life of its own.

In the mid-1960s, FM receivers became more common as FM began to broadcast in stereo, but without original material, FM radio had no real impact. The surprising knight in shining armor in this scenario was the FCC, which decided in July 1965 that FM stations had to carry at least 50 percent original programming instead of replaying material from their AM affiliates. Effectively, the FCC forced radio to increase the diversity of its programming. This was no easy task—radio stations had a fairly simple format that was made up of jingles, promotions, contests, time and temperature, and extremely limited song lists consisting of the Top 15 or 20 three-minute pop hits on the charts.

FM radio struggled for direction only briefly before taking on underground rock music as a source of new material. With the British invasion and the increasing number of rock bands on the scene in the late 1960s, FM was the perfect place for artists to find an audience, and rock was the perfect untapped resource for FM programmers. It was about this time that sales of rock albums began to overtake sales of singles, and the advantage for programming-starved FM stations of playing entire records instead of three-minute songs was obvious.

The transition from AM affiliate to rock station was by no means easy for FM stations, and the process took several years. The man widely credited for the advent of FM as a rock venue was Tom Donahue, a well-known San Francisco concert promoter and DJ who was hired in 1967 to be the new program director for KMPX, a former foreign-language station in the Bay Area. Unlike many radio DJs, who spun the same tunes over and over, Donahue was a real music fan and debuted his own underground rock show on April 7, 1967, promising "no jingles, no talkovers, no time and temp, no pop singles."[2]

Donahue also hired a staff of hip DJs and an all-girl engineering department, and steadily increased the diversity of the station's rock programming with great success; by early 1968, the once struggling station's ad revenues were up 1,000 percent. But like most FM stations, KMPX had a corporate parent, and disagreements between Donahue and his bosses over the station's new direction led to Donahue's resignation in March 1968, an event that could have ended rock's promising new delivery system had Donahue not garnered so much loyalty from his associates. Only two days after Donahue's resignation, almost all of his co-workers went on strike to support him, decrying the station's low pay and the persecution of the largely hippie staff by the station's corporate managers. Despite the huge increase in revenue, most of the employees still made their starting salary—about $100 per week—and many accused the station's management of "interference of artistic and personal freedoms." After the strike, 95 percent of the station's advertisers pulled their spots in support of the strikers.

The entire staff found a home five weeks later at San Francisco's KSAN, a classical station that decided to turn rock, thus becoming the first full-on FM rock station in the country. The popularity of the format and increased revenue for the station led to a quick succession of imitations in 1968 by KSHE in St. Louis, WABX in Detroit, and WNEW in New York. Other FM and even some AM stations began carrying limited progressive programming in 1968, including KFMK Houston; WMBM Miami Beach; WOPA Oak Park, Illinois; WLS Chicago; WAVA Arlington, Virginia; WASH Washington, D.C.; and WIXY Cleveland. Some stations began playing underground rock mostly on weekends, like WBZ Boston, KSFR San Francisco, WMFT Chicago, WSDM Chicago, and WKYC Cleveland. Over the course of 1968, underground rock found a nationwide delivery system for its product, leading to a massive increase in sales, the eventual domination of album sales over single sales, and the death of the formulaic three-minute pop song.

Unfortunately, the FCC sought to undo some of the progress FM radio had made when it began censoring stations in 1970 for obscene language and drug references in the music. Socially acceptable in mainstream society or not, drugs were an intimate aspect of the growing rock culture, particularly the psychedelic and hard-rock scenes that brought FM radio back to life. On March 5, 1970—almost two years after Donahue left KMPX for KSAN—the FCC issued a notice to stations that the DJs would have to know the meaning of the songs that "tend to glorify or promote the use of illegal drugs such as marijuana, LSD, speed, etc." "In short," the statement ran, "we expect licensees to ascertain, before broadcast, the words or lyrics of recorded musical or spoken selections played on their stations."[3]

Finding it virtually impossible to interpret the lyrics to every song they aired, stations began pulling artists from rotation for fear of repercussions from the FCC. A number of songs—some of them fairly innocuous—that had helped break open the underground rock scene were removed, including Jefferson Airplane's "White Rabbit," the Beatles' "Lucy in the Sky with Diamonds," and the Rolling Stones' "Let It Bleed." The Byrds' smash hit "Eight Miles High," which was about fear of flying, was banned at some stations because listeners might interpret it as a "drug song." FM rock stations, essentially, had become victims of their own success. As FM audiences increased dramatically, so too did the complaints from consumers who heard objectionable material in the songs as well as the advertising dollars the stations were pulling in. More profitable stations attracted more corporate attention, which led station managers to remove objectionable material from the airwaves to dissuade complaints from listeners. Even Donahue's KSAN, the country's first major FM rock station, felt the pinch as it let go some of its more controversial programmers. FM survived, of course, and continued to be an alternative to bubble-gum AM pop, but at the same time adopted some of the Top 40 tactics of their AM competitors, ultimately weakening their credibility as a truly underground alternative.

ROCK ON THE BIG SCREEN

Since the early twentieth century, the movie industry has been one of the most dominant cultural forces in America. Single films have inspired near-cultish legacies—witness 1939's *The Wizard of Oz*, 1977's *Star Wars*, or 2001's *The Lord of the Rings*. An essential aspect of film is the soundtrack, which can launch a band to fame or even find a place on the charts itself, which is not an unusual feat—five of the nine albums that reached No. 1 in 1965 were film soundtracks. It follows that the genre of a soundtrack would receive attention proportionate to the popularity of the film, and that the use of a certain type of music in a film would serve as a major promotion tool for that genre.

An offshoot of the movie industry that has been particularly kind to rock and roll is the documentary. Since rock's earliest days, cameramen have been filming concert performances, eventually creating the "rockumentary," which followed top acts on tours, gathering a mishmash of performance and backstage drama to create a real-life narrative of a rock star's world. Below is a brief list of some of the more important rockumentaries and feature films with rock soundtracks from 1967 to 1973.

The Graduate, 1967

One of the great coming-of-age stories in American cinema, The Graduate was only director Mike Nichols' second movie and star Dustin Hoffman's third. The film is centered on Hoffman's character Benjamin Braddock, a promising—though awkward and lost—high school graduate who can't figure out what to do with his future. Doing his best to dodge parental expectations, Hoffman falls into an affair with the much older and married Mrs. Robinson—a friend of the family—but eventually finds himself in love with the Robinsons' daughter.

Nichols' decision to hire the songwriting duo of Paul Simon and Art Garfunkel to compose a soundtrack for the film was a perfect match for the film's mood and subject matter. Simon and Garfunkel were major attractions at college venues, and their young fans could certainly appreciate Braddock's yearning for answers. Nichols initially hired the duo to write an entire soundtrack, but used some of their existing songs during the editing phase to create a similar mood. He found that these tunes worked well with the film and decided to keep them, so the movie actually contains only one new Simon and Garfunkel song, the No. 1 single "Mrs. Robinson," making it one of the first major motion pictures of the era to have a rock soundtrack.

Dont Look Back, 1967

More than just a day in the life of Bob Dylan, this early rockumentary follows Dylan through a three-week tour of England in the spring of 1965, just as he was publicly moving into his electric phase (see Chapter 5, "Folk Rock and Its Successors"). It is not a stretch to say that this time frame is one of the pivotal periods of 1960s rock. Dylan has become the crown prince of folk, but has also generated mass appeal to the point of becoming a commercial figure. He has also just released the important "Subterranean Homesick Blues," sporting a drum backing and electric guitar. It's clear in the film that Dylan is well aware of the contradictions he's embracing—a folk-protest icon who wants to be a rock star.

The film was directed by D. A. Pennebaker, one of rock's most important documentarians of the day, who also directed Monterey Pop and Ziggy Stardust and the Spiders from Mars (both featured later). Pennebaker reportedly designed special microphones for this film rather than use boom mikes so as to be as unobtrusive as possible. The result is a hip-pocket documentary that

Poster for the film *Dont Look Back*, 1967. Leacock Pennebaker/ The Kobol Collection.

captures Dylan's acerbic wit and impatient insolence to his supporters and hangers-on alike, revealing how difficult a transition it was for a budding rocker to be trapped in a world of folk expectations.

Festival, 1967

Another film that captures Dylan during this crucial transition stage is *Festival*, a documentary of the Newport Folk Festival from 1963 to 1966. Featuring Dylan's famous electric performance at Newport '65 (see Chapter 5, "Folk Rock and Its Successors"), the film captures the folk-music elite (both artists and fans) during a time when a certain corner of folk was spinning into the highly successful genre of folk rock and the traditional folkies are trying to hang on.

Featuring interviews and performance excerpts with some of the era's greatest artists—Bob Dylan, Joan Baez, Mike Bloomfield, Son House, Pete Seeger, Johnny Cash, Paul Butterfield, Donovan, Judy Collins, Mississippi John Hurt, and Peter, Paul and Mary among them—the film somehow manages to boil four years of Newport down to ninety-five minutes. Also capturing some of the great blues artists breaking through to young, white crowds, the film truly seizes an important era of rock music, as it crawls out of its blues and folk cradle into a much bigger world.

Yellow Submarine, 1968

In 1964 and 1965, the Beatles made splashes with their "day-in-the-life" film *A Hard Day's Night* and the slightly more bizarre *Help!* Like their music, the Beatles movies inspired a number of American imitations, from Roger McGuinn's 12-string Rickenbacker sound in the Byrds to a TV show for the pop-phenom group the Monkees. Perhaps the strangest Beatles film, however, was their cartoon fantasy adventure *Yellow Submarine*, shot for $1 million and featuring the voices of the Beatles singing the songs of their animated selves.

The ninety-minute feature is centered around the citizens of Pepperland, a playful folk who are invaded by the Blue Meanies. The Meanies steal the Pepperlanders' color and musical instruments, reducing them to grayish figures. Old Fred, who conducts Sgt. Pepper's Lonely Hearts Club Band, escapes to Liverpool in a yellow submarine and enlists the help of the Beatles to fight the Blue Meanies. The somewhat psychedelic film was made at the height of the band's popularity and during the San Francisco acid-rock explosion. The Beatles penned four new tunes for the soundtrack, including "Hey Bulldog," "It's All Too Much," "All Together Now," and "Only A Northern Song."

Animation cel from the motion picture *Yellow Submarine*, 1968. Courtesy of the Library of Congress.

Sympathy for the Devil (originally titled *One Plus One*), 1968

One of the rare English-language movies by French film giant Jean-Luc Godard, *Sympathy for the Devil* is a heady, anti-intellectual polemic against western culture, an argument made by documenting 1960s British and American counterculture as a revolutionary force. Although the extensive political footage is interesting to students of Marxism and revolution, the film is intriguing to rock fans for the way it captures on camera the creation of the title track, one of the greatest Rolling Stones songs ever. The impossible-to-find director's cut *One Plus One* reportedly contains more extensive Stones footage, but as it was released, *Sympathy for the Devil* was a gem for Stones fans and one of the more captivating documentaries of the song process.

Monterey Pop, 1968

Originally shot as a film for ABC television, *Monterey Pop* wound up as an eighty-minute theatrical release and one of the most important film documents of the 1960s rock scene. An abbreviated chronicle of the crucial 1967 Monterey Pop Festival in Monterey, California, the film features electric performances by some of the hottest acts in underground rock, including the Mamas and the Papas, Canned Heat, Simon and Garfunkel, Jefferson Airplane, Big Brother and the Holding Company, the Animals, the Jimi Hendrix

Experience, the Who, and Otis Redding. The footage of Redding, Hendrix, and the Who is especially important—Hendrix and the Who broke out in America largely because of their excellent performances at Monterey, and Redding's show was his first major performance in front of a predominantly white audience, making him an instant crossover success.

Director D. A. Pennebaker admirably captures more than just the performances. The Monterey event was emblematic of a new type of phenomenon: the rock festival, an affair that depended on interaction between the audience and

Poster for the film *Monterey Pop*, 1968. Foundation/The Kobol Collection.

performer (see Chapter 7, "The Festival Is Born"). Pennebaker was lauded for capturing numerous crowd shots in addition to the music, demonstrating as much an "in front of the stage" approach as a "behind the scenes" look. One only has to see the footage of Mama Cass being moved to ecstasy by Janis Joplin's performance to see the impact underground rock festivals were having on their audiences. This attempt at a crowd-oriented approach would be taken a step further—just as the music festival was—when Michael Wadleigh would film the Woodstock affair two years later. But for the most part, *Monterey Pop* is an amazing peep at the music of the San Francisco rock scene when the bands were young and energetic and the spirit of revolution was in the air.

Easy Rider, 1969

The writing and directing debut of actor Dennis Hopper, *Easy Rider* encapsulates for many the disappearance of living as a free spirit in America. Hopper and Peter Fonda (in the role that defined his career) play two motorcycle-riding hippies who travel cross-country, seeking the myth of "America" and encountering a string of unusual characters along the way. As a movie closely tied with rock's counterculture at the end of the 1960s, the film is an extraordinary fictionalization of the hippies' attempt to live outside mainstream consumer society.

Film still from the motion picture *Easy Rider*, 1969. Courtesy of Photofest.

The film's soundtrack is a bold step beyond Simon and Garfunkel's relatively inoffensive folk rock in *The Graduate*. Featuring songs by Bob Dylan, Roger McGuinn (of the Byrds), Jimi Hendrix, the Band, the Electric Prunes, and Electric Flag, the music is a powerful assertion of underground rock as the soundtrack to living free and easy in America's broad heartland. Especially noteworthy is the inclusion of the Steppenwolf song "Born to Be Wild" on the soundtrack, which became the theme song for the movie and permanently created an association between the tune and the film's outlaw biker theme—the song's famous lyrics "heavy metal thunder" (composed more than a year before the film was made) were written specifically to capture the feel of a car or motorcycle rumbling down a desolate highway.

Alice's Restaurant, 1969

A somewhat goofy, almost quaint look at the interaction between naive hippies and "the Man" in Vietnam-era America, *Alice's Restaurant* is a timeless film about the idealism of 1960s youth and the barriers that brought it to an end. Very closely based on Arlo Guthrie's clever, eighteen-plus-minute song *Alice's Restaurant Massacree* (and starring Guthrie as the autobiographical character in the tune), the film tells the story of the ingenuous Arlo, who got arrested for littering after trying to help a friend dump some garbage, and the problems it causes him down the road when he is drafted into the Army. Although the film does not have a rock soundtrack beyond the folkie title song, it remains a staple of the era's counterculture for the deft way it captures hippie innocence and youthful enthusiasm when rock was still in its adolescence.

Woodstock, 1970

One of the cornerstones of the 1960s rock scene in popular memory is the Woodstock Music and Arts Fair in 1969. Woodstock was the "über-festival," the largest and most peaceful music gathering in hippiedom, and either you were there or you were not. If you were, your credibility is intact, but if you were not, maybe you can fake it by watching this highly praised chronicle of the event. *Woodstock*, which won the Oscar for best documentary, is a broad yet detailed look at the festival, from the first tractor coming over the hill a week before the event to the massive cleanup effort afterward. In between the two lies another world, director Michael Wadleigh showing every aspect of the event in vivid detail—naked campers in the lake, free spirits dancing in the mud, the National Guard distributing food and medical supplies, the occasional partaking of banned substances (including Jerry Garcia holding a joint up to the camera and deadpanning "Marijuana. Exhibit A"), and, of course, blistering performances by a who is who of top American acts of the day. Wadleigh ingeniously weaves two and sometimes three camera shots on the screen at once, side by side, giving viewers the feeling that they cannot quite catch everything being shown, and a sense that the festival was just too much for one person to take in. Another advantage of such montage technique is that viewers get to see about eight hours of footage in a three-hour film, so that when they get to the end, they feel like they just endured the actual festival.

Although some of the festival's artists opted not to appear in the film, the footage still contains excellent performances by bands like Santana, the Who, Sha-Na-Na, Ten Years After, Jimi Hendrix, Richie Havens, Joe Cocker, Joan Baez, and Crosby, Stills & Nash. The film serves as a cultural weigh station

Poster for the film *Woodstock*, 1970. Courtesy of the Library of Congress.

between *Monterey Pop* and *Gimme Shelter*, the height of counterculture idealism born of Monterey's good vibes, which all came crashing down months later
at Altamont (see Chapter 7, "The Festival Is Born").

Gimme Shelter, 1970

Between 1966 and 1969, the rock festival grew from the 3,000-member
crowd at San Francisco's Love Pageant Rally in Panhandle Park to the
400,000-plus fans at the Woodstock Music and Arts Fair in upstate New York.
During the same period, the Rolling Stones grew roughly proportionately in
popularity, ending a smashing 1969 American tour with a free concert at Altamont Speedway near Oakland, California (see Chapter 7, "The Festival Is
Born"). If Woodstock was the culmination of 1960s idealism, then the tragedy
at Altamont was the drunk drive home after the victory party.

Although *Gimme Shelter* was originally intended to be a documentary of the
Stones' tour, the Altamont disaster created a whole different beast. The performance footage is excellent, with the Stones at their angsty, bad-boy best,
but it is all a lead-up to the death of Meredith Hunter at the hands of the
Hell's Angels the band had hired as security for the event. Several thousand
were injured by the rowdy Angels that weekend, and the cameramen (including future *Star Wars* creator George Lucas) put themselves right in the middle
of it, capturing not only the Stones at their best but 1960s counterculture at
its worst.

Let It Be, 1970

In stark contrast to the goofy, fun-loving Beatles films of the 1960s, *Let It Be*
is an intimate look at the Beatles drawing their final breaths as a band, tired of
the fame, tired of the drama, and tired of each other. Though originally meant
to be a documentary of the Beatles returning to their happy-go-lucky days as a
fun band amid reports of their demise (the working title was the optimistic *Get
Back*), it turned out to be a valuable record of the group falling apart. With
specters like Billy Preston, George Martin, and Yoko Ono haunting the film,
it's clear that the Beatles have evolved from a rock group to an industry, and
any attempt to return to purity and innocence is futile.

The Beatles continued to produce some excellent work after this film, but it
was clear that their time as a foursome was limited, as the members were already embarking on individual projects by 1970. For fans of the group, the
film is an intimate, must-see document that the band ultimately did not want
to see released, as it often portrays feuds and tensions that undermine the
positive Beatles myth. Still, past all of the drama, the final scene with the
band jamming on a rooftop has achieved legendary status in rock lore, a
thrilling performance that tells viewers that although the group is still capable
of blowing away the competition, maybe this would be a good time to just
let it be.

200 Motels, 1971

A highly stylized look at life on the road with Frank Zappa and the Mothers of Invention, *200 Motels* is Zappa's first feature film (after creating several shorts). Part documentary, part circus, the often bizarre film may be for Zappa fans only, but it is particularly noteworthy in that it is a forerunner to the music video that would become so popular a decade later with the advent of MTV. *200 Motels* was also the first movie to be shot on video and then transferred to film for theatrical release, making it much cheaper to create. Reportedly taking only a week to film, the movie features Ringo Starr as the Zappa-like "Larry the Dwarf," the Who's Keith Moon as a groupie-obsessed nun, and performances by the Royal Philharmonic Orchestra. Like much of Zappa's work, the film is highly original and clever but just plain weird, an oddly psychedelic romp by an artist who was adamantly against drug use.

Fillmore, 1972

Ostensibly a film about the closing of the important concert venue Fillmore West in 1971, the movie is more a biopic of concert guru Bill Graham, rock's most successful promoter, who owned San Francisco's Fillmore West and New York's Fillmore East from 1968 to 1971 (see Chapter 1, "The Psychedelic Experience"). Performances by the likes of the Grateful Dead, Santana, and Jefferson Airplane give the viewer a glimpse at these seminal groups in their heyday, but the historic value of the film lies in seeing Graham as a self-appointed martyr, giving up his dream of being an actor to book shows in the 1960s Bay Area, ultimately enduring the slings and arrows of greedy agents and egotistical performers to get concerts off the ground. Though the closing of the venues was to mark Graham's departure from the promotion business, he continued to run shows out of San Francisco's Winterland through the 1970s.

Ziggy Stardust and the Spiders from Mars, 1973

In 1972, David Bowie created the androgynous, otherworldly character Ziggy Stardust, a science-fiction hero that spoke to every music fan who ever felt like an outsider. The personality launched Bowie to stardom in the United States, making him the sovereign of glam rock. On July 3, 1973, Bowie retired the character at a show in London, captured on film by *Monterey Pop* director D. A. Pennebaker. The concert documentary nets Bowie at his absolute peak, belting out some of his greatest hits before casting off Ziggy for the equally surreal character Aladdin Sane. The filming, unfortunately, does not do Bowie justice, shot from the theater floor in ambient light. The concert footage took ten years to find a distributor, by which time it was relatively passé as a rockumentary. Though even the much-improved remastered version (in 2000) does not hold a candle to the great concert films like *Monterey Pop*, *Woodstock*, and *The Last Waltz*, it is worth a look simply to see David Bowie in his prime.

HIPPIES ON BROADWAY

In late 1971, at least six rock musicals were running on Broadway. Common sense would dictate that the conservative, often stodgy theater scene would be the last bastion against rock influence, but when the walls fell, they came down fast and hard. Only four years earlier, there was no such thing as a rock musical or rock opera. In the fall of 1967, underground rock was seeking to find a place in film; rock's first major magazine, *Rolling Stone*, was just hitting the stands; and Tom Donahue was only beginning to make waves at KMPX. But on October 17, 1967, the rock musical *Hair* landed like an A-bomb on New York's theater scene.

Beginning as the opening production for Manhattan's 1967 Shakespeare Festival, *Hair* ran for eight weeks before moving to a club called Cheetah, then premiered on Broadway at the Biltmore on April 29, 1968. The story is an amalgam of all the counterculture issues of the day—racism, women's liberation, open sexuality, violence, drugs, and, ultimately, acceptance of hippie values by mainstream America. The play follows a group of New York hippies called "the Tribe" as they try to help their friend Claude, who has been drafted to fight in Vietnam. Along the way, the audience is treated to full frontal male and female nudity, a copious amount of filthy language, and regular doses of fairly mild—though shocking by Broadway standards—rock and roll. According to the opening night review by then dean of theater critics, the *New York Times'* Clive Barnes, *Hair* was "the first Broadway musical in some time to have the authentic voice of today rather than the day before yesterday."[4]

Billing itself as "the American Tribal Love-Rock Musical," *Hair* began as somewhat of a novelty on Broadway, a chance for clean, decent theater patrons to go slumming with the hippies and take in the play's controversial nude scene. Before anyone noticed what was happening, the musical had played to thousands of patrons and made millions of dollars. Beyond the original themes and music it brought to Broadway for the first time, *Hair* significantly curtailed censorship in American theater as it fought legal battles over obscene lyrics and desecration of the American flag. Two cases eventually wound up in the Supreme Court, and over time *Hair* became a symbol of free speech in American theater.

By the time it closed on July 1, 1972, the play had run for 1,742 performances and spawned approximately two dozen road company productions, reaching millions of audience members all over the world. In 1979, Milos Forman directed a successful film version of the play. Hundreds of recordings were made of the play's score, and the original cast recording spent thirteen weeks on top of the charts in 1969, making it one of the Top 20 recordings of the 1960s.

Hair paved the way for rock music on Broadway, and its influence was quickly felt. Broadway's second rock musical, *Jesus Christ Superstar*, came hot on its heels, directed by Tom O'Horgan (who also directed *Hair*). Written by Tim Rice and Andrew Lloyd Webber, *Superstar* spent a good deal of time in secondary theaters until reaching the Hellinger Theatre in 1971, and its soundtrack sold more than 3 million copies before the play ever saw the Broadway stage. Though rock critics felt the music was years behind current rock styles, *Rolling Stone* called it "a hell of a show, the *2001* of the stage, a rich, gaudy, vulgar, stupefying spectacle."[5] Soon rock musicals were just another genre of Broadway theater, with shows like *Stomp, Inner City, Godspell, Joseph and the Amazing Technicolor Dreamcoat*, and *Grease* all delivering variations of rock to the theater audience by 1973.

MAGAZINES AND LITERATURE

The Beats

> "Sal, we gotta go and never stop going till we get there."
> "Where we going, man?"
> "I don't know but we gotta go."

This conversation, appearing in Jack Kerouac's seminal work *On the Road*, deftly captures the essence of the beat generation of the 1940s and 1950s—adventurous wanderers who never knew what was around the corner but were always eager to find out. The characters are Sal Paradise and Dean Moriarty, based respectively on Kerouac himself and his friend Neal Cassady, two figures who—along with literary greats William Burroughs, Allen Ginsberg, and a few other unruly figures—captured the imagination of millions with their real-life and fictional exploits along America's long highways and down its dark alleys.

These figures, popularly remembered as "beatniks," or "the Beats," were an enormous influence on the experimental culture of 1960s San Francisco, even coining the term "hippie" to refer to one who is somewhat—but not entirely—hip. Their presence in 1960s San Francisco—some physically, others in myth only—helped foster the sense of experimentation that brought about the great divergence of musical styles discussed within these pages. The passage above was written in the early 1950s, but carried great weight among San Francisco's 1960s counterculture as a mantra for experimentation, particularly among its musical set. Music ceased to be a means through which to obtain the specific end of hearing your three-minute pop song on the radio. Music came to be seen as a journey, an expedition of experimentation with no goal in sight beyond the immediate sensory thrill of the process itself. This reexamination of musical creation gave birth to some of rock music's key innovations in the 1960s—the guitar solo; conversations between instruments; and the hallmark of psychedelic music, the jam session.

If the 1960s had its own beatnik, it was Ken Kesey, the author of *One Flew over the Cuckoo's Nest* and leader of the bizarre assemblage of lunatics called the Merry Pranksters (which, off and on, featured the legendary Neal Cassady himself). Figures like Kesey, Cassady, and Ginsberg were honored heroes of San Francisco's underbelly, revered as true expeditionaries and keepers of the Beat flame. Without their presence and influence, the Bay Area would have been a very different place, and the music that flowed from its shores, shaping all of the genres discussed in this book, would not have been nearly as adventurous. The musicians of 1960s San Francisco did not know where they were going, but it was a good thing they went.

Rolling Stone and the New Rock Criticism

On October 18, 1967, at about 5:30 p.m., the first issue of *Rolling Stone* magazine rolled off the press, dated November 9. The magazine was to be published every other Wednesday, though it took until 1968 to achieve a regular publishing schedule. This premiere issue, only twenty-four pages in length, featured John Lennon in army fatigues and a helmet—a scene from his new film *How I Won the War*, in which John plays World War II British soldier Private Gripweed. The feature stories included a rundown of the finances of the Monterey Pop Festival, an update on the shake-ups of the Bay Area's FM stations, and a look at the progress of Jefferson Airplane's next album.

From such a small start, the magazine became the pinnacle of rock journalism. *Rolling Stone* was a breath of fresh air in the stagnant music press, which up to then consisted of minor fanzines and trade publications that did not come close to reporting the breadth and depth of the new rock scene. San Francisco arts journalist Jann Wenner teamed up with *San Francisco Chronicle* music critic Ralph Gleason to create *Rolling Stone* with $7,500 borrowed from friends and credit from a printing company. Though decidedly centered on the Bay Area scene, the magazine quickly increased its national and international coverage to become the nation's leading rock magazine by 1970, employing some of rock's greatest critics, including Jon Landau, Lester Bangs, and Greil Marcus.

The first U.S. equivalent to British rock journals *Melody Maker* and *New Musical Express*, *Rolling Stone* became known for its in-depth interviews, behind-the-scenes coverage, and authoritative album reviews. Beyond music, *Rolling Stone* covered rock's periphery issues, such as film, politics, television, and theater, even achieving respect from the mainstream press with its penetrating coverage of the Altamont fiasco in 1969 and a feature on the Charles Manson family. With the addition of Hunter S. Thompson to the writing staff in 1970, the magazine pioneered stream-of-consciousness "gonzo" journalism.

Though it lost much of its counterculture cachet as it moved away from music to become a general culture magazine through the 1970s—particularly after its move to New York in 1977—its initial brave, headfirst dive into the music scene served as a catalyst for a golden era of rock criticism between the late 1960s and mid-1970s, within its own pages as well as in those of other publications it inspired. In March 1969, publisher Barry Kramer debuted the hard-edged magazine *Creem* in Detroit, Michigan, covering the Motown sound, the early punk group MC5, and the hard-hitting rock bands emerging from Britain. With its talented writers Robert Christgau, Patti Smith, Cameron Crowe, and Dave Marsh, as well as already renowned critics Lester Bangs and Greil Marcus, *Creem* built a reputation as a populist magazine, focusing on the cutting edge of rock and roll.

Even before *Creem* and *Rolling Stone*, there was *Crawdaddy!*—one of America's first all-rock magazines, having premiered in February 1966. Foregoing the political and social commentary of *Rolling Stone* and its imitators, *Crawdaddy!* focused solely on rock music from a serious fan's perspective, that of publisher Paul Williams. Though it never achieved the mainstream success of its competitors, for serious rock fans, *Crawdaddy!* was the peak of rock journalism.

Crawdaddy! inspired a series of other fanzines around the country, including the *Mojo-Navigator R&R News*. San Francisco's first music magazine, the short-lived *Mojo* was started by David Harris and Greg Shaw in late 1966, and featured some of the first interviews with future rock giants the Grateful Dead, Big Brother and the Holding Company, and Country Joe and the Fish. Subsequent fanzines like *Big Beat*, *Stormy Weather*, *Record Exchanger*, and *Who Put the Bomp*—most of them West Coast publications, and most short-lived—are veritable time capsules of the era, containing music of a time long gone covered by its most ardent fans.

ROLLING STONE COVERS

Since shortly after it appeared in 1967, getting one's face on the cover of *Rolling Stone* was one of the highest honors for a rock musician. In 1972, Dr. Hook and the Medicine Show even wrote a song about it; "The Cover of Rolling Stone" made it to No. 6 on the American charts. Below is a list of the first twenty-five *Rolling Stone* covers, stretching from November 1967 to January 1969.

Issue 1: John Lennon
Issue 2: Tina Turner
Issue 3: The Beatles and staff
Issue 4: Donovan, Jimi Hendrix, and Otis Redding
Issue 5: Jim Morrison
Issue 6: Janis Joplin
Issue 7: Jimi Hendrix
Issue 8: Lou Adler and John Phillips
Issue 9: Cartoons of John Lennon and Paul McCartney
Issue 10: Eric Clapton
Issue 11: Unnamed model for issue on rock fashions
Issue 12: Bob Dylan
Issue 13: Tiny Tim
Issue 14: Frank Zappa
Issue 15: Mick Jagger
Issue 16: The Band
Issue 17: Mickey Mouse
Issue 18: Pete Townshend
Issue 19: Mick Jagger
Issue 20: The Beatles
Issue 21: Cartoon of soldiers
Issue 22: John Lennon and Yoko Ono
Issue 23: Doug and Sean Sahm
Issue 24: The Beatles
Issue 25: Rob Tyner

NOTES

1. Friedlander 1996, 101.

2. www.wfmu.org.

3. Ben Fong-Torres, "Radio: One Toke Behind the Line," *Rolling Stone*, April 15, 1970, 10.

4. Clive Barnes, "'Hair': It's Fresh and Frank," *New York Times*, April 30, 1968.

5. Tom Topor, "Rock and Roll, Dead, Takes Over Broadway," *Rolling Stone*, December 23, 1971, 6.

A-TO-Z OF ROCK, 1967–1973

Bold-faced terms refer to other entries in this A-to-Z chapter.

Abraxas, 1970. Arguably **Santana**'s finest album, following an auspicious start one year earlier with their debut release *Santana*, which heralded a bright new star in frontman Carlos Santana. With timeless tracks such as "Black Magic Woman" and "Oye Como Va," this sophomore effort secured a place for Latin rhythms in the hard-rock era.

Adler, Lou (b. 1933). As a songwriter, producer, manager, and promoter for acts such as Jan and Dean, Sam Cooke, and **Carole King** in the 1950s and 1960s, Adler was already a prominent figure in the West Coast music scene when he founded Dunhill Records in 1964. Dunhill would be a force in the growth of **folk rock** with artists such as Barry McGuire and the **Mamas and the Papas**. After selling Dunhill in 1966, Adler became one of the main organizers of the seminal 1967 **Monterey Pop Festival** before founding Ode Records, the outlet for folk-rock heavies Scott McKenzie and Carole King.

Alice Cooper. Shock rocker Vincent Furnier formed Alice Cooper (later adopting the name for himself) in 1969 when he signed to **Frank Zappa**'s Straight label after several other incarnations in the L.A. club scene. Known for their outrageous stagecraft—including fake executions during their performances—the band released two unnoticed albums on Straight before signing to Warner Brothers in 1970, beginning a string of hits with the single "Eighteen" on *Love It to Death* in 1971. Bigger success with subsequent albums *Killer*, *School's Out*, and *Billion Dollar Babies* elevated the band to metal-god status and established Furnier as an icon of shock rock. (See Chapter 2, "Hard-Rock Lightning, Heavy-Metal Thunder.")

The Allman Brothers Band. Formed in Macon, Georgia, in 1969 by brothers Duane and Gregg Allman, this quintessential **southern rock** group married delta blues with **psychedelia**-inspired improvisation to provide a southern San Francisco sound immortalized in their first two releases, *The Allman Brothers Band* and *Idlewild South*. Powered by two drummers and Duane's awesome slide guitar (showcased in his contribution to the **Derek and the Dominos** album *Layla and Other Assorted Love Songs* in 1970), the group pounded out classics such as "Whipping Post" in live shows that have become legendary. Though producing good albums into the 1970s such as *Eat a Peach* and *Brothers and Sisters*, the band never really recovered from the death of Duane in a motorcycle accident in 1971, seven months after a live show that was captured in their seminal album **Live at Fillmore East**. (See Chapter 4, "The South Rises Again.")

Alpert, Herb (b. 1935). An accomplished producer, trumpet player, and songwriter (co-writing "Wonderful World" with **Lou Adler**), Alpert's main influence was as the cofounder of A&M Records with promoter Jerry Moss. The label scored hits in the 1960s and 1970s with acts such as the **Flying Burrito Brothers, Joe Cocker, Carole King**, and the Carpenters, as well as Alpert himself backed by the Tijuana Brass. In the later 1960s, Herb Alpert and the Tijuana Brass placed five albums at the top of the charts for a total of twenty-six weeks at the No. 1 spot, making him one of the twenty most successful artists of the decade.

Altamont (December 6, 1969). Coming only months after the peaceful festival at **Woodstock**, this free performance at the Altamont Speedway near San Francisco was marred by a number of violent scuffles that brought about the death of eighteen-year-old Meredith Hunter, who was beaten by a group of Hell's Angels hired to provide security at the event. Although the Angels were held responsible, **Rolling Stones** frontman Mick Jagger received much criticism as a main sponsor of the event and for continuing his performance as Hunter was being killed only yards away (though Jagger has contended since that he did not know what was going on). The grisly scene is featured on the film *Gimme Shelter*, released the following year. (See Chapter 7, "The Festival Is Born.")

America. Formed in London in 1970 by sons of military families stationed in England, the **Crosby, Stills & Nash**–influenced trio scored a major hit in the United Kingdom in 1972 with their first single, "A Horse with No Name." The band's debut album *America* rose to No. 1 in the United States, paving the way for future soft-rock hits like "Lonely People" and "I Need You."

***American Pie* (1971).** **Don McLean**'s paean to Buddy Holly on this album's eponymous song is widely regarded as one of the all-time acoustic greats, securing a permanent spot for itself at campfires and jukeboxes around the country. The single reached No. 1 in the United States and No. 2 in the

United Kingdom, where, soon after, another single from the album, "Vincent," topped the charts. (See Chapter 5, "Folk Rock and Its Successors.")

The Animals. Also known as **Eric Burdon** and the Animals and Eric Burdon and the New Animals, this 1960s club-circuit band from England backed up blues legends like John Lee Hooker and Sonny Boy Williamson on UK tours before scoring a major hit around the world with their remake of the traditional "House of the Rising Sun" in 1964. Before disbanding in 1968, the band dabbled in **psychedelia**, scoring with covers like "We Gotta Get Out of This Place" and originals like "Monterey," a Burdon-penned tribute to the famous 1967 festival.

Are You Experienced? (1967). Although this debut album of the **Jimi Hendrix** Experience only reached No. 5 on the charts, partially due to the near-simultaneous release of *Sgt. Pepper's*, it endured in the Top 40 for an amazing seventy-seven weeks—longer than any **Beatles** or **Elvis Presley** album. Timed to follow his legendary live performance at **Monterey Pop**, which launched him to national stardom, the release contains many of Hendrix's all-time classics, including "Purple Haze," "Hey Joe," "Fire," and "The Wind Cries Mary." (See Chapter 2, "Hard-Rock Lightning, Heavy-Metal Thunder.")

Art Rock. See **Progressive Rock.**

The Association. Distinctive for their mellow psychedelic harmonies on songs like "Along Comes Mary," "Never My Love," and "Cherish," this easy-listening staple had a few Top 10 hits but never developed a large fan base for their pop-tinged folk.

The Atlanta Rhythm Section. Composed of studio musicians from Studio One in Doraville, Georgia, this talented southern rock band differed from their contemporaries in that their emphasis was on studio albums rather than live shows. Seeing a slow climb to popularity through the 1970s, the group saw success late in the decade with their hits "So into You" and "Imaginary Lover." (See Chapter 4, "The South Rises Again.")

Baez, Joan (b. 1941). Though not a full-fledged rock-and-roll artist, the folkie Baez was strongly affiliated with the civil-rights and antiwar movements of the period for which rock and folk formed. Achieving critical and commercial success in the early 1960s with covers of traditional and folk tunes, Baez brought many other songwriters to national attention, including **Bob Dylan**, who toured with Baez early in his career and whose songs Baez made into a tribute album with 1968's *Any Day Now*. (See Chapter 5, "Folk Rock and Its Successors.")

The Band. Originally called the Hawks and employed as the back-up and touring band for **Bob Dylan's** notorious electric coming-out period of the mid-1960s, this soulful group changed their name after holing up with the recluse Dylan in upstate New York in 1967 and 1968. The music composed in the house (dubbed "Big Pink") was released by Dylan in 1975 as *The Basement Tapes*. In the meantime, the newly renamed group, including future solo artists Robbie Robertson and Levon Helm, became pioneers of a rootsy, confessional brand of Americana rock with their first album (sans Dylan), **Music from Big Pink**, in 1968, quickly followed by *The Band* in 1969. Although other fine albums followed, they are mostly remembered for this early work and for Martin Scorsese's 1978 film about their final performance, *The Last Waltz*. (See Chapter 5, "Folk Rock and Its Successors.")

The Beach Boys. The legendary California group led by brothers Carl, Dennis, and Brian Wilson suffered the extremes of rock stardom from the mid-1960s to the mid-1970s—artistic coups like 1966's *Pet Sounds* and 1974's *Endless Summer*, as well as personal tragedies involving drug abuse, depression, and major career setbacks. More than just a surf band, the remarkably prolific group (releasing eleven albums in their first four years) felt compelled to compete with the other top acts of the day, including the burgeoning San Francisco bands and the **Beatles**, whom they replaced in the UK music press as the world's favorite group in 1966.[1] Known mainly for their immediately identifiable harmonies, the real engine behind their success—as well as many of their problems—was the deeply troubled Brian Wilson, who was eventually appreciated as one of the great composers of the era.

The Beatles. It would be difficult to overstate the quality of the Beatles' work in the mid-1960s or their importance to the rock era. After establishing themselves as more than just a pop trend with monumental albums like *Rubber Soul* in 1965 and *Revolver* in 1966, the English quartet—**John Lennon**, Paul McCartney, **George Harrison**, and Ringo Starr—released their tour de force **Sgt. Pepper's Lonely Hearts Club Band** in 1967 to critical acclaim and record sales. But as *Sgt. Pepper's* marked their highest peak, it also marked the beginning of their descent. Before the album was even released, they had performed their last official concert together, and their next few albums, though still remarkable works, were more compilations of individual efforts than the real teamwork we see pre–*Sgt. Pepper's*. Outside their music, the members were heavily occupied with film projects such as **Yellow Submarine**, a Beatles boutique in London, their company Apple Corps, and various solo projects. Despite these distractions, the band was able to leave behind excellent albums even as they fell apart, releasing the fantastic *The Beatles* (aka *The White Album*) in 1968 and the remarkable *Abbey Road* in 1969. In 1970, the band released *Let It Be* and a "Greatest Hits" album, *Hey Jude*, but even the five No. 1 singles between the two were not enough to keep the group together as they went their separate ways, but still on top.

Beck, Jeff (b. 1944). Standing alongside **Eric Clapton**, **Jimi Hendrix**, and Jimmy Page as one of the guitar gods of the hard-rock era, Jeff Beck's blistering fretwork and distortion techniques earned him his first major gig as Clapton's replacement in the **Yardbirds**. After walking away from the band in 1966 due to conflicts with fellow Yardbird Page, he formed the Jeff Beck Group with future **Faces** members **Rod Stewart** and Ron Wood, releasing several albums that cemented him as a guitar virtuoso, and providing a sound later mimicked by Page in **Led Zeppelin**. Though a major influence on later **heavy-metal** groups, Beck was a chameleon who continuously reinvented himself, later incorporating styles such as jazz and electronica into his repertoire. (See Chapter 2, "Hard-Rock Lightning, Heavy-Metal Thunder.")

The Bee Gees. Formed by Gibb brothers Barry, Robin, and Maurice while in their mid-teens (the name is short for "Brothers Gibb") and later adding attendant musicians, the Bee Gees are best remembered for their string of disco hits in the mid-1970s, particularly on the soundtracks to *Saturday Night Fever* and *Grease* (for which Barry Gibb wrote the title track). In the 1960s, however, they were a different sound altogether, earning comparison to the **Beatles** for excellent albums like *Bee Gees 1st* and *Horizontal*, and taking stabs at following in the footsteps of **psychedelia** on later, less successful releases. Much like the **Beach Boys**—another major family group of the period—they faced inner strife and occasional breakups, but survived to become one of the most prominent acts of the 1970s.

The Be-In (January 14, 1967). Also known as "the Gathering of the Tribes," the winter solstice festival in San Francisco's Golden Gate Park brought together between 20,000 and 30,000 hippies and "wanna-beatniks" to eschew politics and protest for a day of just "being." The remarkably peaceful assembly (two cops, no fights) featured performances by the **Grateful Dead**, **Big Brother and the Holding Company**, and others, and included the presence of such transcendental luminaries as Allen Ginsberg and Timothy Leary. The event is remembered fondly as the closest idealists of the time ever got to achieving their dreams of peace and love, no strings attached. (See Chapter 7, "The Festival Is Born.")

Big Brother and the Holding Company. See **Joplin, Janis**.

Black Sabbath. Despite a series of changes in their lineup from the mid-1970s to the 1990s, the original Black Sabbath, with singer Ozzy Osbourne at the helm, was one of the prototypical **heavy-metal** bands, scoring instant success with their 1970 debut *Black Sabbath*, which launched them into stardom. A string of consistently powerful releases over the next few years—including *Paranoid*, *Master of Reality*, and *Sabbath Bloody Sabbath*—earned them criticism as Satanists for the dark themes and stage antics (which included Osbourne biting the head off a bat) but secured their place as true legends in the annals of heavy metal. (See Chapter 2, "Hard-Rock Lightning, Heavy-Metal Thunder.")

Blind Faith. This instant supergroup—formed by **Cream**'s **Eric Clapton** and Ginger Baker, Steve Winwood (**Traffic**), and Rick Grech (Family)—launched their very short career at a 100,000-strong free concert in London's Hyde Park in 1969. Despite a successful U.S. tour and a million-selling debut album featuring the Winwood-penned classic "Can't Find My Way Home," the group disbanded the following year in search of other projects.

Blood, Sweat & Tears. Founded by Blues Project alumnus **Al Kooper** in 1967, this large ensemble moved away from the popular guitar-driven rock of the day to a rock-jazz fusion flavored by Kooper's bluesy organ, evident on their 1968 debut *Child Is Father to the Man.* Kooper left the band before the release of their second album—the masterpiece *Blood, Sweat & Tears,* which included the top-selling singles "You've Made Me So Very Happy," "And When I Die," and "Spinning Wheel." Although they had several more moderately successful albums, it was this sophomore effort for which they are remembered.

Bloomfield, Mike (1944–1981). Best remembered as **Bob Dylan**'s electric guitarist during Dylan's electric phase in the mid-1960s, Bloomfield was one of the finest white blues players of his day. His work with the **Paul Butterfield** Blues Band, **Stephen Stills**, and **Al Kooper** earned him respect as America's top gun until **Jimi Hendrix** stole the scene. In 1967, Bloomfield formed the short-lived but influential **Electric Flag**, a soul and blues band that inspired a number of imitators. After two excellent joint albums—*Super Session* in 1968 with Stills and Kooper, and *The Live Adventures of Mike Bloomfield and Al Kooper* in 1969—Bloomfield retired from the public scene, releasing occasional material until his death in 1981.

Blue Cheer. Though overshadowed by other **heavy-metal** pioneers like **Black Sabbath**, **Deep Purple**, and **Led Zeppelin**, Blue Cheer was one of the first "loud" bands, a blues-oriented San Francisco trio influenced by **Jimi Hendrix**'s performance at the **Monterey Pop Festival**. Backed by LSD entrepreneur **Augustus Owsley Stanley** (they got their name from one of Stanley's LSD strains), Blue Cheer was one of the last truly original sounds to come out of San Francisco in the late 1960s.

***Bookends* (1968).** Recorded at the height of **Simon and Garfunkel**'s fame and talent, *Bookends* is considered by many to be their finest album. Featuring **folk-rock** classics such as "America," "Mrs. Robinson," "Hazy Shade of Winter," and "At the Zoo," the album spent seven weeks at No. 1 and influenced a generation of singer-songwriters in the 1970s.

Booker T. and the MG's. The studio sound behind the famous Stax record label, the MG's backed stars such as **Isaac Hayes**, Albert King, **Otis Redding**, Sam and Dave, and Wilson Pickett on hit after hit, almost single-handedly establishing the sound of Memphis soul, in addition to producing many fine albums of their own through the 1960s and lesser releases in the 1970s. Organist Booker T. Jones also helped write hits such as "Born Under a Bad Sign," and guitarist Steve Cropper co-penned the soul standards "In the Midnight Hour,"

"Knock on Wood," and the Otis Redding hit "(Sittin' on) the Dock of the Bay," which Cropper finished recording after Redding's untimely demise.

Bowie, David (b. 1947). Born David Jones, Bowie changed his name in 1966 to avoid being confused with the popular Monkee. After being largely ignored in his UK homeland, he hit it big in 1969 with "Space Oddity"— released to coincide with the first lunar landing—though his failure to immediately follow up relegated him to one-hit-wonder status. But Bowie rebounded in the early 1970s with a string of powerful albums, including *The Man Who Sold the World*, *Hunky Dory*, ***The Rise and Fall of Ziggy Stardust and the Spiders from Mars***, and *Aladdin Sane*, cementing his status as a futuristic, otherworldy artist. His hypnotic voice and surreal sound were aided by his sexual ambiguity and feminine presence, appearing on album covers and in magazines in dresses, elaborate costumes, and makeup—a challenge to the testosterone-driven rock that preceded him, ushering in a new decade of thoughtful, reflexive music and establishing **glam rock** as the new **psychedelia**. (See Chapter 3, "Glamour Kings: The Birth of Glitter Rock.")

Bread. A soft-rock staple formed in 1968, Bread broke through with their 1970 No. 1 "Make It with You," followed by other candle-lit-evening tunes over the next few years, including "Baby I'm-a Want You" and "Guitar Man."

Brown, James (b. 1928). Always accompanied by epithets such as "soul brother number one," "the godfather of soul," and "the hardest working man in show business," James Brown deserved every one of them, making music a physical act beyond **Elvis Presley**'s hip thrusts and Mick Jagger's strut by incorporating over-the-top vocals and acrobatic dance moves reminiscent of his Pentecostal Baptist roots. The patron saint of the black pride movement of the period, Brown had already become a legend in the early 1960s for his live performances and string of hard-driving funk albums, but created black anthems in the late 1960s with recordings such as *Cold Sweat* and *Say It Loud, I'm Black and I'm Proud*, ultimately releasing an amazing thirty-nine albums in his first ten years of recording.[2]

Browne, Jackson (b. 1948). Jackson Browne's 1972 debut *Jackson Browne: Saturate Before Using* introduced him to the world of 1970s acoustic rock, a genre to which he contributed consistently excellent albums for the remainder of the decade. Browne's songwriting talent also extended to hits for other acts, including "Doctor My Eyes" for the **Jackson Five**, and the Eagles' "Take It Easy," which he co-wrote with Glenn Frey.

Buffalo Springfield. Rivaling the **Byrds** as an influential **folk-rock** group of the 1960s, this short-lived band launched the careers of **Neil Young** and **Stephen Stills** (both later members of **Crosby, Stills, Nash & Young**) and Jim Messina and Richie Furay (both later of Poco). After creating a stir in the Los Angeles club scene shortly after they formed in 1966, the group hit it big with the folk anthem "For What It's Worth," a naked look at the Vietnam protest era. Though only together for two short years, the strong songwriting of Young, Stills, and Furay secured the band status as progenitors in folk-rock history.

Burdon, Eric (b. 1941). Made famous by his guttural vocals in the **Animals'** early hit "House of the Rising Sun" in 1964, Burdon spent the remainder of the decade churning out originals and covers with the band until their demise in 1968. After a few unsuccessful years as an actor, Burdon teamed up with Lee Oskar and a backing band in 1970 to form War, a group that later went on to great success without Burdon, who soon left the band. Burdon attempted several later reunions with the Animals but never regained the status he held in the mid-1960s.

Butterfield, Paul (1942–1987). One of the greatest white blues players of the 1960s, Butterfield is best remembered for his Paul Butterfield Blues Band, which backed up **Bob Dylan** at the 1965 Newport Folk Festival, when Dylan chose to debut his electric sound. Butterfield worked with many of the greats, including Howlin' Wolf, Muddy Waters, Elvin Bishop, and **Mike Bloomfield**, eventually releasing a string of his own albums, among which his debut *Paul Butterfield Blues Band* and sophomore effort *East-West* remain his most memorable.

The Byrds. The originators of folk rock, this Los Angeles quintet was immediately hailed as America's answer to the **Beatles** with their 1965 debut *Mr. Tambourine Man*, featuring the eponymous **Bob Dylan**–penned single that shot to No. 1 in the United States even before Dylan released his own version. After their excellent second album of the same year *Turn! Turn! Turn!*—whose title track, a biblical Pete Seeger tune, also went to No. 1—critical hits including "Eight Miles High" and "So You Want to Be a Rock and Roll Star" followed. But the original band was short-lived, with David Crosby departing in 1967 to later join the Byrds-influenced **Crosby, Stills, Nash & Young**, and Gene Clark exiting the band twice due to his fear of flying. Remaining member Roger McGuinn was left to juggle a series of new members, resulting in the surprisingly powerful *The Notorious Byrd Brothers* and ***Sweetheart of the Rodeo***, the latter planting the seeds of the country-rock movement, which grew into 1970s acts like the Eagles and Fleetwood Mac. (See Chapter 5, "Folk Rock and Its Successors.")

Canned Heat. Founded in 1966 by blues aficionados Bob "the Bear" Hite and Al "Blind Owl" Wilson, this white blues group was a hit at the **Monterey Pop** and **Woodstock** festivals, but never achieved large commercial success. Their moderate 1968 hit "Going Up the Country" was a highlight at Woodstock and became an unofficial anthem of the festival.

Capricorn Records. Largely responsible for the growth of **southern rock** from a regional style to a national phenomenon, Capricorn Records brought to prominence such acts as the **Allman Brothers Band**, Wet Willie, and the **Marshall Tucker Band**. Capricorn was founded in Macon, Georgia, in 1969 by Phil Walden—who had managed **Otis Redding**, Percy Sledge, and Sam and Dave—and funded by Atlantic Records through Jerry Wexler; the label was named after Wexler and Walden's mutual birth signs. (See Chapter 4, "The South Rises Again.")

Captain Beefheart. Both a band name and the adopted moniker for founder Don Van Vliet, Captain Beefheart was known early on for impenetrable lyrics and bizarre anti-harmonies, making the group the darling of the underground after their 1967 debut *Safe as Milk*. Their third release—1969's *Trout Mask Replica*, produced by **Frank Zappa**—is almost painful to listen to, hailed by some as one of the great psychedelic albums, and criticized by others as one of the greatest musical practical jokes of all time. (See Chapter 6, "Rock Goes Progressive.")

The Charlatans. Considering their almost nonexistent recording career and the fact that none of their members went on to any great musical success, the Charlatans had a remarkable influence on the future of rock and roll. They were the progenitors of the San Francisco psychedelic scene, essentially the first to treat music as a visual experience, dressing as Wild West outlaws and promoting themselves with the first psychedelic posters—a medium that itself became an independent cultural phenomenon. Starting out as the house band at the Red Dog Saloon in Virginia City, Nevada, in 1965, they were already underground heroes when they moved to San Francisco later that year, influencing such acts as **Big Brother and the Holding Company, the Grateful Dead**, and **Jefferson Airplane**. The band did not last long and released only one song with its original lineup, "The Shadow Knows." (See Chapter 1, "The Psychedelic Experience.")

***Cheap Thrills* (1968).** Though **Big Brother and the Holding Company** was an adequate band, they did not become a national act until they introduced **Janis Joplin** to the world. Because of this fact, this album—the group's major label debut and only release with Joplin at the mic—still survives as one of the great classics of its time, featuring Joplin's unforgettable interpretations of "Summertime," "Piece of My Heart," and "Ball and Chain." Tensions were so high during its recording that even though it launched the band to national prominence, Joplin quickly left after its release, going on to become a major rock star while Big Brother was left in the dust. (See Chapter 1, "The Psychedelic Experience.")

Chicago. Founded in 1966 in its namesake city, the Chicago Transit Authority (renamed Chicago in 1970) was a jazz-rock band similar to its predecessors **Electric Flag** and **Blood, Sweat & Tears**, but with much more stamina and many more hits. After debuting in 1969 with *Chicago Transit Authority*, this horn-heavy band released an average of one album a year over the next decade—every one making the Top 20 list, five of them hitting No. 1. The band continued to have milder success with various lineups into the 1990s.

Chicago Transit Authority (1969). The debut album of the Chicago Transit Authority (later renamed **Chicago**), this early incarnation of jazz rock not only presented long-lived singles such as "Does Anybody Really Know What Time It Is" and "Beginnings," but introduced a band that would shape the mellower range of 1970s rock.

Clapton, Eric (b. 1945). One of the single greatest figures in late 1960s and early 1970s rock, Eric Clapton played in an assortment of popular bands, including the **Yardbirds**, John Mayall's Bluesbreakers, **Cream**, **Blind Faith**, and **Derek and the Dominos**. Despite his resistance to being the center of attention, his remarkably evocative blues guitar made him the focus of almost every group he was in, earning him the nickname "God" before he was twenty-one years old. Over the years, Clapton found roles in many of rock's great moments, including playing lead on **George Harrison**'s "While My Guitar Gently Weeps" on *The Beatles*, performing at the 1971 **Concert for Bangladesh**, and guest appearing at the **Band**'s famous Last Waltz concert, in addition to playing at one time or another with **John Lennon**, **Bob Dylan**, Phil Collins, Duane Allman, **Aretha Franklin**, Roger Daltrey, **Stephen Stills**, and many other rock luminaries. After his many friends rallied to bring him back from a two-year, heroin-fueled depression in the early 1970s, he went on to craft great music for decades, making him one of the most consistent hitmakers in rock, with chart-toppers like "For Your Love" and "Strange Brew" in the 1960s, "Layla" and "Cocaine" in the 1970s, "I Can't Stand It" and "Tearing Us Apart" in the 1980s, and "Tears in Heaven" and an acoustic version of "Layla" in the 1990s. History will undoubtedly record Clapton as one of rock's most enduring icons. (See Chapter 2, "Hard-Rock Lightning, Heavy-Metal Thunder.")

Cocker, Joe (b. 1944). Joe Cocker burst onto the scene in 1968 with his cover of the **Lennon**/McCartney song "With a Little Help from My Friends," which was a major hit in the United Kingdom and paved the way for his debut album of the same name the following year, through which he was introduced to U.S. audiences, mainly through an appearance on the Ed Sullivan Show and a powerful performance at **Woodstock**. This Sheffield, England native is considered one of the great white soul singers, a label he proved on his subsequent 1969 album *Joe Cocker!* and 1970 *Mad Dogs and Englishmen*, completing a trio of strong releases that saw him interpreting Dave Mason's "Feelin' Alright" and **Leon Russell**'s "Delta Lady" with his guttural, gospel-tinged delivery. Although heavy drinking resulted in a series of forgettable releases through much of the 1970s, he bounced back after drying out in 1982 with several decent albums and a few minor hits.

Concert for Bangledesh (August 1, 1971). The first of the mega-benefit concerts, the Concert for Bangladesh was the brainchild of **Beatle George**

Harrison and revered sitar player **Ravi Shankar**, who asked Harrison to help ease the suffering of refugees from the 1971 India-Pakistan war. The concert, held in New York's Madison Square Garden, featured some of rock's top names, including Harrison, Shankar, Ringo Starr, **Eric Clapton**, and a surprise appearance from the then-reclusive **Bob Dylan**. The concert spawned a film and a live album, and influenced future benefits such as Rock for Kampuchea in 1979 and Farm Aid and Live Aid in 1985.

Cooder, Ry (b. 1947). A self-taught blues player from Los Angeles who formed a short-lived band in 1965 called Rising Sons, Cooder was an extremely flexible studio guitarist, performing with such acts as **Captain Beefheart**, Paul Revere and the Raiders, **Randy Newman**, Little Feat, and the **Rolling Stones**. While his own albums—which included a range of styles such as blues, jazz, dixie, reggae, and Hawaiian—failed to catch on with the wider public, he is acknowledged within the musical community as one of rock's most versatile guitarists, later in his career earning some fame for his work composing movie soundtracks.

Cosmo's Factory (1970). Widely hailed as **Creedence Clearwater Revival**'s finest work, the fifth CCR album spent nine weeks at No. 1 and spawned three gold singles—"Travelin' Band," "Up Around the Bend," and "Lookin' Out My Back Door." This essential rock classic also included a lengthy remake of the **Motown** hit "I Heard It Through the Grapevine," and was one of the top-selling albums of the year.

Country Joe and the Fish. Initially a jug band centered around folkie Country Joe McDonald, the politically active group were a rallying point for the anti-Vietnam protest movement of the late 1960s in San Francisco. Perhaps most famous for the F-I-S-H cheer featured in the documentary of **Woodstock** and the antiwar anthem "I Feel Like I'm Fixin' to Die Rag," the band went through a constantly changing lineup, preventing them from ever achieving major sales success beyond the Bay Area. (See Chapter 1, "The Psychedelic Experience.")

Crawdaddy! One of America's first rock magazines in 1966, *Crawdaddy!* helped inspire later heavyweights *Rolling Stone* and *Creem* to take on the dynamic rock world of the late 1960s. Though *Crawdaddy!* never saw the mainstream success of its followers, it was widely respected as one of America's best fanzines, eschewing general cultural commentary to focus on rock music from a fan's perspective.

Cream. The most hard-hitting rock trio of their time, Cream featured classically trained bassist Jack Bruce (Manfred Mann), blues guitar phenom **Eric Clapton** (the **Yardbirds** and John Mayall's Bluesbreakers), and self-taught drummer Ginger Baker. Already well-respected artists (the band took its name from an off-the-cuff comment by Clapton: "We are the cream"), the band focused on its signature sound in Bruce's stinging harmonica and bass, Baker's powerful drumming, and Clapton's mesmerizing technical guitar work. In their short time together between 1966 and 1969, they produced four amazing albums, including *Wheels of Fire*—a partially-live double album featuring an eleven-night improv-fest at the **Fillmore** West. In 1969, they sold out Royal Albert Hall for two farewell concerts.

Creedence Clearwater Revival. The West Coast band that brought southern rockabilly to the San Francisco scene, Creedence made a reputation for themselves producing hit after hit from three excellent albums in 1969, including "Proud Mary" from their sophomore effort *Bayou Country*, "Bad Moon Rising" and "Green River" from *Green River*, and "Down on the Corner" from *Willy and the Poorboys*, all of which charted in the Top 5. Their fifth album—*Cosmo's Factory*, with three Top 5 singles—is generally considered their finest and last great work before rivalries between the lead songwriters, brothers Tom and John Fogerty, led to the band's eventual demise in 1972, but not before influencing future artists like **Lynyrd Skynyrd** and Bruce Springsteen.

Creem. Founded in March 1969 by publisher Barry Kramer, the Detroit-based *Creem* magazine covered rock music in an irreverent style with some of the period's greatest critics, including Greil Marcus, Cameron Crowe, Robert Christgau, Patti Smith, and Dave Marsh.

Crosby, Stills, Nash & Young. Formed in 1969 by David Crosby (**the Byrds**), Graham Nash (the Hollies), and **Stephen Stills (Buffalo Springfield)**, Crosby, Stills & Nash released an excellent debut their first year before adding another Buffalo Springfield alum, **Neil Young**, to make one of the most successful and critically acclaimed bands of the period. Rising from the ashes of burnt-out mid-1960s hippie idealism, this harmonically perfect quartet seemed determined to prove that the peace and love movement was more than just a passing phase, releasing eternal anthems such as "Almost Cut My Hair," "Teach Your Children," a reworking of Joni Mitchell's "**Woodstock**," and Young's powerful and enduring "Ohio," written and recorded within days of the Kent State shooting. Their 1970 sophomore release *Déjà vu* was their masterpiece, one of three CSN&Y albums to reach No. 1 on the charts. Their ability to nimbly stretch their vocal harmonies over soft acoustic pieces and layered electric guitars alike made them one of the top acts of the early seventies, but their independent projects took over, and the group only did sporadic work through the later 1970s and 1980s. (See Chapter 5, "Folk Rock and Its Successors.")

Daniels, Charlie (b. 1936). This North Carolina fiddler made his name in Nashville doing studio work for other artists, most notably appearing on **Bob Dylan's** *Nashville Skyline* in 1969. His own star rose when he formed the **southern-rock** group the Charlie Daniels Band, which achieved hits through the 1970s and 1980s with songs about the south and patriotism. Frequently performing with the **Marshall Tucker Band**, Daniels established the annual

Volunteer Jam in 1974 with Marshall Tucker and the **Allman Brothers Band**. (See Chapter 4, "The South Rises Again.")

***Dark Side of the Moon* (1973).** Although this eighth **Pink Floyd** album spent only one week in the top spot of the charts, it lingered for sixty-three weeks on the Top 40, and an astonishing fourteen years in the Top 200, where it still pops up from time to time, making it one of the best-sellers in music history. Already known for its experimental use of electronica, Pink Floyd took it to a new level in this album, combining long periods of tonal stillness with steady driving rhythms and powerful lyrics to create a theme album that did not greatly differ sonically cut to cut, yet produced a number of singles that could stand on their own.

***Days of Future Passed* (1967).** The Moody Blues' first album to combine rock and classical influences to create a **progressive** sound, *Days of Future Passed* used the London Festival Orchestra to produce a lush classical arrangement of blues-based rock. Featuring their most memorable song, "Nights in White Satin," *Days of Future Passed* rose to No. 3 on the American charts and kindled an interest in the recording studio as an instrument in itself rather than a means to capture music the way it was performed on stage.

Deep Purple. Formed in London in 1968, this early **progressive** band and **heavy-metal** progenitor was once declared by the *Guinness Book of World Records* to be the world's loudest band.[3] Their deafening sound came mainly from distortion-heavy collaborations between organist Jon Lord and guitarist Ritchie Blackmore, complemented by regular solos from drummer Ian Paice. Though the group went through several lineups in their decade-long career (not counting later incarnations), the members took the unique sound with them as they formed other metal bands such as Rainbow, Whitesnake, and **Black Sabbath**. (See Chapter 2, "Hard-Rock Lightning, Heavy-Metal Thunder.")

***Déjà vu* (1970).** The first album from **Crosby, Stills, Nash & Young** (though CSN had one release prior to **Neil Young**'s arrival and several more after his departure), this is the opus of a quartet that only managed to turn out two records in their short history and yet became one of the most important American acts of their time. Combining powerful political lyrics (one song, "Ohio," was banned on some stations) with intricate guitar work and dead-on harmonies, the album features masterpieces by all four members, including Crosby's "Almost Cut My Hair," **Stills**' "Carry On," Nash's "Teach Your Children," and Young's "Helpless."

Derek and the Dominos. **Eric Clapton**'s short-lived follow-up to his previous band **Blind Faith**, Derek and the Dominos produced only one album before breaking up, the highly acclaimed *Layla and other Assorted Love Songs*. The 1970 album was moderately successful, most notably producing the title track—a memorable partnership between Clapton and the **southern-rock** legend Duane Allman.

Donahue, Tom (1928–1975). An influential DJ in San Francisco, initially at **KMPX** and then later at KSAN, "Big Daddy" Donahue was a major factor in bringing rock music to the FM dial. His progressive programming created a massive increase in ad revenue for KMPX, and other stations began to follow suit, bringing rock music to a mainstream audience. Donahue also supported the burgeoning 1960s San Francisco scene by managing bands, promoting shows, and creating the touring revue "Medicine Ball Caravan," as well as introducing an album format at KSAN during a time when albums were beginning to dominate singles in sales.

Donovan (b. 1946). Initially hailed as a Scottish **Bob Dylan** and despite his fairly fluffy material, Donovan Leitch became a "psychedelic troubadour" and honorary hippie for the drug references in his lyrics and his association with the Maharishi (**the Beatles'** meditation mentor). After early hits such as 1966's "Sunshine Superman" and 1967's "Mellow Yellow," Donovan fell out of favor with a harder-edged rock scene, losing widespread appeal but continuing to record and perform for decades.

The Doors. The seminal L.A. band of the late 1960s, the Doors' self-titled debut was heralded by a billboard on Sunset Boulevard—the first of its kind. Singer Jim Morrison's dark, brooding poetry framed by organist Ray Manzarek (an art-school friend) and complemented by Robby Krieger's creative guitar work and John Densmore's skilled drumming were just the right combination to create a unique, acid-infused sound in an age of rehashed **psychedelia**. Jim Morrison's erotic stage antics captured the public's attention, but the stark, intelligent music—songs of sex and death after the **summer of love**—held it captive. Four years and seven albums later (all seven of which hit the Top 10), Morrison retired to Paris, where he hoped to leave music behind and become a writer, but died in 1971 at the age of twenty-seven of a heart attack brought on by excessive drug use. The band attempted to continue without him, but to fans, Jim Morrison *was* the Doors; after two mediocre albums, the remaining group dissolved. (See Chapter 1, "The Psychedelic Experience.")

***The Doors* (1967).** This debut album of the eponymous band thrust Jim Morrison into the national spotlight and added a moody, dramatic element to 1960s pop. While later albums were equally powerful, their first release spent the longest time on the charts—fifty-three weeks in the Top 40—and featured classics such as "Break On Through" and "The End" as well as their first No. 1, "Light My Fire."

Dr. John (b. 1940). Also known as Malcolm Rebennack—a growling, bayou-funk pianist from New Orleans—Dr. John worked as a session player through the 1950s and 1960s before releasing his creole/R&B debut *Gris Gris* in 1968 to little sales but critical acclaim. Releasing about an album a year for the next fifteen years, he built a reputation as a talented showman, getting artists like Mick Jagger and **Eric Clapton** to guest-appear, but only charting one song in the Top 10, 1973's "Right Place, Wrong Time" from the album *In the Right Place*, his most successful release.

Dylan, Bob (b. 1941). Already a folk favorite by the late 1960s, Dylan released some of his most highly acclaimed albums—*Highway 61 Revisited, Blonde on Blonde, John Wesley Harding*—after he had remade himself into a rocker in 1965 with *Bringing It All Back Home*. The album, whose title betrays Dylan's flirtations with early rock before he became a folkie, featured future rock legends **Michael Bloomfield** and **Al Kooper**. Bloomfield played lead guitar for Dylan at the 1965 Newport Folk Festival, the somewhat mythical event at which Dylan was supposedly booed offstage for going electric. By 1966, exhausted from overcommitments, Dylan retired from public life for almost two years, rumored to have quit music for good. In 1968 he reunited with the Hawks, a rock group that had briefly backed him up before his hiatus. The Hawks became **the Band** and continued to back Dylan, eventually appearing at **Woodstock** without him and launching the careers of Robbie Robertson and Levon Helm. Through the late 1960s and early 1970s, Dylan released interesting but mostly inaccessible albums as he again receded from the public eye, playing only one show between 1970 and 1974. (See Chapter 5, "Folk Rock and Its Successors.")

Electric Flag. A short-lived but highly respected group formed in 1967 that featured blues-guitar heavy **Michael Bloomfield** and established pros Harvey Brooks, Barry Goldberg, Nick Gravenites, Peter Strazza, Marcus Doubleday, Herbie Rich, and Buddy Miles. One of the first groups to mix horns, **psychedelia**, and R&B, they debuted at the **Monterey Pop Festival** to great acclaim, but only released one good album, *A Long Time Comin'*, before they began to fall apart. An attempted reunion in 1974 was absent many of the members.

Emerson, Lake & Palmer. One of the archetypal **progressive** bands of the early 1970s, ELP masterfully reworked compositions by classical artists such as Mussorgsky, Bartók, and Copland for a popular audience by combining lyrics and rock sounds with spectacular visuals. Releasing four albums in their first eighteen months to moderate chart success followed by an extensive touring schedule made them one of the top grossing acts of the mid-1970s.[4] But as **punk** and new wave began to take over the common tastes, the members spent more time on outside projects, leaving ELP a legacy along with groups like **Yes**, **Pink Floyd**, and Electric Light Orchestra as originators of 1970s art rock. (See Chapter 6, "Rock Goes Progressive.")

Faces. Formed in 1969 from the defunct British mod group the Small Faces and refugees **Rod Stewart** and Ron Wood from the **Jeff Beck** Group, Faces got off to a slow start with their enjoyable but sloppy debut *First Step*, but quickly recovered in 1971 with the excellent *Long Player*, helped out by Stewart's near simultaneous solo success with *Every Picture Tells a Story*, which spent four weeks in the No. 1 spot. The band soon became little more than a backing group for the popular Stewart, who led them to success with bluesy party songs for largely drunk crowds until 1975, when Stewart left the band to continue his solo career.

Festival (1967). Featuring interviews and performance excerpts with artists including **Bob Dylan**, **Joan Baez**, **Mike Bloomfield**, Son House, Pete Seeger, Johnny Cash, **Paul Butterfield**, **Donovan**, Judy Collins, Mississippi John Hurt, and Peter, Paul and Mary, the documentary *Festival* covers the famous Newport Folk Festival through its pivotal years of 1963 through 1966. The film is especially important historically for capturing the introduction of many black blues artists to white folk audiences, and the 1965 Bob Dylan performance that largely brought about the **folk-rock** revolution. (See Chapter 8, "Rock and the Media.")

The 5th Dimension. A Los Angeles soul group, the 5th Dimension rose to prominence in 1967 with the help of songwriters Jimmy Webb and Laura Nyro, who put them on the charts with songs like "Up, Up and Away," "Stoned Soul Picnic," and "Wedding Bell Blues." Perhaps best remembered for their 1969 chart-topping medley "Aquarius/Let the Sunshine In" from the Broadway musical *Hair*, the group continued making lesser albums until 1976, when singers Marilyn McCoo and Billy Davis Jr. went on to successful duet and solo careers.

The Fillmore. Originally a second-story ballroom in San Francisco, the Fillmore rose to prominence when **Bill Graham**, then manager of a performance troupe, began renting it out for parties and concerts, promoting local bands such as **Jefferson Airplane**, the Great Society, and **Big Brother and the Holding Company**, and exposing white audiences to black acts such as B. B. King, Miles Davis, and Muddy Waters. In 1968, Graham bought the larger Carousel Ballroom in San Francisco and a movie theater in New York, renaming them Fillmore West and Fillmore East, respectively. "The Fillmore" became an icon of the psychedelic era, where every event was an *event*—the Fillmore West featuring such legendary performances as **Cream**'s eleven-day residency captured on **Wheels of Fire** and Ken Kesey's acid parties with the Warlocks (later renamed **the Grateful Dead**). Graham closed both East and West down in 1971. (See Chapter 1, "The Psychedelic Experience.")

The Flying Burrito Brothers. Founded in 1968 by former **Byrds** Gram Parsons and Chris Hillman, the Flying Burrito Brothers are often credited as the first country rock band, which is not surprising considering that Parsons and Hillman left the Byrds after the 1968 record *Sweetheart of the Rodeo*, which is credited as the first country-rock album. These alt-country forerunners never hit it big, and their music was rarely critically praised, peaking early with their 1969 debut *The Gilded Palace of Sin*, but they were a major influence on later bands and artists like the Eagles, Uncle Tupelo, and the **Rolling Stones'** Keith Richards.

Folk Rock. A hybrid of Greenwich Village folk and the West Coast sound coming out of 1960s California, folk rock saw its development through acts like the Los Angeles–based bands the **Byrds** and **Buffalo Springfield**. Though many believe that folk rock was born when **Bob Dylan** plugged in his guitar at the 1965 Newport Folk Festival, its strains could be heard months earlier when Dylan released his famous "Subterranean Homesick Blues," a folkie song with a rock groove. With the advent of folk rock, women began to play a more significant role in the rock world, and musicians gained much more creative control, giving birth to the singer-songwriter boom of the 1970s. (See Chapter 5, "Folk Rock and Its Successors.")

Franklin, Aretha (b. 1942). Though Aretha Franklin had made a living singing a wide range of styles on a dozen albums for Columbia through the 1960s, this gospel-influenced daughter of a Pentecostal pastor did not find her voice until she moved to Atlantic in 1966. There she met producer Jerry Wexler and, backed by the remarkable Muscle Shoals studio band, she recorded a string of immortal hits, including "Respect," "Do Right Woman, Do Right Man," "(You Make Me Feel Like) a Natural Woman," "Chain of Fools," and "Think," charting eight songs in the Top 10 within two years of her arrival. Between 1967 and 1970, she released a remarkable fifteen albums, most of them of high quality, earning her diva status among the great female blues singers of the century.[5]

Free. A London-based group heavily influenced by the likes of **Cream** and **Jimi Hendrix**, Free had a run from 1968 to 1973 as a raw, bluesy, good-time band, known for energetic live performances with plenty of feedback and sustain. Their 1970 hit "All Right Now"—a staple party song through the 1970s—was their only song that charted, reaching No. 2 in England and No. 4 in the United States.

Gaye, Marvin (1939–1984). Though Marvin Gaye was already the biggest selling male artist at **Motown** in the mid-1960s and continued to record until his death in 1984, he really did not come into his own until tragedy struck in 1970 when his duet partner, Tammi Terrell, died of a brain tumor, two years after collapsing onstage into his arms. Devastated, Gaye spent the remainder of 1970 in seclusion, emerging the following year with one of the greatest **Motown** recordings ever, *What's Going On*, which spawned three Top 10 singles. Gaye's mix of jazz and soul to address social evils influenced subsequent black artists, and after the moderately successful soundtrack *Trouble Man*, Gaye released the powerfully sensual *Let's Get It On* in 1973, whose eponymous single was Gaye's second solo No. 1. Despite fine work with Diana Ross and the occasional hit over the following decade, including 1977's "Got to Give It Up" and 1982's "Sexual Healing," Gaye sunk into a spiral of cocaine abuse, tax problems, contract disputes with **Motown**, and eventually fights with his family, bringing about a sad end to his brilliant career when his father shot him to death in 1984.

***Gimme Shelter* (1970).** Using footage meant for an upbeat documentary of the **Rolling Stones'** 1969 American tour, *Gimme Shelter* leads the viewer down a path of powerful performances to what has become known as rock's worst day—the concert at **Altamont** Speedway on December 6, 1969, when the young Meredith Hunter was murdered by Hell's Angels right in front of the stage during the band's last concert. For many, the event marks the death of hippie idealism and the positive contribution rock and roll made to the 1960s peace movement. (See Chapter 8, "Rock and the Media.")

Glam Rock. Also known as "glitter rock," glam was more of an attitude than a style of music. Although it was associated with some **punk** and **heavy metal** of the early 1970s, the style was a flashy, androgynous look created by **David Bowie**, who played on his background in art and theater to create musical characters such as Major Tom and Ziggy Stardust, who were meant to represent singular outsiders. Bowie created the model for this look on the cover of his 1970 album *The Man Who Sold the World*, which pictures him lounging in a dress and holding a queen of diamonds in his limp wrist. The spiked hair, makeup, and flashy clothes sported by Bowie onstage influenced future "outsider" acts such as **T. Rex** and the **New York Dolls**, leading to later, heavier theatrics from bands such as KISS and **Alice Cooper**. (See Chapter 3, "Glamour Kings: The Birth of Glitter Rock.")

Graham, Bill (1931–1991). Perhaps the greatest concert promoter in rock history, Graham had a hand in launching the careers of the **Grateful Dead**, **Quicksilver Messenger Service**, **Big Brother and the Holding Company**, **Jefferson Airplane** (for whom he briefly served as manager), and many other bands of the psychedelic era. As owner of the **Fillmore** West (in San Francisco) and Fillmore East (in New York), Graham popularized music benefits, light shows, and mixed-media events, and brought many of the great black performers of the period to receptive white audiences. After closing both Fillmores in 1971, Graham continued promoting tours for **Bob Dylan** and **Crosby, Stills, Nash & Young**, as well as occasional benefits, such as the American portion of the famous 1985 Live Aid. Graham tragically died in a helicopter crash in 1991 after a Huey Lewis and the News concert. (See Chapter 1, "The Psychedelic Experience.")

Grand Funk Railroad. A hard-rock trio from Flint, Michigan, Grand Funk Railroad (sometimes shortened to Grand Funk) experienced a steep popularity curve by playing a number of large festivals after they formed in 1968. Within two years they had four albums on the charts, each reaching higher than the one before, and were a major concert draw, for which manager Terry Knight's publicity skills are often credited. Although not appreciated by the press, the band continued to draw large audiences, becoming the second band ever to sell out New York's Shea Stadium (after the **Beatles**). After Knight was replaced by John Eastman (Linda McCartney's father) in 1972, the band had their first No. 1 single with "We're an American Band," followed the next year by a No. 1 remake of "The Loco-Motion." But their popularity ebbed as quickly as it had crested, and by 1975 the band had fallen apart, with some members leaving and the rest becoming the unsuccessful group Flint.

The Grateful Dead. Perhaps the most enduring band in rock history— certainly the most traveled—the Grateful Dead existed for many (and still does for some) as an icon of **Woodstock**-era hippie bohemia. Originally the War- locks, a bluesy Bay Area rock group, the quintet was transformed after becom- ing the "house band" for Ken Kesey's LSD parties, originating all-night improv sessions and long, rambling trips into unknown territory (captivatingly recorded in Tom Wolfe's book *The Electric Kool-Aid Acid Test*). Their first few albums tried to capture their live sound, to good and bad effect, but by the time their finest live work, ***Live/Dead***, appeared in 1969, they were cult giants (with the addition of several more members). Followed by throngs of fans from show to show, they established a gypsy phenomenon that lasted well into the 1990s, a mythical experience centered around jolly, beloved, Santa-like front- man Jerry Garcia. Their subsequent, format-friendly albums *Workingman's Dead* and *American Beauty* are considered their finest, showcasing their appreciation for bluegrass and rural American sounds. Although their recording output grew and shrank from the 1970s through the 1990s, rarely reaching the quality of their earlier work, and although they never made it big on the charts, they are perhaps the most successful touring band of all time, consistently selling out large tours year after year for almost three decades, until Garcia died of heart failure in 1995 after a lifelong battle with drug addiction. In his honor, the mayor of San Francisco flew a tie-dye flag from city hall. (See Chapter 1, "The Psychedelic Experience.")

Grossman, Albert (1926–1986). A top folk manager of the 1960s, Grossman helped bring **Bob Dylan** to a national audience and managed major acts like Peter, Paul and Mary and **Big Brother and the Holding Company**. Grossman also helped found the annual Newport Folk Festival in 1959, at which Dylan revealed his heavier side in 1965.

The Guess Who. Although the Guess Who were one of the most successful bands in their native Canada in the late 1960s, it was not until their No. 1 Cana- dian single "These Eyes" reached No. 6 on the American charts in 1969 that they really broke ground in the United States. Several hits followed from their next three albums, including "No Time," "Share the Land," and their only U.S. No. 1, "American Woman." The band fell from the charts at about the same time guitarist Randy Bachman left the group in 1970. Bachman returned to the charts in 1974 with major hits from his new band Bachman-Turner Overdrive.

Guthrie, Arlo (b. 1947). It would be hard to grow up in the shadow of the greatest folkie ever and not become one yourself, which is what happened to the son of Woody Guthrie, known by every acoustic musician in the country before he even picked up a guitar. Arlo proved himself worthy of that attention when he released his eighteen-minute story-song "Alice's Restaurant Massacree" in 1967, which grew to be almost as famous as his father's "This Land Is Your Land." None of his fine follow-up albums achieved near the fame or moderate chart success as this debut, but Guthrie became a favorite on the folk circuit for decades. (See Chapter 5, "Folk Rock and Its Successors.")

Haight-Ashbury. The de facto home of the hippies, this Victorian San Francisco neighborhood was the center of the 1960s psychedelic scene, and spiritual (and often physical) home to some of the biggest bands of the day, including the **Grateful Dead**, the **Charlatans**, the Great Society, **Jefferson Airplane**, and **Quicksilver Messenger Service**. Major events such as the Merry Pranksters' acid parties and the 1967 Human **Be-In** took place in and near "the Haight." By 1968, overrun by tourists and "weekend beatniks," the Haight was deserted by many who made it what it was, though it still lives in the minds of many as the birthplace of much experimental rock. (See Chapter 1, "The Psychedelic Experience.")

Hair **(1968).** Originally a 1967 off-Broadway musical that became a long-playing Broadway hit (over 1,700 consecutive shows), the original cast album that was released the following year spent thirteen weeks at No. 1, lasted fifty-nine weeks in the Top 40 (second only to 1964's *Fiddler on the Roof* for original cast recordings), and became one of the biggest selling albums of the rock era. The story is set in Greenwich Village, and touches on many themes, from the immediate context of rock music and the Vietnam War to larger moral issues of race, sex, violence, drugs, and the conflict between individual freedom and social responsibility. (See Chapter 8, "Rock and the Media.")

Harrison, George (1943–2001). After major success following the dissolution of the legendary **Beatles** in 1970, George Harrison was somewhat vindicated for the years he spent in the shadows of senior Beatles **John Lennon** and Paul McCartney. Although signs of his talent were apparent in his limited contributions to Beatles albums, including "While My Guitar Gently Weeps" and the No. 1 "Something," it was not until his third solo effort—1970's triple album *All Things Must Pass*—spent seven weeks at the top of the charts and spawned the No. 1 single "My Sweet Lord" that he became a bankable solo artist. Harrison's long-standing interest in Indian culture and friendship with **Ravi Shankar** led to his next project, the highly successful **Concert for Bangladesh**—a live series of charity concerts at Madison Square Garden featuring friends **Bob Dylan**, **Eric Clapton**, Ringo Starr, **Leon Russell**, and others. After the chart-topper *Living in the Material World* in 1973, Harrison continued solo works and outside projects through the 1970s and more sporadically afterward.

Havens, Richie (b. 1941). Although Richie Havens was regarded as a fine folk songwriter, this Brooklyn native was better known for excellent covers of artists ranging from **Gordon Lightfoot** to **Bob Dylan** to the **Beatles**. His open-E tuning and percussive playing style gave him a unique sound best brought forth on his 1967 debut *Mixed Bag* and 1969's *Richard P. Havens, 1983*. He is perhaps best remembered as the opening act at **Woodstock**, well-captured in Michael Wadleigh's documentary of the event.

Hayes, Isaac (b. 1942). A Memphis, Tennessee native, Hayes spent the better part of the 1960s as a writer for Stax Records, co-writing such hits as "Soul Man" and "I Thank You" for Stax's top artists. Hayes established himself as a major talent with his 1969 sophomore release *Hot Buttered Soul*, a complex jam-fest that revealed his potential. Though many of his later releases were only of average quality, he scored another major success with the 1971 soundtrack to the blacksploitation film *Shaft*, whose "Theme from Shaft" became Hayes's best-known song.

Heavy Metal. Originally a blues-dominated power rock, heavy metal was born in the 1960s out of blues-based hard-rock bands such as **Cream** and the **Yardbirds** and furthered by distortion and volume by the likes of **Jimi Hendrix** and the **Who**. As heavy metal evolved (there are many beliefs about the phrase's origin, the most reliable credited to rock journalist Mike Saunders), the aggressive style focused less on lyrics and more on volume, sometimes using inane lyrics simply to support loud guitars. In Britain, heavy metal was brought into its own at the turn of the decade by **Black Sabbath**, **Deep Purple**, and **Led Zeppelin**, and in the United States by **Blue Cheer**, **Alice Cooper**, and **Iron Butterfly**, whose 1968 hit "In-A-Gadda-Da-Vida" is considered by some to be the first truly heavy-metal song. (See Chapter 2, "Hard-Rock Lightning, Heavy-Metal Thunder.")

Hendrix, Jimi (1942–1970). Believed by many critics to be the finest rock guitarist ever, James Hendrix was one of the great characters of the late 1960s—a self-taught, left-handed guitarist playing a right-handed guitar, a black southern blues aficionado screeching psychedelic rock with a mostly white band. A virtual unknown until **Animals** bassist Chas Chandler took him to England in 1966 and helped him create the Jimi Hendrix Experience, Hendrix blew away the rock cognoscenti, impressing such luminaries as Mick Jagger, Pete Townshend, and **Eric Clapton** with his unusual style, fiery licks, and heavily textured distortion prowess. Within three years Hendrix was a legend, setting fire to his guitar at the **Monterey Pop Festival**, closing **Woodstock** with a wildly electric "Star-Spangled Banner," and releasing three of the period's most exciting albums—***Are You Experienced?***, *Axis: Bold as Love*, and *Electric Ladyland*. Sadly, Hendrix's flame blew out as quickly as it had ignited. By 1970, he had reformed his group into the less exciting Band of Gypsies. As drug use and management problems sapped his energy, Hendrix's playing became more erratic, sometimes just poor. In September 1970, he took too many sleeping pills and suffocated in his sleep. In less than four years, Hendrix had gone from a small club player to one of rock's most enduring icons. (See Chapter 1, "The Psychedelic Experience" and Chapter 2, "Hard-Rock Lightning, Heavy-Metal Thunder.")

Hot Tuna. Formed in San Francisco in 1969 as a side project for **Jefferson Airplane**'s guitarist Jorma Kaukonen and bassist Jack Casady, Hot Tuna sought to explore their more folksy blues side, often opening for Airplane itself. As Jefferson Airplane's material got weaker, Hot Tuna got louder and more careless, releasing a number of unremarkable albums through the 1970s.

Ian, Janis (b. 1951). A folk-rock singer-songwriter from a very young age, Ian's 1967 debut album included the remarkably mature "Society's Child," which made her instantly famous at the tender age of sixteen. Her intensely personal and honest lyrics made her a folk favorite of the period, and she spent the 1970s recording and writing for other artists. Her best-selling and most famous song was "At Seventeen" from 1975's chart-topping *Between the Lines*.

Iggy and the Stooges. See **The Stooges**.

In-A-Gadda-Da-Vida **(1968).** The second release of the proto-**heavy-metal** band **Iron Butterfly**, this album's title track is believed by some to be the first heavy-metal song. A seventeen-minute roller coaster of organ, bass, drums, and feedback, the song made the album Atlantic Records' biggest seller for years. (See Chapter 2, "Hard-Rock Lightning, Heavy-Metal Thunder.")

In the Court of the Crimson King **(1969).** Some look back on the British band **King Crimson**'s debut, *In the Court of the Crimson King*, as the beginning of **progressive rock**. The complex album, featuring Robert Fripp's classically influenced guitar work, was an experimental melding of classical and rock styles that gave rise to a host of imitators throughout the 1970s. (See Chapter 6, "Rock Goes Progressive.")

Iron Butterfly. A briefly successful act from the late 1960s, Iron Butterfly is chiefly remembered as the first full-on **heavy-metal** band (some believe the term "heavy metal" was coined just for them). Their biggest hit—the seventeen-minute title track to their 1968 sophomore album *In-A-Gadda-Da-Vida*—was Atlantic Records' biggest seller for years. (See Chapter 2, "Hard-Rock Lightning, Heavy-Metal Thunder.")

The Jackson Five. In 1968 the five Jackson brothers—Tito, Jermaine, Jackie, Marlon, and future king of pop Michael—were signed on to Berry Gordy's **Motown** label. They became one of the most successful pop/soul groups of the early 1970s, scoring No. 1 spots early in their career with hits like "I Want You Back," "ABC," and "I'll Be There." Though their early releases were penned by writers at Motown, the group began covering older soul hits and eventually composing most of their own material by the mid-1970s, paving the way for individual careers when the group left Motown in 1975 and dissolved as a family act soon after.

Jefferson Airplane. One of the original "West Coast rock" (a punchy folk/rock blend) acts in 1960s San Francisco, Jefferson Airplane brought enough attention to the psychedelic scene to earn major contracts for other groups such as the Steve Miller Band and **Quicksilver Messenger Service.** Singer Grace Slick, who left the Great Society to join the group, contributed two of her former band's songs to Airplane's landmark sophomore release *Surrealistic Pillow* (1967). Both songs, "Somebody to Love" and "White Rabbit," landed in the Top 10 and became hallmarks of psychedelic rock. The band also brought attention to the **Haight-Ashbury** neighborhood, where they lived in a communal home near a similar setup for the **Grateful Dead,** and they were present at many of the great musical moments of the period, including gigs at **Monterey, Woodstock,** and **Altamont.** Several of Airplane's late 1960s acid-rock albums are now classics of the genre, including *After Bathing at Baxter's, Crown of Creation,* and *Volunteers.* Though the members moved on to outside projects by the early 1970s, part of the band re-formed into the very successful science-fiction themed Jefferson Starship. (See Chapter 1, "The Psychedelic Experience.")

Jethro Tull. Known for the distinctive voice and flute playing of frontman Ian Anderson, Jethro Tull first hit the charts in their native England with their 1968 debut *This Was,* a highly stylized blues-oriented album that sold largely because of Anderson's reputation as an exciting live performer. Anderson's voice, flute, obscure lyrics, and disheveled appearance were so unique and central to the band's identity that many thought "Jethro Tull" was his name. Within four years of the band's formation, Anderson was the only original member left, but with several excellent albums behind him—including the 1971 classic *Aqualung*—Anderson continued with new bandmates to release Tull's first U.S. No. 1 *Thick as a Brick* in 1972. Several more successful albums followed, and Anderson continued releasing tracks as Jethro Tull throughout the 1990s, but it was their early work for which the band is best known. (See Chapter 6, "Rock Goes Progressive.")

John, Elton (b. 1947). One of rock's true international superstars and most famous keyboardists, Elton John began as a staff writer for a music publishing house after playing piano in English pubs throughout the 1960s. Though his 1969 debut *Empty Sky* was largely ignored—and for good reason—his sophomore *Elton John* released the following year was a smash, reaching No. 4 on the U.S. charts, with the single "Your Song" reaching No. 8 in the United States and No. 2 in the United Kingdom. Two mediocre releases later, he could have been reduced to a one-hit wonder, but he returned to the charts in 1971 with the excellent *Madman across the Water,* followed by *Honky Chateau,* which spawned a string of five No. 1 albums in less than three years, making him a rock legend. John also became known for his extravagant and campy stage outfits and the consistently excellent quality of his performances. He continued to record albums for decades, between average and excellent in quality, and placed an album in the American Top 40 every year until the mid-1980s.[6]

Joplin, Janis (1943–1970). Janis Joplin is widely regarded as perhaps the best white female blues singer ever. Originally a folk musician playing the clubs in southern Texas, she relocated to San Francisco in 1966 to front **Big Brother and the Holding Company**, a somewhat improvisational blues/rock act that gave Joplin the freedom to develop the boisterous, expressive singing style that would make her famous. After a legendary performance at the **Monterey Pop Festival** in 1967—at which, it is said, Joplin raised people from their seats with a wave of her hand during "Ball and Chain"—critics claimed Big Brother was simply not worthy of Joplin's talents, and despite the excellent release *Cheap Thrills*, which topped the charts for eight weeks, she left the band in 1968. A string of mishaps followed as Joplin's supporters tried to organize bands for her, including bad shows, overproduced tracks, and problems from Joplin's growing drug use. In 1970 Joplin died from an overdose, but not before she recorded enough tracks for *Pearl*, arguably her best work, with her minimally arranged Full Tilt Boogie Band. Some of her most memorable tracks appear on the No. 1 album, including "Cry Baby," "Get It While You Can," and what has become the definitive interpretation of the Kris Kristofferson classic "Me and Bobby McGee." (See Chapter 1, "The Psychedelic Experience.")

Kick Out the Jams (1969). This seminal live album from **MC5** (Motor City 5), a quintet from Detroit, Michigan, is celebrated in hindsight as one of the earliest live **punk** albums. The band's first of only three commercial releases, *Kick Out the Jams* was loud, energetic, electric, and occasionally obscene. The album was banned at some music stores, and subsequently the band was dropped from their label, Elektra, though they were later signed to Atlantic for two more albums.

King, Carole (b. 1942). One of the most prolific Brill Building songwriters of the 1960s, Carole King finally earned her own star in 1971 with her massive selling third album, *Tapestry*, the fifth-longest charting album in history in any genre. Featuring some of her most enduring hits like "So Far Away," "It's Too Late," and "You've Got a Friend" (made even more famous by her friend **James Taylor**), *Tapestry* made King a major act in the 1970s and an icon of the burgeoning singer-songwriter movement. (See Chapter 5, "Folk Rock and Its Successors.")

King Crimson. Along with **Yes** and the **Moody Blues**, King Crimson helped popularize the **progressive-rock** sound in the late 1960s with their stunningly sophisticated 1969 debut *In the Court of the Crimson King*. Internal strife, however, saw all but one of the band members leave after the first album, including Greg Lake, who went on to found another major progressive rock group, **Emerson, Lake & Palmer**. Guitarist Robert Fripp re-formed the band several times for both excellent and average albums, and the group built a reputation by 1973 as somewhat of a **heavy-metal** symphony with incredible live performances. By 1974, Fripp had declared the band dead, though he resurrected it again in the 1980s and 1990s for several lesser albums. (See Chapter 6, "Rock Goes Progressive.")

The Kinks. One of the earliest hard-rock bands, the Kinks are believed by some to have invented **heavy metal** when they slashed their amplifiers with razor blades to create distortion. Their first hit singles included future **punk** staples "You Really Got Me" and "All Day and All of the Night" in 1964. Temporarily banned from the United States for violent performances, their most influential albums didn't even chart in the American Top 100, including 1967's *Something Else*, 1968's *The Kinks Are the Village Green Preservation Society*, and 1969's *Arthur Or the Decline and Fall of the British Empire*, all of which established the group as working-class heroes and frontman Ray Davies as one of England's greatest songwriters. The band returned to popularity in 1970 with their most famous track, "Lola"—a Top 10 single in the United States, which paved the way for major American tours. (See Chapter 2, "Hard-Rock Lightning, Heavy-Metal Thunder.")

KMPX. KMPX was the first underground FM radio station to bring rock music to a commercial audience when **Tom Donahue** took over programming. From 1967 to 1968, Donahue turned the foreign-language station into a progressive contemporary rock medium, increasing ad revenues 1,000 percent and influencing the spread of rock music on FM stations. The trend was followed in 1968 by KSHE in St. Louis, WABX in Detroit, WNEW in New York, and eventually dozens of stations around the country. (See Chapter 8, "Rock and the Media.")

Kooper, Al (b. 1944). After making a name for himself in the Blues Project and **Blood, Sweat & Tears**, Al Kooper played for or produced artists such as **Bob Dylan**, **Jimi Hendrix**, **Stephen Stills**, Carlos **Santana**, and the **Rolling Stones**. When Kooper heard the music coming out of the **southern-rock** label **Capricorn** in Macon, Georgia, he became hooked on the southern sound. With the help of MCA, Kooper founded the Sounds of the South label in Atlanta in 1972, signing what was to become one of southern rock's greatest bands, **Lynyrd Skynyrd**.

Led Zeppelin. Formed in 1968 as the New Yardbirds by session guitarist and **Yardbirds** member Jimmy Page, who took on veteran session musician John Paul Jones and unknowns Robert Plant and John Bonham, these English kings of blues-based heavy rock quickly became one of rock's most enduring phenomena. Their first four albums, *Led Zeppelin* through *Led Zeppelin IV* (1969–1971), ruled the airwaves through the 1970s and established them as one of the top touring acts in the world. Though remembered mainly as a powerful and skilled **heavy-metal** band, the members brought all of their remarkable talents to bear, recording subtle and complicated blends of rock, reggae, folk, and blues through an eleven-year career. (See Chapter 2, "Hard-Rock Lightning, Heavy-Metal Thunder.")

***Led Zeppelin* (1969).** The self-titled debut of a band that would change the face of rock, *Led Zeppelin* was an unparalleled work of hard British blues that featured blistering guitar work by Jimmy Page and scorching vocals by the unknown singer Robert Plant. Page also produced the album, demonstrating a studio prowess that complemented the band's thick grooves and masterful instrumental work. *Led Zeppelin* instantly earned the band a teen fan base that would make them one of the most successful acts in rock history.[7]

***Led Zeppelin IV* (1971).** Also known as the Runes, Zoso, and Four Symbols (the album was not given an official title), this fourth outing by British heavy-blues act **Led Zeppelin** has become immortalized simply for its song "Stairway to Heaven," perhaps the best-known rock anthem of all time. The other tracks proved nearly as enduring and equally compelling, including the party song "Rock and Roll," the wistful acoustic "Going to California," and the folk-mystical "Battle of Evermore." The album spent an incredible 259 weeks on the charts (among rock albums, third only to Pink Floyd's 1973 *Dark Side of the Moon* and Carole King's much softer 1971 release *Tapestry*).

Lennon, John (1940–1980). Even before the **Beatles** began breaking up in the late 1960s, frontman John Lennon was making music with his wife Yoko Ono in what came to be called the Plastic Ono Band. After several unremarkable avant-garde releases and a well-received live album, the group (often featuring guitarist **Eric Clapton**) had several hit songs through the early 1970s, including "Whatever Gets You Thru the Night," "#9 Dream," and the immortal classic that has been forever paired with the artist, "Imagine."

***Let It Be* (1970).** The Beatles' most serious film after sillier outings such as *A Hard Day's Night* and *Yellow Submarine*, *Let It Be* captures the band in their final stages before their breakup. A must-see for Beatles fans, the rooftop performance at the end of the film has become a classic moment in rock lore. (See Chapter 8, "Rock and the Media.")

***Let It Bleed* (1969).** Though it is difficult to proclaim a single **Rolling Stones** album their "best," *Let It Bleed* captured the band at their absolute peak, as well as capturing a "where do we go from here?" moment in rock. Released in the middle of a tumultuous period for both the Stones and the American rock scene, the raw album defiantly declared the end of hippie idealism with classic songs like "Let It Bleed," "You Can't Always Get What You Want," and "Gimme Shelter," and marked a period of the band's finest work with the preceding album, 1968's *Beggars Banquet*, and subsequent releases, 1971's *Sticky Fingers* and 1972's *Exile on Main St.*

Lightfoot, Gordon (b. 1938). Though generally regarded as a folk musician, the Canadian Gordon Lightfoot was a strong draw for American rock fans, having penned tunes for artists like **Elvis Presley**, **Bob Dylan**, and Jerry Lee Lewis, as well as folkies Peter, Paul and Mary and country star Marty Robbins. Lightfoot was considered a masterful lyricist by his peers, and released several well-regarded albums before *Sit Down Young Stranger* hit the charts in 1970 with its No. 5 single "If You Could Read My Mind," paving the way for a number of successful albums through the mid-1970s.

***Live at Fillmore East* (1971).** In March 1971, the **Allman Brothers Band** played four shows over two days at **Bill Graham's Fillmore** East, which were captured for an album now hailed as one of the greatest live recordings in rock. Showing the band at their absolute peak—only months before the tragic death of Duane Allman—*Live at Fillmore East* was an announcement to the rock community that the new genre of **southern rock** should be taken seriously. The performance was released as a very successful double album, and earned the band the right to play Fillmore East's last show that June, a gig that lasted until 7:00 in the morning. (See Chapter 4, "The South Rises Again.")

***Live/Dead* (1969).** Though this early **Grateful Dead** album failed to even chart in the Top 40, it is regarded as one of the finest and most revolutionary live albums in rock, by what is probably the most successful live act in rock history. Although the Grateful Dead had incorporated elements of their live act into earlier albums, *Live/Dead* was the first to completely capture the remarkable feel of a live Dead show, with its wandering acid-jazz improv, including the critically praised twenty-three-minute "Dark Star."

Lynyrd Skynyrd. One of **southern rock**'s biggest acts, Lynyrd Skynyrd picked up where the **Allman Brothers Band** left off after the death of two of its members in 1971 and 1972. With their debut on **Al Kooper**'s new Sounds of the South label, 1973's *Pronounced Leh-Nerd Skin-Nerd* was one of the genre's major works, introducing tunes like "Gimme Three Steps," "Simple Man," and the group's signature song, "Freebird." (See Chapter 4, "The South Rises Again.")

The Mamas and the Papas. As major players in the burgeoning California music scene of the 1960s, this harmony **folk-rock** act jumped onto the charts with the singles "California Dreamin'" and "Monday, Monday" in advance of their well-received 1966 debut *If You Can Believe Your Eyes and Ears*. Despite a string of follow-up hits, the band broke up in 1968, but not before frontman and songwriter John Phillips played a larger hand as organizer of the very important **Monterey Pop Festival** in 1967, as well as launching the career of Scott McKenzie by penning for him the hippie anthem "San Francisco (Be Sure to Wear Flowers in Your Hair)." (See Chapter 5, "Folk Rock and Its Successors.")

The Marshall Tucker Band. A Spartanburg, South Carolina, act that got their start as regular openers for the **Allman Brothers Band** in 1971, Marshall Tucker produced **southern-rock** classics such as "Can't You See," "Ramblin'," and "Heard It in a Love Song." The band got its name from a key ring they found in their rehearsal space—no one in the band was named Marshall Tucker. (See Chapter 4, "The South Rises Again.")

Mayfield, Curtis (b. 1942). A major R&B lyricist of the 1960s, Mayfield brought a black consciousness to soul music, emulated by later giants such as **Stevie Wonder** and **Marvin Gaye**. After penning hits such as "Gypsy Woman" and "People Get Ready" for his group the Impressions, Mayfield went solo in 1970, scoring a number of excellent soul albums, including the blaxploitation soundtrack *Superfly* in 1972, one of the most enduring soul recordings of the period.

MC5. An experimental proto-**punk**/jazz improv group that explored music as confrontational social commentary, MC5 (Motor City 5, a Detroit quintet) were known for their association with radical social groups, which gave them major cachet with antiestablishment punk groups of the 1970s. Like **the Velvet Underground** and **the Stooges**, their critical acclaim far outweighed their commercial success. *Kick Out the Jams*, their landmark 1969 live debut album, was successful locally but boycotted in several stores, causing the band to be dropped from their label. The band survived with another label for two more lesser albums before disbanding in 1972.

McLean, Don (b. 1945). Author of lyric masterpieces "Vincent," "And I Love You So," and the legendary "**American Pie**," McLean was a virtual unknown when his sophomore release *American Pie* unexpectedly topped the charts for seven weeks in 1972. The album's title track was also No. 1 in the United States and No. 2 in the United Kingdom, where "Vincent," off the same album, hit No. 1. McLean was an instant lyrical giant, and though he achieved little subsequent chart success, he held steady for many years as not only a gifted songwriter but a talented cover artist as well.

Miller, Steve (b. 1943). Although the Steve Miller Band arrived in San Francisco in 1966—after the psychedelic movement was well underway—the Wisconsin native took his group (originally named the Miller Blues Band) to the forefront of the scene when they signed with Capitol Records for $50,000, a large sum at the time for a Bay Area band. Their success not only helped bring national attention to the area's musical scene but launched the band's own successful career, with their unique sound that was simultaneously commercial and psychedelic. (See Chapter 1, "The Psychedelic Experience.")

Mitchell, Joni (b. 1943). Although mainly remembered as an archetypal coffeehouse singer-songwriter, Mitchell's connections to rock music cannot be ignored. Her excellent 1968 debut *Song to a Seagull* was produced by boyfriend

David Crosby in between his stints with the **Byrds** and **Crosby, Stills, Nash &
Young**. Mitchell's "Both Sides, Now" and "**Woodstock**" became major hits for
Judy Collins and CSN&Y. Established as a songwriter, she came through as a
performer with a string of acclaimed jazz- and rock-laced albums in the 1970s,
including *Blue, Court and Spark*, and *Ladies of the Canyon*, which featured one
of her best-known tunes, "Big Yellow Taxi." (See Chapter 5, "Folk Rock and Its
Successors.")

Moby Grape. A rock/blues/folk hybrid ensemble formed mostly from California bar bands in 1966, Moby Grape's self-titled debut was hailed as the arrival of an incredibly talented new group that was destined to shape rock music
in the coming decade. But sabotaged by manager conflicts, an overly zealous
record company that released five singles at once, and the mental illness of one
of its members, the band disappeared by 1971 after recording five fairly unsuccessful albums. The group's legend has only grown as the decades have passed,
phrased generally in terms of "what might have been," though several attempted reunions have failed to live up to expectations. (See Chapter 1, "The
Psychedelic Experience.")

The Monkees. One of pop's first successful corporate-constructed boy
bands, the four Monkees—Peter Tork, Michael Nesmith, Davy Jones, and
Micky Dolenz—were chosen from a field of 400 applicants for a TV show about
a struggling pop group. The show was inspired by the **Beatles** films *A Hard
Day's Night* and *Help!* and was a hit soon after it appeared in 1966, setting the
group up as an American version of the Fab Four. Although the group's initial
albums were major successes, spawning the No. 1 singles "Last Train to
Clarksville" and "I'm a Believer," the band and their fans were upset that the
Monkees simply dubbed in vocals while writers and studio musicians provided
the real talent. Despite the fact that the formula worked—their sophomore album *More of the Monkees* eclipsed even the Beatles' tour de force *Sgt. Pepper's
Lonely Hearts Club Band* for most weeks at No. 1 in 1967—the group insisted
on more control over their music. After gaining some artistic freedom, the
band released several more, fairly successful albums as the TV show drew to a
close in 1968, followed by the group's demise in 1969.

Monterey International Pop Festival (June 16–18, 1967). On par with
Woodstock for its importance in rock history, this California festival ushered
in a new era of experimental styles and diverse musical interests. Produced by
Lou Adler and run by John Phillips of the **Mamas and the Papas**, the festival
introduced to the larger public such figures as **Jimi Hendrix, Janis Joplin**, the
Who, and **Otis Redding**. The event was captured in **D. A. Pennebaker**'s
eighty-minute film *Monterey Pop*. (See Chapter 7, "The Festival Is Born.")

The Moody Blues. Evolving from a mid-1960s R&B band, the Moody
Blues reemerged in 1967 with an altered lineup that brought about their first
Top 5 album *Days of Future Passed*, which featured the hit "Nights in White

Satin" (which appeared on the charts as a single in both 1972 and 1979). As one of the early **progressive-rock** bands, the group brought a classical quality to their songs with heavy use of the mellotron, an early electronic keyboard that produced pretaped orchestral sounds. Part symphony, part psychedelic rock, the Moody Blues released a steady stream of well-received albums, including *A Question of Balance* and *Seventh Sojourn*, until they temporarily disbanded in 1974 to pursue solo efforts. (See Chapter 6, "Rock Goes Progressive.")

Morrison, Van (b. 1945). One of the legends of Irish music, the Belfast-born Morrison emerged on the U.S. scene in 1967 with the hit single "Brown Eyed Girl," followed over the next few years by a string of famous tunes such as "Moondance," "Domino," and "Tupelo Honey," which established him as an original artist who could combine blues, jazz, and rock for a truly unique sound. His 1968 sophomore release *Astral Weeks* did not sell well initially, but came to be considered an underrated classic from the era.

Motown. Already a hit machine through the 1960s with acts like the Supremes, the Miracles, and the Four Tops, the Motown record label expanded in the late 1960s to gain artists such as Diana Ross and the Isley Brothers. Founder Berry Gordy maintained tight control over the creative process, leading to the loss of several key people in the organization, including his hit-songwriting team known as Holland/Dozier/Holland in 1967. Motown rebounded in 1969 when the **Jackson Five** paid off big for the label, but the success was short-lived, as the label that was once the home of soul music in America had relatively few hit makers in the 1970s.

Mountain. Led by vocalist/guitarist Leslie West's guttural banshee yells, Mountain was one of the early crop of **heavy-metal** bands with obvious **Cream** and **Deep Purple** influences. The power-rock group led off in 1970 with the relatively successful *Mountain Climbing*, featuring their biggest hit, "Mississippi Queen." Several follow-up albums were minor hits, as the group continued to depend heavily on weighty blues riffs and long guitar and keyboard solos. The band dissolved after a poor selling live album in 1972, and re-formed several times since with little success.

***Music from Big Pink* (1968).** The Band was originally know as **Bob Dylan**'s backing group during his electric period after 1965 (when they were known as the Hawks), but this debut album saw the emergence of a new blend of rock music and traditional folk that would influence a generation of Americana. Recorded after a period in the late 1960s that the group spent sequestered with Dylan in his upstate New York home (these recordings were later released by Dylan as *The Basement Tapes*), the album is about as raw and straightforward as rock music gets. (See Chapter 5, "Folk Rock and Its Successors.")

***Nashville Skyline* (1969).** After a significant absence from the music scene in the late 1960s, **Bob Dylan** followed his excellent 1968 album *John Wesley*

Harding with a relatively new kind of country-rock sound portrayed on *Nashville Skyline*. Although **the Byrds** had introduced country rock a year earlier with ***Sweetheart of the Rodeo***, Dylan's foray into Americana helped make it more than a passing fad, bringing roots music to the forefront of rock. (See Chapter 5, "Folk Rock and Its Successors.")

The New York Dolls. One of the earliest and most audacious incarnations of **glam rock** in the United States, the New York Dolls were **MC5** with a sense of humor. This early lipstick-and-big-hair **punk** band made a name for themselves in the New York clubs in the early 1970s, but failed to reach commercial success elsewhere. Their 1973 debut ***New York Dolls*** is a seminal punk album. Despite the efforts of come-lately manager Malcolm McLaren (founder of the Sex Pistols), alcoholism, rivalries among band members, and poor production of their second album led to the group's demise in 1976. (See Chapter 3, "Glamour Kings: The Birth of Glitter Rock.")

New York Dolls* (1973).** The eponymous band's debut album was critically lauded but commercially minor, and now stands alongside **MC5**'s ***Kick Out the Jams and the **Velvet Underground**'s ***The Velvet Underground & Nico*** as one of **punk rock**'s foundation albums. Incorporating the bluesy swagger of the **Rolling Stones** and the impudent audacity of the **Stooges**, the **New York Dolls** lay it bare on this influential gem.

Newman, Randy (b. 1943). One of the most versatile and subtle songwriters in American music, Newman is best known for a series of soundtracks he wrote for hit films through the 1980s and 1990s. Although most of his own albums sold poorly since his self-titled 1968 debut, he wrote hit songs such as "Love Story" and "Mama Told Me Not to Come" for a litany of other artists, including **Three Dog Night**, Judy Collins, **Eric Burdon**, Manfred Mann, **Blood, Sweat & Tears**, Liza Minnelli, Ringo Starr, and Ray Charles.

Nilsson (1941–1994). Born Harry Nelson, Nilsson achieved fame initially for penning songs for other artists, then later for covering songs written by other composers. Artists who sang his material in the late 1960s included **the Monkees**, the Turtles, **the Yardbirds**, **Blood, Sweat & Tears**, and **Three Dog Night**, who struck gold with Nilsson's "One" on their 1969 debut album. Nilsson translated his writing fame to recording fame with his own covers of songs by **Randy Newman**, Fred Newman, and Badfinger, whose song "Without You" earned Nilsson a Grammy in 1972.[8]

Ochs, Phil (1940–1976). Often billed as a "singing journalist"—his first album in 1964 was called *All the News That's Fit to Sing*—Phil Ochs was one of the more vocal protest musicians of the 1960s, often beating other folkies to the punch writing political songs about American policies. One of the first to sing out about America's involvement in the Vietnam War, Ochs rivaled even **Bob Dylan** for a period of time before he gradually disappeared from the forefront of the 1960s **folk-rock** scene, eventually succumbing to schizophrenia and hanging himself in 1976.

Paxton, Tom (b. 1937). One of the most resilient of the 1960s Greenwich Village folkies, Tom Paxton was an erudite songwriter in the scene, penning clever ditties such as "Goin' to the Zoo" as well as more sophisticated social commentary like "Lyndon Johnson Told the Nation" and "I'm the Man Who Built the Bridges." Not as politically biting as his friend **Phil Ochs**, who remained in New York with Paxton when many other folkies fled to Los Angeles, Paxton nonetheless built a remarkably enduring career as a folksinger that has lasted for decades, still earning him Grammy nominations after more than forty years of performing.

Pennebaker, D. A. (b. 1925). Director of more than a dozen documentaries on rock music, Pennebaker is probably best known for his 1968 *Monterey Pop*, an important archive of the 1967 **Monterey Pop Festival**. He also directed the 1967 **Bob Dylan** vehicle *Dont Look Back*, covering Dylan's 1965 tour of England, as well as *Ziggy Stardust and the Spiders from Mars*, a recording of the 1973 **David Bowie** concert that was his last as Ziggy. (See Chapter 8, "Rock and the Media.")

Pink Floyd. One of the earliest and most celebrated **art-rock** bands, Pink Floyd released seven albums between 1967 and 1972, shaping the British psychedelic sound with improvised performances and light shows well ahead of their time. Minor chart successes with early songs like "Arnold Layne" and "See Emily Play" gave them enough clout to tour and record, and enough brilliance shines through on albums like 1968's *A Saucerful of Secrets* and 1971's *Meddle* to turn them into a large concert draw, but their work was still inconsistent. In 1973, they released their tour de force ***Dark Side of the Moon***—the longest-charting album of all time and a remarkable achievement that made the band a legend, opening the door to a string of excellent albums through the 1970s and 1980s, such as *Wish You Were Here*, *Animals*, and *The Wall*. (See Chapter 6, "Rock Goes Progressive.")

Pop, Iggy. See **The Stooges**.

Presley, Elvis (1935–1977). Already reigning as the king of rock, Presley had taken time off from serious recording in the 1960s to release a string of successful, if unremarkable, movies. Most of his recordings were hasty soundtracks, and as the **Beatles** and the **Rolling Stones** signaled a new era, Elvis in his early thirties was a dinosaur. In December 1968, he made a remarkable comeback with a one-hour television special that saw him dressed like the rock and roller of his youth and playing every bit the part. The concert was critically praised and put Elvis back on top for several years, with continuous performances in Las Vegas and several well-regarded hits such as "Suspicious Minds" and "In the Ghetto." This personal renaissance lasted until the mid-1970s, when increased weight and extensive barbiturate use reduced his performance abilities, eventually taking his life in 1977.

Procol Harum. This progressive British band was a one-hit wonder that permanently lived in the shadow of its early single "Whiter Shade of Pale," a worldwide smash in 1967 that featured an opening penned by Bach. Though producing an occasional well-received tune over the next few decades with a constantly changing lineup, the group never regained its early success. They are, however, held up as an example of early 1970s **progressive rock**, largely on the strength of their 1972 release *Live in Concert with the Edmonton Symphony Orchestra*, which reached No. 5 on the U.S. charts. (See Chapter 6, "Rock Goes Progressive.")

Progressive Rock. In the late 1960s, some musicians took rock and roll in more avant-garde directions. Also known as "**art rock**" and "prog rock," progressive music incorporated jazz, classical, and electronica into blues-based rock in experimental ways. Largely a British movement, progressive rock found its earliest home in bands like the **Moody Blues, Jethro Tull, Yes, King Crimson**, Genesis, and **Pink Floyd**. Progressive rock in the United States was more reserved and earned little attention, with the exception of the brilliant **Frank Zappa** and the constantly changing lineup in his band the Mothers of Invention. (See Chapter 6, "Rock Goes Progressive.")

Psychedelia. Perhaps no other style of music in America is so inextricably linked to its birth city as psychedelic music is to San Francisco, California. Home of the beatniks that preceded the hippies in this liberal, arts-oriented community, San Francisco in the 1960s gave rise to the peace, love, and freedom movement that manifested itself musically in the improvisation, Indian-influenced experimentation, and drug-enhanced visual presentation that was psychedelic music. All-night musical acid parties were common (predecessors to later "raves"), played by such bands as the **Grateful Dead, Quicksilver Messenger Service, Country Joe and the Fish**, and **Jefferson Airplane**, all of whom became known for their surreal music, long improvisational sets, and trance-inducing live performances. (See Chapter 1, "The Psychedelic Experience.")

Punk Rock. The term "punk rock" is practically redundant; rock in the 1960s was largely about rebellion against the status quo, and punk rock was an extension of that. Essentially a combination of urban poetry and youthful angst, punk rock grew out of garage bands in the mid-1960s, many of whose members were amateur musicians but eager to produce loud, raw music for club audiences. Leading the way in the United States were Lou Reed and the **Velvet Underground**, Iggy Pop and the **Stooges**, the **New York Dolls**, and Detroit's **MC5**. British punk came much later in the form of the Clash and the Sex Pistols in the mid-1970s.

Quicksilver Messenger Service. One of the centerpiece bands of the San Francisco psychedelic movement in the mid-1960s, QMS did not achieve the nationwide success of flower-power comrades like the **Grateful Dead** or **Jefferson Airplane**, but were solidly rooted in the sound of the generation. Their album covers were highly regarded works of art, and their sophomore effort, 1969's *Happy Trails*, is now considered a classic of the genre. (See Chapter 1, "The Psychedelic Experience.")

Redding, Otis (1941–1967). A well digger from Macon, Georgia, whose hits included "Mr. Pitiful" (giving him his nickname) and "Respect" (covered by **Aretha Franklin**), his 1965 album *Otis Blue* broke the white music charts and brought him into the limelight. In 1967, he replaced **Elvis Presley** as the world's top male vocalist in *Melody Maker*'s annual poll, and shone at the **Monterey Pop Festival** that summer. Redding died in a plane crash in December 1967, only three days after recording "(Sittin' on) the Dock of the Bay," which later became his only million seller and No. 1 hit.

Reed, Lou. See **The Velvet Underground**.

The Rise and Fall of Ziggy Stardust and the Spiders from Mars, 1972. After challenging the stereotypical persona of the testosterone-laden rock star with his 1970 *The Man Who Sold the World*, **David Bowie** established the new effeminate model with his extraordinary character Ziggy Stardust, in this album that was as much theater as it was music. Through this fictional rock star, the audience experiences the end of the world, coinciding with the rise and fall of his career. Following on the heels of his excellent 1971 album *Hunky Dory*, *Ziggy Stardust* earned Bowie enough critical praise to begin a performance career that dominated 1970s rock, as well as production stints for acts such as **Lou Reed** and Mott the Hoople. (See Chapter 3, "Glamour Kings: The Birth of Glitter Rock.")

Rolling Stone. Destined to become the authoritative word in rock music, *Rolling Stone* magazine's first issue rolled off the press October 18, 1967 (although it is dated November 9, 1967), featuring **John Lennon** in army fatigues and a helmet—a scene from his new film *How I Won the War*.[9] Published irregularly for the first few years, the magazine was decidedly San Francisco–centric, largely reporting on Bay Area bands, events, and issues until it took on a national focus as it picked up readership. The publication was not afraid to be controversial, publishing personal interviews and taking stands on social and political issues of the time. Although it lost much of its brashness and integrity in later years, the first decade of the magazine is without parallel in rock journalism, making legends of critics Greil Marcus, Lester Bangs, Ralph Gleason, and others. (See Chapter 8, "Rock and the Media.")

The Rolling Stones. Undeniably one of rock's greatest icons, the Rolling Stones have always been the stereotype of rock and roll—loud, bratty, blues-tinged, and infused with sex and drugs in their lyrics and lifestyle. Formed in London in 1962, the group released almost twenty albums by the mid-1970s, many of them brilliant and some absolute classics, such as *Aftermath, Beggars*

Banquet, **Let It Bleed**, *Sticky Fingers*, and *Exile on Main St*. Though their music was critically praised, their over-the-top rock-star persona was often the center of controversy, fueled by drug arrests, the mysterious death of their guitarist Brian Jones a month after leaving the band, and tragedy at the **Altamont** concert in 1969, when a spectator was murdered by Hell's Angels, whom the band had hired to provide security for the event. Such irresponsibility only fueled their reputation as the ultimate rock band, and with the demise of the **Beatles**, they found themselves kings of the genre, soon influencing new movements such as **punk**, **glam**, and **heavy metal**. (See Chapter 2, "Hard-Rock Lightning, Heavy-Metal Thunder.")

Russell, Leon (b. 1941). Though achieving limited success as a solo musician in the early 1970s, Russell was an important background figure in rock history as a session guitarist and pianist for a litany of artists since the 1950s, including Jerry Lee Lewis, Frank Sinatra, **Herb Alpert**, the **Byrds**, and Phil Spector, later recruiting top artists to play on his own albums, such as Charlie Watts, Steve Winwood, **Eric Clapton**, **George Harrison**, Ringo Starr, and Bill Wyman. After organizing the famous Mad Dogs and Englishmen tour with **Joe Cocker**, Russell achieved brief fame with his autobiographical 1972 release *Carney*, which spent four weeks in the U.S. No. 2 spot. Further forays in the 1970s as a producer, performer, and songwriter established him as one of rock's great unsung heroes.

Santana. Santana the band is embodied in the style of its frontman and namesake Carlos Santana, who has managed to maintain a fairly consistent sound for the group despite a number of lineup changes over its thirty-plus-year career. The pioneers and undeniable kings of Latin rock in the United States, Santana introduced a fusion of rock, blues, salsa, and samba to a stunned crowd at the **Woodstock** Festival in 1969, featuring Carlos's clean and expressive guitar work and a powerful backing group. Immediately following up with their debut album *Santana* and the excellent *Abraxas*, *Santana III*, and *Caravanserai* over the next three years, the group achieved immediate chart success, with their second and third albums spending a combined eleven weeks at No. 1. Many of their major hits are the definitive versions of the songs, such as Peter Green's "Black Magic Woman," Tito Puente's "Oye Como Va," and one of rock's most divine instrumentals, "Samba Pa Ti." (See Chapter 1, "The Psychedelic Experience.")

***Sgt. Pepper's Lonely Hearts Club Band* (1967).** By some estimations the greatest rock album ever, this **Beatles** classic was their best-seller, spending fifteen weeks at No. 1 and sixty-three weeks in the Top 40, despite the fact that it spawned zero No. 1 singles, as had almost every Beatles album before and since. A bizarre and ambitious combination of visual artistry; tracks linked by background noise; loosely related themes of drugs, eastern mysticism, and western pop culture; orchestras; steam organs; sitars; farm animals; and a new concept in pop music, printed lyrics, the album was as much a coup for über-producer George Martin as it was for the band. Besides blending pop, rock, **psychedelia**, world music, and electronica in truly innovative ways, the album spawned imitations and parodies, including **Jefferson Airplane**'s 1967 *After Bathing at Baxter's*, the **Rolling Stones**' 1967 *Their Satanic Majesties Request*, and a 1978 film version of the album starring the **Bee Gees**. (See Chapter 1, "The Psychedelic Experience.")

Shankar, Ravi (b. 1920). Through his relationship with the **Beatles**, particularly **George Harrison**, Shankar is largely responsible for bringing the sitar into rock music in the mid-1960s. His fame as a performer in the United States was brought about through his appearances at the **Woodstock** and **Monterey** music festivals, but on a larger scale he influenced rock musicians such as Harrison, the **Yardbirds**, the **Byrds**, and the **Rolling Stones** to experiment with world-music styles. It was at Shankar's request that Harrison organized the famous **Concert for Bangladesh** in 1971.

Simon and Garfunkel. Though not rockers in the traditional sense, the late-1960s folk duo of Paul Simon and Art Garfunkel was enormously popular among college students, and their records were at home in between **Cream** and **Jimi Hendrix** on dorm bookshelves. Their albums *Sounds of Silence*, *Bookends*, and *Bridge over Troubled Water* are classics of the period, with cerebral lyrics and soaring harmonies addressing themes of alienation and freedom common in contemporaneous rock music.

Sly and the Family Stone. Sly Stone (born Sylvester Stewart) worked in the music industry for twenty years before forming this soul/funk group in 1967, scoring a series of excellent albums over the next five years, including 1969's *Stand!* and 1971's *There's a Riot Goin' On*. The band brought an energetic combination of soul, funk, and **psychedelia** to the world of dance music, influencing fellow and future R&B artists such as the Temptations and George Clinton.

Southern Rock. Largely a combination of delta blues and country and western, southern rock was essentially born with the **Allman Brothers Band** in 1969, a Macon, Georgia, outfit that utilized psychedelic-inspired improvisation just as psychedelic music was getting lazy and rock was ready for a new breath of life. That breath came with the Allman Brothers Band's first two albums in 1969 and 1970, and their 1971 double album ***Live at Fillmore East***, one of the finest live recordings in rock. Groups that followed suit, such as the **Charlie Daniels** Band, the **Marshall Tucker Band**, and **Lynyrd Skynyrd**, took southern rock into the 1970s and established it as a nationally recognized regional style. (See Chapter 4, "The South Rises Again.")

Stanley, Augustus Owsley (b. 1935). Nicknamed "the Bear" by friends in San Francisco's early 1960s music scene, Stanley made a name for himself manufacturing and selling LSD to Bay Area bands and their fans while it was still legal, helping to launch the phenomenon of **psychedelia**. The early **heavy-metal** band **Blue Cheer** took its name from one of Stanley's potent LSD strains, and Stanley supplied the required LSD for Ken Kesey's famous acid tests. More than just a drug dealer, Stanley was also a pioneering sound engineer, creating one of the finest sound systems in the country for the **Grateful Dead** and designing a system that allowed the artist to hear what the audience was hearing. (See Chapter 1, "The Psychedelic Experience.")

Steppenwolf. This once Canadian group re-formed in Los Angeles and reached their peak early with their self-titled debut album in 1968, featuring the hard-rock anthem "Born to Be Wild," made immortal by its inclusion in the cult-classic film *Easy Rider*. Other hits, such as "Magic Carpet Ride" and "The Pusher," varied little in style, but defined the band's gritty, power-blues sound. Personnel changes limited their success after 1970, but the group defined its own small niche on the late-1960s airwaves.

Stewart, Rod (b. 1945). One of the most popular British musicians of the 1970s, Stewart did double duty in the early part of the decade as both a solo artist and the leader of **Faces**. After a brief stint with the **Jeff Beck** Group in 1968, Stewart joined Faces and began his solo career with a 1969 debut. His third solo album—1971's *Every Picture Tells a Story*—put him at the top of the charts for four weeks and gave him his first No. 1 single, "Maggie May," leading to a string of moderately to very successful releases through the 1970s.

Stills, Stephen (b. 1945). Often remembered simply as a member of **Buffalo Springfield** and **Crosby, Stills, Nash & Young**, Stills made important contributions to rock with his solo work, and his compositions for these two bands—including the folk-rock anthem "For What It's Worth"—are worthy of homage. After narrowly missing a spot as one of the **Monkees** and serving a brief stint with Buffalo Springfield in the late 1960s, Stills joined with Crosby and Nash to form CSN, with **Neil Young** joining soon after. During this supergroup's reign, Stills embarked on the excellent solo recordings *Stephen Stills* (1970) and *Stephen Stills 2* (1971), on which he brought together rock heavyweights including **Eric Clapton**, **Jimi Hendrix**, and John Sebastian, as well as bandmates David Crosby and Graham Nash. Later releases ranged from excellent to spotty, but the guitar and compositional talents Stills brought to his bands largely made them what they were. (See Chapter 5, "Folk Rock and Its Successors.")

The Stooges. One of America's original **punk** bands, the Stooges were formed in the late 1960s as the Psychedelic Stooges by punk godfather Iggy Pop (called Iggy Stooge at the time). Dropping the "Psychedelic" from their name before their first album, this young, loud garage band became known for their **Doors**-like stage antics and drug-addled performances, releasing three critically acclaimed albums before their breakup in 1973. Iggy later became a legend in the 1970s for his self-destructive behavior and his association with fellow godfather (of **glam**) **David Bowie**. (See Chapter 3, "Glamour Kings: The Birth of Glitter Rock.")

Summer of Love. A phrase reserved for the summer of 1967, remembered as the apex of the peace, love, and music movement of hippie culture, largely centered on **Haight-Ashbury** activities in San Francisco. Events during this period included the **Beatles'** zenith *Sgt. Pepper's Lonely Hearts Club Band*, the Scott McKenzie single "San Francisco (Be Sure to Wear Flowers in Your Hair)," **Jefferson Airplane's** *Surrealistic Pillow*, the Human **Be-In** in Golden Gate Park (actually a January event whose good vibes resonated that summer), and the launch of **KMPX's** new rock format. The attention on "the Haight" that summer brought wanna-be hippies in droves, and by 1968, the neighborhood was more a tourist attraction than the cradle of rock experimentation it once was. (See Chapter 1, "The Psychedelic Experience.")

***Surrealistic Pillow* (1967).** **Jefferson Airplane's** sophomore album and debut with singer Grace Slick, the album spawned the singles "Somebody to Love" and "White Rabbit," which Slick brought from her previous band the Great Society. The latter track, recalling the adventures of Alice in Wonderland (with LSD-themed overtones), provided the psychedelic slogan "Feed your head." The album was one of the centerpieces of **psychedelia's** heyday in mid-1967, bringing nationwide attention to the band's neighborhood of **Haight-Ashbury**. (See Chapter 1, "The Psychedelic Experience.")

***Sweetheart of the Rodeo* (1968).** Coming on the heels of their brilliant recordings *Younger Than Yesterday* and *The Notorious Byrd Brothers*, the **Byrds** astonished their fans with the countrified rock of *Sweetheart of the Rodeo*, now seen as the foundation album for the Americana movement. Largely a product of talented newcomer Gram Parsons taking control of the group, the album preceded **Bob Dylan's** western styled *Nashville Skyline* by a year and influenced a generation of musicians to explore roots-music styles. (See Chapter 5, "Folk Rock and Its Successors.")

Taylor, James (b. 1948). One of the leaders of the 1970s singer-songwriter movement, James Taylor became an instant household name when his 1970 sophomore release *Sweet Baby James* rose to the Top 5, taking his cover of **Carole King's** "You've Got a Friend" to No. 1 the following year. Catchy, enduring classics such as "Fire and Rain," "Carolina in My Mind," and "Country Road" put Taylor in the upper echelon of 1970s lyricists and made him a symbol of the decade's more sensitive side. (See Chapter 5, "Folk Rock and Its Successors.")

Ten Years After. Guitarist Alvin Lee made this British quartet stand out from other English blues bands with his lightning-fast fretwork, captured in the documentary about **Woodstock** in the band's performance of "Goin' Home," one of the highlights of the film. The band toured the United States almost incessantly from 1968 until their breakup in 1975, landing several albums on the Top 40 charts and earning a reputation as a full-tilt-boogie live outfit.

Three Dog Night. Registering ten Top 10 hits in the United States between 1969 and 1974, Three Dog Night was a major hit maker for other songwriters, including Laura Nyro's "Eli's Coming," **Randy Newman**'s "Mama Told Me Not to Come," Hoyt Axton's "Joy to the World," and **Nilsson**'s "One." Their strength lay in their harmonies and arrangements, which gave life to great songs often overlooked by critics and mainstream artists.

***Tommy* (1969).** The Who's first major hit in America, *Tommy* spent forty-seven weeks in the Top 40, establishing the band's reputation in the United States as artists to be taken seriously after years of chart success in their native United Kingdom. *Tommy* is a high-concept rock opera about a deaf, dumb, and blind pinball player in search of an ultimate truth. One of hard rock's all-time classics, *Tommy* was later made into a film, a Broadway play, and a symphony. (See Chapter 2, "Hard-Rock Lightning, Heavy-Metal Thunder" and Chapter 6, "Rock Goes Progressive.")

Traffic. Although this British **progressive**/psychedelic group broke up and re-formed after almost every album and their live performances were said to be erratic, their studio work was highly respected, and some of their singles— "Low Spark of High Heeled Boys" and "Light Up or Leave Me Alone"—are classics of the British psychedelic movement. Frontman Steve Winwood, who later enjoyed a very successful solo career, was largely responsible for the band's sound, a combination of rock, **psychedelia**, and world music.

T. Rex. Founded by singer and poet Marc Bolan as Tyrannosaurus Rex (later shortened) in 1967, the band found fame in the UK underground for their acoustic and bongo sound and Bolan's impenetrable, fantasy-thick lyrics. After some changes, the band found themselves more mainstream popularity with a slimmed-down, electric version in 1970, leading to a string of hit singles in the United Kingdom. Bolan became a pop icon, later embracing **punk** and **glam** in the 1970s, though only scoring one single in the American Top 10, 1972's "Bang a Gong (Get It On)."

***Trout Mask Replica* (1969).** Captain Beefheart's most celebrated album, *Trout Mask Replica* stands as a sign of how bizarre avant-garde music could get in the 1960s. Hailed by some as a work of genius and derided by others as a massive practical joke, the nonsensical, antiharmonic album, produced by avant-garde wunderkind **Frank Zappa**, made Beefheart one of the most celebrated figures in the musical underground at the turn of the 1970s. (See Chapter 6, "Rock Goes Progressive.")

***200 Motels* (1971).** After creating several short feature films, avant-garde musician **Frank Zappa** released *200 Motels*—his first full-length work—chronicling life on the road with his band the Mothers of Invention. The bizarre, heavily stylized film is more a predecessor to the music video than it is a documentary. *200 Motels* was the first film shot on video and transferred to film to be released in theaters, making it a much cheaper endeavor. (See Chapter 6, "Rock Goes Progressive.")

The Velvet Underground. Although they never scored on the charts and were generally panned by the critics, the VU had enormous influence on later **punk** and new-wave movements, and frontman **Lou Reed** has come to be seen as a godfather of moody, anticommercial music. With the help of financier Andy Warhol (who also designed their first album cover and set the group up with one-off singer Nico), the band recorded their 1967 debut *The Velvet Underground & Nico*, a poorly received album that is now an experimental punk classic. While the West Coast was steeped in an acid-heavy flower-power sound, Reed indulged his id in heroin-flavored New York gloom, recording three more excellent albums before leaving the band in 1970 to pursue a very successful solo career through the 1980s. (See Chapter 3, "Glamour Kings: The Birth of Glitter Rock.")

The Velvet Underground & Nico (1967). Introduced to **Velvet Underground** frontman **Lou Reed** by Andy Warhol, the singer-actress Nico joined the band for its first album, the groundbreaking *The Velvet Underground & Nico*, produced by Warhol himself. Though Nico's deep voice gave some of the songs a spectral quality, the real gold was Lou Reed's outstanding songwriting, tackling the darker side of drugs and sex while the optimistic flower-power scene was exploding on the West Coast. Often referred to as "the banana album" for Warhol's peel-off-banana cover art, *The Velvet Underground & Nico*, though largely ignored at its release, has become one of the most appreciated albums of the 1960s, influencing dozens of later **punk** and experimental acts.

What's Going On (1971). After a year of seclusion following the death of singing partner Tammi Terrell, **Marvin Gaye** emerged with an album that **Motown** initially declined releasing due to its seeming lack of commercial appeal, but *What's Going On* proved to be Gaye's most successful solo effort, spawning three Top 10 singles. The social consciousness of the album, addressing poverty, ecology, and faith, was a new direction in soul music, and this album has become one of the must-haves of the genre.

Wheels of Fire (1968). Although it can easily be argued that **Cream**'s second album, *Disraeli Gears*, represented their finest work, Cream was born to be a live band, and *Disraeli* was all studio. *Wheels of Fire*, their third effort, was a double album featuring one entire record of Cream at their visceral best, playing an eleven-night residency at the **Fillmore** West. This power-blues jam-fest set a new standard for live recordings and was the band's only No. 1 album.

The Who. Though their remarkable talents were often overshadowed by their onstage and offstage antics—including destroying their instruments set after set and hotel rooms show after show—these former modsters hold a place in history as the third front of the British invasion after the **Beatles** and the **Rolling Stones**. What the Beatles had in charm and the Stones in sexuality, the Who had in the raw emotion of Pete Townshend's guitar, Roger Daltrey's vocals, John Entwistle's bass, and Keith Moon's drums, fueling hard rock in the late 1960s and beyond with anthems like "My Generation" and "I Can See for Miles." A string of rebellious albums, including *The Who Sell Out*, *Live at Leeds*, *Who's Next*, and the first rock opera, **Tommy**, cemented this group as originators of hard rock and progenitors of the 1970s **punk** and **heavy-metal** movements. (See Chapter 2, "Hard-Rock Lightning, Heavy-Metal Thunder.")

Wonder, Stevie (b. 1950). One of the most successful artists to come out of **Motown**, Wonder combined pop and soul to create songs that were both upbeat and socially conscious. After scoring a string of Top 40 hits for Motown through the 1960s, Wonder gained more artistic freedom in 1971 and began recording some of his most enduring material, including 1972's *Talking Book*, 1973's *Innervisions*, and 1974's *Fulfillingness' First Finale*—all Top 5 albums, spawning six Top 10 singles among them.

Woodstock Music and Art Fair (August 15–17, 1969). Woodstock was not the first big rock festival nor the largest, but it marked a moment in history when rock music was diverging in a dozen new directions with original and spectacular artists leading the way, and the ideals of peace, love, and music that the festival championed seemed—briefly—within our grasp. Held on a dairy farm in upstate New York and attended by some 400,000 people (the largest festival gathering at the time), Woodstock featured some of the top acts of the day, including **Jimi Hendrix; the Who; Jefferson Airplane;** the **Grateful Dead; Crosby, Stills, Nash & Young; Santana; Janis Joplin;** and **Blood, Sweat & Tears**. In a larger context, Woodstock was the zenith of the early era of music festivals, bookmarked on one end by the original and serene **Monterey Pop Festival** in 1967 and on the other by the tragic concert at **Altamont** only months after Woodstock, which for many marked an end to hippie idealism. (See Chapter 7, "The Festival Is Born.")

The Yardbirds. The Yardbirds were one of the seminal British rock groups of the mid-1960s—if not for their brilliant, scorching blues concoctions, then at least for the fact that they, mostly at different times, held three of the world's greatest guitarists in their fold—**Eric Clapton, Jeff Beck,** and Jimmy Page. After giving the rock world such memorable tracks as "For Your Love," "Still I'm Sad," and "Heart Full of Soul," the band dissolved in 1968 but was immediately resurrected by Page as the New Yardbirds, which soon became known as **Led Zeppelin**. (See Chapter 2, "Hard-Rock Lightning, Heavy-Metal Thunder.")

Yellow Submarine (1968). A ninety-minute animated feature film made for $1 million and featuring the **Beatles** singing their own songs, *Yellow Submarine* involves the fantastical plot of the band members battling the Blue Meanies, who have stolen the color and music from the citizens of Pepperland. The Beatles penned four new songs for their third film, including "Hey Bulldog," "It's All Too Much," "All Together Now," and "Only A Northern Song." (See Chapter 8, "Rock and the Media.")

Yes. One of the earlier and more successful of the United Kingdom's **progressive rock** bands, Yes made its mark on the music world with highly stylized and lyrically obtuse albums that incorporated classical music, rock guitars, and synthesizers to create long, self-indulgent sonic experiments. After little success with their first two albums, their third and fourth ventures, 1971's *The Yes Album* and 1972's *Fragile*, found widespread popularity, and subsequent albums became major sellers as well as benchmarks in **art rock**. (See Chapter 6, "Rock Goes Progressive.")

Young, Neil (b. 1945). A prolific and highly respected singer-songwriter from Canada, Young first made his mark in the short-lived L.A. band **Buffalo Springfield**, an influential folk-rock group he founded with **Stephen Stills** in 1966. Though the band only lasted two years, its success and Young's lyrical contributions earned him a spot in another respected and influential group, **Crosby, Stills, Nash & Young**, to which he contributed the folk-rock anthems "Helpless" and "Ohio." CSN&Y had to function intermittently without Young as he simultaneously pursued a successful solo career, penning classics such as "Heart of Gold," "Cinnamon Girl," and "Southern Man," the latter provoking future **southern-rock** legends **Lynyrd Skynyrd** to write their mega-hit "Sweet Home Alabama." Young continued to perform and make excellent albums throughout the 1970s with his backing band Crazy Horse and through collaborations with old friend Stills.

Zappa, Frank (1940–1993). A musician well ahead of his time, Frank Zappa was a gifted avant-garde composer and America's first (and some would argue only) **progressive** rocker at the turn of the decade. His loyal fans believe he was pure genius, while his detractors regard much of his work as smut and juvenile humor. But fan or not, his range of work and influence is too great to simply be dismissed. Part rock, part jazz, part baroque, part parody, Zappa's music demanded much from his rotating lineup of backup musicians he dubbed the Mothers of Invention, as well as other artists he incorporated along the way, including Jack Bruce, **Captain Beefheart**, Tina Turner, Steve Vai, Adrian Belew, and the London Symphony Orchestra. His work ranged from the serious (his acclaimed recordings with the LSO) to the bizarre (a touring show in 1967 that included rotting vegetables and a giraffe that sprayed whip cream at the audience) to the hilarious (a riff on *Sgt. Pepper*'s album cover on his 1968 *We're Only in It for the Money*). What Mark Twain was to American literature, Frank Zappa was to music—simply one of the most colorful and creative artists in rock. (See Chapter 6, "Rock Goes Progressive.")

NOTES

1. Larkin 1997, 102.
2. Larkin 1997, 188–189.
3. *Guinness World Records*, 1975.
4. Larkin 1997, 429.
5. Larkin 1997, 490.
6. Larkin 1997, 676.
7. www.riaa.com.
8. Larkin 1997, 902.
9. *Rolling Stone*, November 9, 1967, cover.

APPENDICES

List of Top-Ranking Albums, 1967–1973

Twenty-five top-ranking albums, 1967–1973, and number of weeks in the Top 40 and at No. 1. These are ranked in order of total weeks spent at No. 1.

Artist	Album	At #1	Top 40	Chart Debut
The Monkees	*More of the Monkees*	18	45	2/11/67
Carole King	*Tapestry*	15	68	4/24/71
The Beatles	*Sgt. Pepper's Lonely Hearts Club Band*	15	63	6/24/67
Original Cast	*Hair*	13	59	11/23/68
The Beatles	*Abbey Road*	11	32	10/25/69
Simon and Garfunkel	*Bridge over Troubled Water*	10	24	2/28/70
Simon and Garfunkel	*The Graduate* (soundtrack)	9	47	3/23/68
Creedence Clearwater Revival	*Cosmo's Factory*	9	27	7/25/70
The Beatles	*The Beatles* (White Album)	9	25	12/14/68
Janis Joplin	*Pearl*	9	23	2/6/71
Chicago	*Chicago V*	9	20	7/29/72
Elton John	*Goodbye Yellow Brick Road*	8	53	10/20/73
The Beatles	*Magical Mystery Tour* (soundtrack)	8	30	12/30/67

(continued)

Artist	Album	At #1	Top 40	Chart Debut
Big Brother and the Holding Company	*Cheap Thrills*	8	29	9/14/68
Blood, Sweat & Tears	*Blood, Sweat & Tears*	7	66	2/1/69
Simon and Garfunkel	*Bookends*	7	40	5/25/68
Led Zeppelin	*Led Zeppelin II*	7	29	11/15/69
Don McLean	*American Pie*	7	26	12/11/71
George Harrison	*All Things Must Pass*	7	22	12/19/70
Santana	*Abraxas*	6	40	10/10/70
Chicago	*Chicago VI*	5	27	7/21/73
Roberta Flack	*First Take*	5	26	3/25/72
Elton John	*Honky Chateau*	5	25	6/24/72
Allman Brothers Band	*Brothers and Sisters*	5	24	8/25/73
Carly Simon	*No Secrets*	5	23	12/23/72

Source: Whitburn 1987, 314–315.

List of Most Significant Rock Albums, 1967–1973

The Doors
The Doors
January 1967

The Velvet Underground
The Velvet Underground & Nico
January 1967

Jefferson Airplane
Surrealistic Pillow
February 1967

The Beatles
Sgt. Pepper's Lonely Hearts Club Band
June 1967

Jimi Hendrix
Are You Experienced?
August 1967

Moody Blues
Days of Future Passed
November 1967

Simon and Garfunkel
Bookends
April 1968

Iron Butterfly
In-A-Gadda-Da-Vida
July 1968

The Band
Music from Big Pink
July 1968

The Byrds
Sweetheart of the Rodeo
August 1968

Big Brother and the Holding Company
Cheap Thrills
September 1968

Led Zeppelin
Led Zeppelin
January 1969

MC5
Kick Out the Jams
February 1969

Bob Dylan
Nashville Skyline
April 1969

The Who
Tommy
May 1969

King Crimson
In the Court of the Crimson King
October 1969

The Rolling Stones
Let It Bleed
November 1969

The Grateful Dead
Live/Dead
November 1969

Crosby, Stills, Nash & Young
Déjà vu
March 1970

Santana
Abraxas
September 1970

The Allman Brothers Band
Live at Fillmore East
July 1971

Led Zeppelin
Led Zeppelin IV (aka Untitled, The Runes, Zoso, Four Symbols)
November 1971

David Bowie
The Rise and Fall of Ziggy Stardust and the Spiders from Mars
June 1972

Pink Floyd
Dark Side of the Moon
March 1973

The New York Dolls
New York Dolls
July 1973

REFERENCE GUIDE

PRINT

Barnard, Stephen. *Rock: An Illustrated History*. New York: Schirmer, 1986.

Bashe, Philip. *Heavy Metal Thunder: The Music, Its History, Its Heroes*. New York: Dolphin, 1985.

Bego, Mark. *The Rock and Roll Almanac*. New York: Macmillan, 1996.

Bowie, Angela. *Free Spirit*. London: Mushroom Books, 1981.

Brant, Marley. *Southern Rockers: The Roots and Legacy of Southern Rock*. New York: Billboard, 1999.

Brick, Howard. *Age of Contradiction: American Thought and Culture in the 1960s*. New York: Twayne, 1998.

Bromell, Nick. *Tomorrow Never Knows: Rock and Psychedelics in the 1960s*. Chicago: University of Chicago, 2000.

Bronson, Fred. *The Billboard Book of Number One Hits*. New York: Billboard, 1985.

Buckley, Peter. *Rough Guide to Rock*. New York: Rough Guides, 1999.

Burroughs, William. *Nova Express*. New York: Grove Press, 1964.

Cagle, Van M. "Trudging through the Glitter Trenches." In *The Seventies: The Age of Glitter in Popular Culture*, edited by Shelton Waldrep. New York: Routledge, 1999.

Campbell, Michael, and James Brody. *Rock and Roll: An Introduction*. New York: Schirmer, 1999.

Carlin, Richard. *Rock and Roll: 1955–1970*. New York: Facts on File, 1988.

Charlton, Katherine. *Rock Music Styles: A History*. Dubuque, IA: Wm. C. Brown, 1989.

Christgau, Robert. "Anatomy of a Love Festival." *Esquire*, January 1968.

Curry, Jack. *Woodstock: The Summer of Our Lives*. New York: Weidenfeld & Nicholson, 1989.

Curtis, Jim. *Rock Eras: Interpretations of Music and Society, 1954–1984*. Bowling Green, OH: Bowling Green State University Popular Press, 1987.

Dalton, David, and Lenny Kaye. *Rock 100*. New York: Putnam, 1976.

Dasher, Richard T. *History of Rock Music*. Portland, ME: J. Weston Walch, 1985.

DeCurtis, Anthony. *In Other Words*. Milwaukee: Hal Leonard, 2005.

Du Noyer, Paul, ed. *The Story of Rock 'N' Roll: The Year-by-Year Illustrated Chronicle*. New York: Schirmer, 1995.

Farber, David, ed. *The Sixties: From Memory to History*. Chapel Hill: University of North Carolina, 1994.

Flippo, Chet. *On the Road with the Rolling Stones*. New York: Dolphin, 1985.

Friedlander, Paul. *Rock and Roll: A Social History*. Boulder, CO: Westview, 1996.

Goldman, Albert. *Sound Bites*. New York: Random House, 1992.

Guinness Book of World Records. London: Guinness World Records, 1975.

Halfin, Ross, and Pete Makowski. *Heavy Metal: The Power Age*. New York: Putnam, 1982.

Helander, Brock. *The Rockin' '60s: The People Who Made the Music*. New York: Schirmer, 1999.

Hendler, Herb. *Year by Year in the Rock Era*. Westport, CT: Greenwood, 1983.

Henke, James, ed. *I Want to Take You Higher: The Psychedelic Era, 1965–1969*. New York: Rock and Roll Hall of Fame and Museum, 1997.

Herman, Gary. *Rock and Roll Babylon*. New York: Perigee, 1982.

Hibbert, Tom. *The History of Rock*. New York: Putnam, 1983.

Hopkins, Jerry. *Hit and Run: The Jimi Hendrix Story*. New York: Perigee, 1983.

Hoskyns, Barney. *Glam: Bowie, Bolan, and the Glitter Rock Revolution*. New York: Pocket Books, 1998.

Hutchinson, Roger. *High Sixties: The Summers of Riot and Love*. London: Mainstream Publishing, 1992.

Huxley, Aldous. *The Doors of Perception*. New York: Harper and Row, 1963.

Isserman, Maurice, and Michael Kazin. *America Divided: The Civil War of the 1960s*. Oxford: Oxford University Press, 2000.

Kaplan, Mike, ed. *Variety's Who's Who in Show Business*. New York: Garland, 1983.

Kolloge, René. *The Times They Are a-Changin': The Evolution of Rock Music and Youth Cultures*. Frankfurt, Germany: Peter Lang, 1999.

Larkin, Colin, ed. *The Virgin Encyclopedia of Popular Music*. London: Muse UK, 1997.

Lescroart, John. *Rock Guitarists: Volume II*. San Mateo, CA: Guitar Player, 1978.

London, Herbert I. *Closing the Circle: A Cultural History of the Rock Revolution*. Chicago: Nelson-Hall, 1984.

Makower, Joel. *Woodstock: The Oral History*. New York: Doubleday, 1989.

Marsh, Dave, and John Swenson. *The New Rolling Stone Record Guide*. New York: Random House, 1983 (1979).

Marsh, Dave, and Kevin Stein. *The Book of Rock Lists*. New York: Dell/Rolling Stone, 1981.

Martin, Bill. *Listening to the Future: The Time of Progressive Rock, 1968–1978*. Chicago: Carus, 1998.

McAleer, Dave. *The All Music Book of Hit Singles*. San Francisco: Miller Freeman Books, 1994.

———. *The Omnibus Book of British and American Hit Singles, 1960–1990*. New York: Omnibus, 1990.

McDonough, Jack. *San Francisco Rock*. San Francisco: Chronicle Books, 1985.

Miller, Jim. *The Rolling Stone Illustrated History of Rock and Roll*. New York: Rolling Stone, 1980.

Nite, Norman N. *Rock On Almanac: The First Four Decades of Rock and Roll*. New York: Perennial Library, 1989. .

Pareles, Jon, and Patricia Romanowski. *The Rolling Stone Encyclopedia of Rock and Roll*. New York: Rolling Stone, 1983.

Pollock, Bruce. *Hipper Than Our Kids: A Rock and Roll Journal of the Baby Boom Generation*. New York: Schirmer, 1993.

Rock Facts. New York: Rock and Roll Hall of Fame and Museum, 1996.

Sarig, Roni. *The Secret History of Rock*. New York: Billboard, 1998.

Sculatti, Gene, and David Seay. *San Francisco Nights: The Psychedelic Music Trip, 1965–1968*. New York: St. Martin's, 1985.

Scully, Rock, and David Dalton. *Living with the Dead: Twenty Years on the Bus with Garcia and the Grateful Dead*. Boston: Little, Brown and Company, 1996.

Sheff, David, and G. Barry Golson. *The Playboy Interviews with John Lennon and Yoko Ono*. New York: Putnam, 1981.

Stuessy, Joe. *Rock and Roll: Its History and Stylistic Development*. Englewood Cliffs, NJ: Prentice Hall, 1994 (1990).

Stump, Paul. *The Music's All That Matters: A History of Progressive Rock*. London: Quartet, 1997.

Szatmary, David. *A Time to Rock: A Social History of Rock and Roll*. New York: Schirmer, 1996 (1987).

Tobler, John. *100 Greatest Albums of the Sixties*. New York: Overlook Press, 1994.

Troy, Sandy. *Captain Trips: A Biography of Jerry Garcia*. New York: Thunder's Mouth, 1994.

———. *One More Saturday Night: Reflections with the Grateful Dead, Dead Family, and Dead Heads*. New York: St. Martin's, 1991.

Waksman, Steve. *Instruments of Desire: The Electric Guitar and the Shaping of Musical Experience*. Cambridge, MA: Harvard University Press, 1999.

Waldrep, Shelton. *The Seventies: The Age of Glitter in Popular Culture*. New York: Routledge, 1999.

Ward, Ed, Geoffrey Stokes, and Ken Tucker. *Rock of Ages: The Rolling Stone History of Rock and Roll*. New York: Rolling Stone Press, 1986.

Warner, Jay, ed. *Billboard's American Rock 'N' Roll in Review*. New York: Schirmer, 1997.

Weinstein, Deena. *Heavy Metal: The Music and Its Culture*. New York: Da Capo Press, 2000 (1991).

Whitburn, Joel, ed. *The Billboard Book of Top 40 Albums*. New York: Billboard, 1987.

———. *The Billboard Book of Top 40 Albums, 1955–1992*. New York: Billboard, 1993.

———. *The Billboard Book of Top 40 Hits*. New York: Billboard, 1996.

———. *Joel Whitburn Presents a Century of Pop Music*. New York: Billboard, 1999.

York, William, ed. *Who's Who in Rock Music*. New York: Scribners, 1982 (1978).

WEB SITES

All Music. http://www.allmusic.com.
    Created by the *All Music Guide* (AMG) staff. Provides detailed information on albums, artists, and songs from its vast database.

Council for the Summer of Love. "The Summer of Love 30th Anniversary." http://www.algroup.co.uk/wpb/people/fraser/blurbal.htm.
   A look back at the 1967 summer of love from the perspective of thirty years later.

Creem Magazine Archives. http://www.creemmagazine.com.
   Web site for the rock-music magazine *Creem*, originally founded in Detroit in 1969. Provides reviews, articles, links, and products.

Hippies on the Web. "Haight-Ashbury in the 1960s. Music and Images." Rockument. http://www.rockument.com/haimg.html.
   An audio and visual tour of San Francisco's Haight-Ashbury district in the mid/late 1960s, with commentary by Tony Bove with Allen Cohen and Raechel Donahue.

Pop Matters Media. Pop Matters. http://www.popmatters.com.
   An alternative online magazine covering popular culture in America, with an extensive archive of album reviews.

Powis, Neville. "The Human Be-In and the Hippy Revolution." Radio Netherlands. http://www.rnw.nl/special/en/html/031221be-in.html.
   Contains audio clips and links to other events of the 1960s in the San Francisco era.

Rate Your Music. http://www.rateyourmusic.com.
   A free, online community for rating music of all genres.

Recording Industry Association of America. http://www.riaa.com.
   A Web site for the trade group that represents the U.S. recording industry. Provides information on issues facing the industry, including computer piracy; information on gold and platinum record winners; statistics; a glossary of terms; and links to other sites.

Rocklist.Net. http://www.rocklist.net.
   Provides critics' lists of favorite albums and singles—as well as lists from magazines such as *Mojo*, *New Musical Express*, *Rolling Stone*, *Spin*, and *Melody Maker*—stretching as far back as 1952.

Rock's Back Pages. The Online Library of Rock and Roll. http://www.backpages.com.
   Offering "the best writing on rock music," this site provides a subscription database to reviews, interviews, and features.

Rolling Stone online. http://www.rollingstone.com.
   An original-content Web site produced by *Rolling Stone*, America's premiere rock magazine in the 1970s.

Rough Guides. *Rough Guide to Rock*. http://www.roughguides.com/music/rock.html.
   An online version of the successful book *The Rough Guide to Rock*, this site provides extensive rock biographics and album recommendations.

Song Facts. http://www.songfacts.com.
   This music trivia site provides lyrics to songs, information on song lyric meanings and tidbits of information about your favorite tunes through its searchable database.

WFMU. http://www.wfmu.com.
> The Web site for WFMU, an independent, free-form radio station in New York City.

MUSEUMS OR SPECIAL COLLECTIONS

The Rock and Roll Hall of Fame and Museum
One Key Plaza
Cleveland, OH 44114
http://www.rockhall.com

The Virtual Museum of the City of San Francisco
PMB 423
945 Taraval Street
San Francisco, CA 94116
http://www.sfmuseum.org

FILMS

In chronological order.

Dont Look Back. Directed by D. A. Pennebaker. Leacock-Pennebaker, 1967.
Festival. Directed by Murray Lerner. Patchke Productions, 1967.
Yellow Submarine. Directed by George Dunning. Apple Corps, 1968.
Sympathy for the Devil. Directed by Jean-Luc Godard. Cupid Productions, 1968.
Monterey Pop. Directed by D. A. Pennebaker. The Foundation, 1968.
Woodstock. Directed by Michael Wadleigh. Wadleigh-Maurice, 1970.
Gimme Shelter. Directed by Alfred and David Maysles. Maysles Films, 1970.
Let It Be. Directed by Michael Lindsay-Hogg. Apple Corps, 1970.
200 Motels. Directed by Tony Palmer, Charles Swenson, and Frank Zappa. Bizarre Productions, 1971.
Fillmore. Directed by Richard T. Heffron. Median Films, 1972.
Ziggy Stardust and the Spiders from Mars. Directed by D. A. Pennebaker. Pennebaker Productions, 1973.
Jimi Hendrix. Directed by Joe Boyd, John Head, and Gary Weis. Warner Brothers, 1973.
The Last Waltz. Directed by Martin Scorsese. FM Productions, 1978.
Jimi Plays Monterey. Directed by Chris Hegedus and D. A. Pennebaker. Pennebaker Films, 1986.
It Was 20 Years Ago Today. Director uncredited. 1987.

INDEX

About the Author

CHRIS SMITH is a Vancouver-based writer and photographer who has served as music editor for *Performing Songwriter*, editor-in-chief for *Inside New York*, and associate editor for *University of Chicago Magazine*. His work has appeared in dozens of publications, including *Rolling Stone*, *Billboard*, *Time Out New York*, *Sydney Morning Herald*, *Texas Music*, *Village Voice*, and the *Journal of Visual Anthropology*. In addition to music and film journalism, Chris has worked as a combat correspondent, a festival producer, a wildlife photographer, and a musician, and is the primary author of Volume 4 of this series.